FROELICH

NAVAL HISTORY
AND
MARITIME STRATEGY

The U.S. Naval War College, Newport, Rhode Island
(*Photo by Rear Admiral Ronald J. Kurth, USN [Ret.]
President, Naval War College, 1987-90*)

NAVAL HISTORY
AND
MARITIME STRATEGY

Collected Essays

John B. Hattendorf
Ernest J. King Professor of Maritime History
Naval War College

KRIEGER PUBLISHING COMPANY
MALABAR, FLORIDA
2000

Original Edition 2000

Printed and Published by
KRIEGER PUBLISHING COMPANY
KRIEGER DRIVE
MALABAR, FLORIDA 32950

Copyright © 2000 by Krieger Publishing Company

Library of Congress Cataloging-In-Publication Data

Hattendorf, John B.
    Naval history and maritime strategy : collected essays /
John B. Hattendorf.
        p.   cm.
    Includes bibliographical references and index.
    ISBN 1-57524-127-7 (cloth : alk. paper) — ISBN
1-57524-128-5 (pbk. : alk. paper)
        1. Naval strategy. 2. Naval history. 3. Naval strategy—Study and teaching. 4. Naval history—Study and teaching. 5. United States—History, Naval. I. Title.

V165 .H38 2000
359'.009—dc21
                                                    99–047385

10   9   8   7   6   5   4   3   2

Contents

List of Illustrations

Preface

In the Anglo-American tradition of maritime strategic thought, historical studies have often played an important role. The most famous theorists in this field have consistently used historical analysis as the starting point for understanding the role of navies in the broader context of maritime affairs. In looking at the relationship of naval history and maritime strategy, there are several interrelated aspects: the intellectual history of its development, the use of history within navies as a means of understanding strategy, and the history of navies and their activities. In addition, a full understanding of this interrelationship must involve a definition of maritime strategy as well as an appreciation of naval history as a subspecialty within the broader field of maritime history.

Founded in 1884, the U.S. Naval College in Newport, Rhode Island, is the oldest continuing institution founded to promote such studies. This volume is designed to provide a foundation for further studies in the field by gathering some fruits of past and recent research. These essays are explorations into the various aspects of the interrelationship between history and maritime strategy and its various dimensions. The essays and addresses in this collection were written over more than a quarter of a century during my association with the U.S. Naval War College, some dating back to 1970. All the older essays have been brought up to date with more recent scholarship in the field and have been selected from a larger group of my writings to create a single theme. They are republished now, in this form, with the thought that they represent some sustained work on various aspects of a single theme and may serve as a foundation for new research and writing in this area.

I have done this work as a civilian academic employed by the U.S. Navy, but the opinions expressed are entirely my own and not official statements of any agency of the U.S. government.

I am grateful to the following for permission to reprint revised versions of articles originally published elsewhere: to the Militärgeschictliches Forschungsamt, Potsdam, for permission to pubx   NAVAL HISTORY AND MARITIME STRATEGY

lish an English-language version of Chapter 1, which was originally prepared for publication in German; to the *Naval War College Review* for Chapters 2, 7, and 12; to Rutgers University Press and the *Naval War College Review* for Chapter 3; to Praeger Publishing, an imprint of Greenwood Publishing Group, Inc, Westport, CT, for Chapter 4; to the *American Neptune* for Chapter 5; to J. A. B. Crawford and the New Zealand Armed Forces Historical Office for Chapter 8; the United States Naval Institute for Chapters 9 and 11; to the University of British Columbia Press for Chapter 10; to the Maritime Studies Program, Royal Australian Navy, and the Strategic and Defence Studies Centre, the Australian National University for Chapter 13; to the Maritime Studies Program, Royal Australian Navy, and the *Journal of the Australian Naval Institute* for Chapter 15.

I am grateful to the following for permission to publish the illustrations in this volume: to The Naval Historical Collection and Naval War College Museum, U.S. Naval War College for the portraits of Colbert, Luce, Mahan and McCarty Little; Bill Ray for the portrait of Wylie; Rear Admiral Ronald J. Kurth USN (ret.) for the photograph of the Naval War College; the U.S. Naval Institute Photo Archive for the photograph of the Standing Naval Force, Atlantic; and the Graphic Arts Department, Naval War College, for the maps.

1

History and Technological Change: The Study of History in the U.S. Navy, 1873–1890

For the United States Navy, as for most navies in the world, the period between 1870 and 1890 was a time of dramatic technological change. In these two decades, the United States Navy was rapidly changing from a minor navy to one that was becoming important in world terms, but, by and large, it was not one of the major naval powers and it was not the technological leader of the time. When we think about historical study in the Navy at this time, we turn naturally to the work of Rear Admiral Alfred Thayer Mahan, whose Naval War College lectures were published in 1890 under the title, *The Influence of History Upon Sea Power, 1660–1783*. Quite rightly, we remember Mahan and his book as the foundation of the modern approach to naval historical study, yet, we often forget that there were others in the U.S. naval service who were also thinking about naval history. Mahan was not alone; he wrote within a context that is important to understand and there were several other important figures who contributed to historical studies in the U.S. Navy of his time.[1]

In the United States, the academic and professional study of history was just beginning during the last quarter of the nineteenth century. At the University of Michigan, Charles Adams introduced the seminar method in 1869, and was followed at Harvard from 1871, and at Johns Hopkins University and Columbia University from 1880. Much of the early work in historical studies in America was highly influenced by the methods of German historical scholarship. German examples also influenced the establishment of the American Historical Society in 1884 and the establishment of its *Re-*

view from 1895.[2] In this period, historians, like naval officers, in America were just beginning to see themselves as professionals, developing basic approaches and standards to training and education for their specific work, while also creating professional organizations to develop a literature for their areas of expertise.

Naval officers established the United States Naval Institute as their professional organization in 1873 and began publishing their journal, *Proceedings,* in the following year.[3] The Naval Institute was not the first professional organization within the U.S. Navy. In 1833, the New York Navy Yard established a library, which, in 1838, the Naval Lyceum incorporated into its Library. In 1836, the Naval Lyceum began to publish a journal, *The Naval Magazine,* but it lasted for only two years.[4] The Boston Naval Library and Institute was established in 1842. Another Lyceum was established at Annapolis in 1845 and, yet another, at the Mare Island Navy Yard in California. All these were the predecessors of the U.S. Naval Institute, but they lasted only up to the Civil War and tended to serve local needs for a library and for discussion rather than for service-wide professionalization.

Only in 1873, when American naval officers began to be more aware of their common interests, their need for mutual education, and their need to systematize knowledge for professional purposes, could the Naval Institute begin to serve as a catalyst to help naval officers define the elements of their profession. The fact that this development took place during a period of great technological change had a profound effect on the way that naval men looked at their profession.

Even while all these technological changes were taking place, there was also a parallel move toward emphasizing historical study. In 1873, the same year that naval officers at Annapolis gathered to form the Naval Institute, the U.S. Naval Academy's Department of English Studies, History and Law changed its curriculum. Under its new head of department, a twenty-three-year-old Harvard graduate, James R. Soley,[5] the Academy added lectures on naval history to its two-semester course on Western Civilization and U.S. History.[6] Four years later, now commissioned as a lieutenant in the naval corps of mathematics professors, Soley moved on to establish a twelve-lecture semester course in naval history for third-year cadets. In this course, cadets were required to have a "tactical familiarity" with fourteen famous naval battles in world naval history, ranging from Lade in the year 494 B.C. to the most recent major fleet battle at Lissa in 1866.[7]

At the same time that these curricula changes were taking place at the Naval Academy, there were several highly influential, progressive naval officers who saw direct value in studying naval history as a guide to the future. Among the most influential of them was Commodore Foxhall Parker, who had been the leading force behind the establishment of the Naval Institute in 1873. Earlier in his career, Parker had commanded the frigate USS *Columbia,* during the U.S. Navy's mission to the North German Confederation in 1848. Having later commanded the Potomac Flotilla during the American Civil War in 1861–62, he had gone on to write two books on naval tactics under steam.[8] Through the latter, he became well known in the Unites States Navy, as well as in other navies, for advocating the use of the ram. This practical application paralleled his interest in naval history. Parker had given the lecture at the first meeting of the Annapolis chapter of the newly established Naval Institute in 1873 on "the battle of Lepanto." Rather than publish it in the Institute's newly established journal, he withheld it until he could include it in his book-length study, *Fleets of the World: The Galley Period,* published in 1876. This was to be the first of a three-volume naval history which, due to the author's early death three years later in 1879, never came to fruition.

Reading Parker's book today, one can see little clear connection between historical study and the technological changes and tactical questions of the day. Yet, noting the great differences between sail and steam warships, naval officers were beginning to see a similarity in the maneuverability which steam-powered vessels had with the maneuverability that the oared galley had in ancient naval history. Taken out of this intellectual context, Parker's history appears only as an antiquarian study. Yet, it represents the connections which the leading naval thinkers were beginning to make as they examined recent experience in the first battles between ironclad warships carrying rams, in Hampton Roads in 1862 and off Lissa in 1866. One of Parker's friends and colleagues in founding the Naval Institute, Captain Stephen B. Luce, stressed the important connection between historical insight and modern thinking for those who did not otherwise see it. Luce, himself, had already gained a reputation as an historically minded officer with a series of six articles on "Modern Navies" in the weekly service newspaper, *The Army and Navy Journal.*[9] In a lengthy review for the Naval Institute, Luce made a direct connection between the actual tactical signals in Parker's *Fleet Tactics* and the description of galley battles in Parker's *Fleets of the World.* Luce observed, "we are forced to the

conclusion that the true way to study naval tactics is to do so in connection with the study of Military and Naval history and of the science of war as taught in the best military schools."[10] Driving home
his point, Luce concluded his commentary of Parker's two books by
saying,

> Full of historical research as these works undoubtedly are, the author
> himself teaches us, perhaps unwittingly, the best and most practical les-
> son, in affording by his own scholarship a brilliant illustration of the
> change from the 'rough and tough old commodore' to the higher culture of
> the modern school.[11]

One of the most important and most enduring features of the
Naval Institute has been its annual prize essay contest on a subject
of immediate importance to the service as a whole. First announced
in June 1878, the Naval Institute's board of control established the
topic of the competition as "Naval Education," an issue of great concern to the service at that time. At the very moment that the announcement was made, the Institute's secretary, Professor James
Soley, was in Europe, where he had been assigned to duty from April
through December 1878 in connection with the American educational exhibit at the international exposition in Paris. At the same
time, he had also been ordered to prepare an official report on foreign systems of naval education.

By the January 1879 essay competition deadline, ten officers had
submitted essays to the Naval Institute. To judge them, the Institute
appointed an independent panel of judges that included Charles W.
Eliot, the President of Harvard University, Rear Admiral Daniel Ammen, recently retired as Chief of the Bureau of Navigation, and En-
gineer-in-Chief W. H. Shock, U.S. Navy.[12] The panel selected as win-
ner the essay written by Lieutenant Commander Allan D. Brown,
who argued for abolishing the distinctions between line and engineer
officers in the service, while recommending a revised curriculum for
professional education. Strongly emphasizing the importance of
steam engineering for all officers, he included a seven-year program
of education and training for officers which included two years of history in the first and second years.

The judges awarded second honorable mention to Commander A.
T. Mahan, for his essay, which, as a result of the competition, became
his very first published work. Although he did not reveal any strong
passion in this early essay for historical study that presaged his later
career, he did reveal his predilection against overemphasizing the
study of scientific and technological subjects. If handling and fight-

ing a ship is a naval officer's business, Mahan argued, the cry to increase scientific and technical study is delusive. There are three
other areas in which the mental acquirements of a naval officer fall:
English, naval tactics, and foreign languages. "If I be asked, in my
own words, how the English studies or the acquirements of Foreign
Languages help a man handle and fight his ship, I will reply," he
said:

> A taste for these two pursuits tends to give breath of thought and loftiness
> of spirit; the English directly, the foreign languages by opening their lit-
> erature. The ennobling effect of such pursuits upon the sentiment and in-
> tellect of the seamen helps, I think, to develop a generous pride, a devo-
> tion to lofty ideals, which cannot fail to have a beneficial effect upon a
> profession which possesses, and its past history has illustrated in a high
> degree, many of the elements of heroism and grandeur. The necessarily
> materialistic character of mechanical science tends rather to narrowness
> and low ideals.[13]

In the following year, Soley's official report on foreign systems of
education appeared.[14] The Naval Institute explicitly encouraged
more historical work, when the Secretary of the Institute, Lieutenant Charles Belknap, reported in his annual report for 1880, "no
more fitting place can be found for monographs on Naval Biography
and Naval History than in a journal written and maintained by
naval officers. In fine, it is the desire of the executive committee to
make the proceedings of the Naval Institute, a complete record of the
workings of the naval mind."[15] Belknap had made some broad use of
historical argument that same year in his own prize-winning essay,
"The Naval Policy of the United States,"[16] but there was no immediate rush to answer his call.

Returning from his European trip, Soley continued his historical
work, publishing in 1881 his study of "The Naval Campaign of
1812."[17] In it, Soley showed that earlier American accounts of the
American naval actions in the war were too filled with "brag and
bluster"[18] and should not have been presented as victories won in the
face of heavy odds.[19] At the same time, he believed that the prevailing standard accounts published in England were inaccurate and
highly biased against Americans. In his attempt to correct the
record, Soley was careful to point out that American commanders followed a cautious system of tactics and, on several occasions chose,
for good reason, to avoid combat. In particular, Soley equally con-
demned the earlier work of the English naval historian, William
James, and the American writer, James Fenimore Cooper, whose

works in regard to the U.S. Navy,[20] he felt, were neither founded on careful research in the documents nor reached dispassionate conclusions. While looking to improved quality in naval history, Soley stressed the singular importance of the Navy in national defense, making a point that would soon become a major political issue that fueled the flames of inter-service rivalry with the Army.[21]

At this point, there was one competitor in the Naval Institute's Prize essay contest whose work presaged some of Mahan's "elements of sea power."[22] Writing on the theme set for 1882, "Our Merchant Marine: The causes of its decline and the means to be taken for its remedy," Ensign William G. David opened his discussion with several pages of historical discussion, broadly surveying Venetian, Spanish, Dutch, and British maritime history. From this, he concluded "the past teaches us that any state to be a great ocean carrier must have (1) a favorable relative geographical position, (2) the ability to run ships cheaply, (3) a strong navy. Other conditions, such as a great commerce, and rich colonies, are without doubt desirable, but they can not be called requisite."[23]

As this issue of the *Proceedings* was appearing in 1882, James Soley left the Naval Academy to take up duties as Librarian of the Navy Department, located in the State, War and Navy Building (now the Executive Office Building) next to the White House in Washington. The valuable seven thousand volume collection of books dated to 1800, but little had been done with them in recent years. Upon assuming his duties, Soley set about cataloging and organizing them, gathering rare materials from the various other bureau offices and conserving them, collecting prints, photographs, and manuscripts. At the same time, he initiated moves to establish a budget and policies for new book acquisitions in the general field of naval history and naval affairs, all in order to have a major research base for professional naval matters.[24] Working closely with the Chief of the Bureau of Navigation, Captain John G. Walker, Soley initiated the first serious attempt to establish an archive for the U.S. Navy, collecting and preserving its official records. His first priority was to gather the naval records relating to the Civil War. There was a great deal of difficulty in doing this. The official reports of fleet commanders and vessels acting singly were found on file in Navy Department offices, but the correspondence of commanders with their subordinates and with other commanders was missing. Missing too were the records of the Confederate States Navy, which many believed to have been destroyed when the building housing the military departments in Richmond burned at the end of the war.[25] In June 1884, Congress authorized the Navy to establish the Office of Library and War Records. Appointing Soley as its head, Congress also gave the Navy funds to hire a clerk and two copyists to begin to prepare the naval documents of the Civil War for publication. As material for serious professional study, Soley believed that they were particularly important for American naval officers. Undoubtedly influenced, if not written by Soley, an official report some years later declared:

> The Civil War is not only the first war in which naval operations on a great scale have been conducted since the introduction of steam, but it is the only war in which those modern appliances have been used which have revolutionized the art of naval warfare. The only operations of any magnitude with rams, with torpedoes, with ironclads, with rifled ordnance, and it might be added, with steam vessels, that can be studied by the professional man are those of the war of 1861-'65.[26]

Soley's interest in promoting the study of contemporary naval history was not limited to publishing documents. In late 1882, the New York book-publishing firm of Charles Scribner's Son commissioned a three-volume series entitled "The Navy in The Civil War". Soley wrote the first volume in the series, *The Blockade and the Cruisers,*[27] which also included a general discussion of events leading up to the war. Rear Admiral Daniel Ammen wrote the second volume, *The Atlantic Coast.*[28] Commander Mahan wrote the final volume: *The Gulf and Inland Waters.*[29] His first effort at writing a book, Mahan finished it in June 1883, after only six months of work. Together, these three volumes provided both the professional reader and the layman with a broad and readable narrative with which to understand the navy's contribution in the war. Equally important, although these books were quickly put together, they provided a soundly based, general guide for the documentary project, capturing original insights and new information from key participants, while also unearthing the locations of some new documentary material for the *Official Records* project.

In 1882–83, while Soley, Ammen, and Mahan were engaged in writing their naval history of the Civil War, another key figure, Commodore Stephen B. Luce, began to put into action his long maturing thoughts on advanced professional education for naval officers. Luce's experience of joint operations during the Civil War had led him to think that there were basic principles of warfare that were applicable to both military and naval affairs. Later, in 1877, he had the opportunity to visit the Artillery School at Fort Monroe, Hampton Roads in Virginia. Then under the command of Brigadier General Emory Upton, the school became a model institution for higher education in the American armed forces. Its curriculum merged reflections from American military experience in its Civil War with the new trends in military thought that were just reaching the United States in the years following Prussia's success in her wars with Austria and France.

Immediately after his visit, Luce sent a formal letter to the Secretary of the Navy recommending that the U.S. Navy establish a similar postgraduate course. "Extraordinary as it may appear," Luce wrote:

> the naval officer whose principal business is to fight is not taught the higher branches of his profession. The U.S. is not singular in this respect. The defect is common to nearly all navies and is an inheritance of a past and less enlightened age. But with the recent revolution in naval warfare comes a demand for a higher order in the conduct of naval operation.[30]

Luce believed that the technological revolution navies were currently experiencing and the great increase in the speed with which contemporary warfare was being conducted required that the modern officer must be both a strategist and a tactician. A commander in chief could no longer limit his focus to tactics and the simple handling of a fleet. The basic principles of strategy remain the same, on land or at sea, and they should be taught that way, Luce argued. For the Navy, "this difference, however, should undoubtedly obtain— that the rules of the Art [of Warfare] should be applied to naval operations, and that the course should be combined with the study of naval history—another branch which has been singularly neglected in our profession."[31]

Professor Soley's 1880 report on *Foreign Systems of Naval Education* had not resulted in the Navy Department taking any action to establish any form of higher education. Between 1877 and late 1882, Luce had been concentrating on improving training for naval apprentices. While serving as senior member of a board to investigate the navy yard establishments, Luce returned to his old idea. The Navy's recent acquisition of Coaster's Harbor Island in Narragansett Bay, Rhode Island, as a base for apprentice training happened also to have a stone building that could be, in Luce's opinion, the ideal location for a Naval College. In November 1882, Luce wrote to a friend, William C. Church editor of the *Army and Navy Journal,* asking him to publish an anonymous squib that, he hoped, could raise interest for the idea among younger officers "and thus start a controversy and—a BOOM."[32] At the same time, he wrote a formal letter to Secretary of the Navy W. E. Chandler, citing the examples of the Army's Artillery School at Fort Monroe and the Infantry and Cavalry Schools at Fort Leavenworth and recommending a naval school for "the higher branches of the naval profession: the science of war, naval tactics, military and naval history, international law, military and naval law, modern languages, and such elective branches as might be found desirable."[33]

A few months later, 4 April 1883, Luce was the key figure in establishing a Newport Branch of the Naval Institute. Meeting on Coaster's Harbor Island, Luce gave a talk entitled "War Schools,"[34] designed to raise discussion of the whole issue of higher education for naval officers. In his talk, Luce congratulated the Naval Institute on its accomplishments in leading naval officers to higher and broader fields of investigation. Praising these accomplishments as a healthy and hopeful sign that the Navy would systematize an effort for professional improvement, he turned to explain in detail the course of study at the U.S. Army's schools. In his descriptions, he explained the full range of interests from scientific investigations to historical study.

In concluding his remarks, he stressed the fact that a naval officer must prepare for the higher duties of his profession by study and reflection on the fundamental aspects of warfare as taught at the military schools. In doing this, Luce declared, a naval officer

> should be led into a philosophic study of naval history, that he may be enabled to examine the great battles of the world with the cold eye of professional criticism, and to recognize where the principles of the science have been illustrated, or where a disregard for the accepted rules of the art of war has lead to defeat and disaster.[35]

This approach to historical study, Luce concluded, "might well occupy the very best thoughts of the naval officer, for they belong to the very highest branch of his profession."[36]

Following on from this lecture and its publication in the Naval Institute *Proceedings,* Luce had the opportunity to raise the subject of a naval war school in private conversations with Secretary of the Navy Chandler and Admiral of the Navy David Dixon Porter. As a result of these conversations, Luce sent to Chandler a draft of a general order that he could sign immediately to establish such a school in March 1884. Not wishing to rush into the question quite so quickly, Chandler replied by ordering Luce to serve as president of a board to consider and to report on the subject. At Luce's suggestion, Chandler appointed as board members, Lieutenant Commander Caspar Goodrich and Captain William T. Sampson. In preparation for duty on the board, Luce asked each of the more junior officers to read both his "War Schools" article for the substance of the proposed curriculum and Professor Soley's report on *Foreign Systems of Naval Education,* with particular reference to the organization of the Royal Naval College at Greenwich.[37]

In the Board's report to the Secretary of the Navy, its members proposed a six-month long course of instruction which included the study of modern political and general naval history. Even while the board was meeting and before the institution was established, Luce began to cast around for possible instructors. He first approached Board member Caspar Goodrich to take up the position in naval history. When it proved impossible for him to do it, Luce considered others and eventually wrote to Alfred Mahan in July 1884, offering him the position.

It took six weeks for Luce's letter to reach Mahan, then in command of USS *Wachusett* on the Pacific coast of South America, and a full year from that point for the Navy Department to order Mahan to duty at the Naval War College. From the outset, Mahan felt himself unready to deal with the assignment without some detailed study: "I believe that I have the capacity and perhaps some inherited aptitude for the particular study;" Mahan replied, "but I do not on questioning myself find that I have the special accurate knowledge that I should think necessary. I fear you give me credit for knowing more than I do."[38] Mahan requested a full year of research and reading time at his home in New York City to prepare himself for his assignment in Newport at the Naval War College. It would not be until 26 August 1886 before Mahan arrived to take up his duties at the Naval War College. By that time, the Navy Department had ordered Luce back to sea as commander-in-chief of the North Atlantic Squadron. Mahan was ordered to assume the additional duties as College's second president, while also giving eighteen lectures on naval history and naval battles in his first year.[39] By this time, Admiral Luce had clearly framed the institutional and intellectual framework of the Naval War College, forming the context and foundation for Mahan to move forward and to develop them further through his own original insights into naval history.

When the Naval War College opened its doors to its first class in September 1885, the students and faculty listened to the inaugural lecture from Rear Admiral Daniel Ammen. In it Ammen, the distinguished Civil War officer and author, told the students to compare and contrast the needs of the service of that day with what had been needed fifty years before, when technological change was not so apparent. As he related some of his own experiences, his comparison showed both changes and similarities.[40] Another key figure in the development of historical studies, Professor James Soley came for several weeks from the Office of Library and Naval War Records in Washington to be the first civilian professor to lecture at the Naval War College. In the midst of part-time law studies at Columbian University (later renamed, The George Washington University), he gave a series of fourteen lectures in international law, lectures which clearly reflected an historical appreciation of his topic.

Leading up to and during the College's first academic session, Admiral Luce, himself, clearly laid out and widely disseminated his fundamental ideas on higher professional education for the Navy. First, he published an article in *The United Service*[41] and, then, gave two lectures at the College, both of which were later published and widely read in the Naval Institute *Proceedings*.[42] Luce sent his lectures on to Mahan, even before they were published, instructing him to read them carefully in preparation for coming to Newport.[43] When Luce returned to Newport with the North Atlantic Squadron in the autumn of 1886, during Mahan's first year as president, Luce again delivered slightly revised versions of the same lectures at the College.

In these lectures, Luce clearly demonstrated the intellectual forces which had motivated and defined his outlook in establishing the College. As such, they were also the initial foundation upon which Mahan built and which Luce laid out for historical studies. Luce brought with him a complex intellectual heritage. It derived from his wide reading and self-education and was profoundly influenced by American, British, and French professional and cultural literature.

Among the key influences on Luce's thinking was the work of the British historian, Thomas Buckle (1821–1862), author of *The History of Civilization in England* (1857–61). This book had a large impact on contemporary American historical thinking and was largely the source for the idea that human progress was regulated by immutable principles, similar to the scientific laws that reflected the physical universe. In particular, Buckle attempted to determine the nature of these laws through an inductive study of history,[44] an idea which Luce related to naval history and which he expected Mahan would carry through his work.

In addition to Buckle, another major influence on Luce were the ideas of Professor Friedrich Max Müller (1823–1900). Born in Dessau, Müller eventually went on to become Professor of Compar-

ative Philology at the University of Oxford. One of his most widely
read books, and one which Luce seems to have been well acquainted
with, was *Lectures on the Science of Language* (1862). Luce was particularly impressed with Müller's explanation of the comparative
method of investigation and his assertion that "all higher knowledge
is gained by comparison and rests on comparison."[45] Seeing other
contemporary nineteenth-century scholars using this method, such
as Louis Aggasiz in the field of natural science and Hutcheson
Macauley Posnett in comparative literature, Luce went on to apply
the idea to naval tactics and strategy. In this field, Luce believed that
intellectual progress for naval science should be based in the comparative examination of naval and military actions.

In finding and developing the basic principles and laws of naval
science through comparative methods, Luce believed that historical
study of naval operations was the most important area of focus. In
this, Luce directly accepted the ideas of Professor Sir John Knox
Laughton (1830–1915) of the Royal Navy, and, later, King's College,
London. Luce was well acquainted with Laughton's important article on "The Scientific Study of Naval History"[46] as well as some of his
other writings on naval tactics. On a visit to London, Luce had met
Laughton and they had been corresponding for many years. Later,
Luce introduced Mahan to Laughton's work and acted as the original mediator between them,[47] subsequently arranging for Laughton
to write one of the earliest reviews of Mahan's *Influence of Sea Power
Upon History, 1660–1783,* which appeared in the *Edinburgh Review.*

After 1890, Alfred Mahan's public success with his book on *The Influence of Sea Power Upon History,* and with the three subsequent
Sea Power books,[48] fundamentally altered and dominated the course
of naval historical studies in the United States and in other countries
for many years to come. Mahan's public success emphasized the public role of naval historians to a degree that was not present earlier.
The way in which Mahan and others writing on naval history after
1890 reacted to the initial foundation for the professional study of
naval history in the United States Navy and the degree to which they
worked within and beyond that context is a broad subject that deserves more careful analysis. It is a subject that goes beyond the
scope of this essay.[49]

In the years between the founding of the Naval Institute in 1873
and the publication of Mahan's first *Sea Power* book, the U.S. Navy
had a group of men who were promoting historical study as one of
the principal approaches for dealing with technological change.
Among the key figures, Daniel Ammen, Stephen Luce, Alfred Mahan,

and James Soley, each showed differing contributions to promoting historical study. Ammen was a widely respected and experienced figure of the Old Navy, who could attest to the value of new approaches to modern, technical warfare. Luce served as the incubator of new ideas and, as a senior flag officer, he had the connections and authority to translate effectively new ideas into bureaucratic change. Mahan was the original thinker who carried these initial ideas forward, modifying and popularizing them in the process. Soley provided the foundation work in promoting naval historical studies at the Naval Academy, in founding the Navy's archives, in publishing its official operational records and writing its first, well-researched naval histories for the public. Together, they shared a principal interest in studying history, using it in a critical and analytical way that would lead to improved professional understanding of the fundamental characteristics, uses, and limitations of naval power. For these early innovators in the American practice of naval history, the historical approach was a means to establish and to define the role and function of a navy, at a time when technological imperatives were leading others to disregard these fundamental factors and to think only of technological improvement for the sake of technological improvement alone. In its initial conception, historical study within the U.S. Navy was designed primarily for professional understanding of the theory and practice of naval warfare and, to a lesser degree, to explain the role of the Navy to the public.

NOTES

1. This essay was originally prepared for publication in German; it appeared as "Geschichte und technologisher Wandel: Das Studium der Marinegeschichte in der US-Marine 1873-1890" in *Seemacht und Seestrategie im 19. und 20. Jahrhundert,* Im Auftrag des Militärgeschichtlichen Forschungsamt herausgegeben von Jörg Duppler (Hamburg, Berlin, Bonn: E. S. Mittler & Sohn, 1999), pp. 105–120.
2. For recent comment on this connection, see Patrick J. Geary, *Medieval Germany in America.* Annual Lecture series, no. 8. (Washington: German Historical Institute, 1996), pp. 7–8 and Ernst Shulin "German and American Historiography in the Nineteenth and Twentieth Centuries" in Hartmut Lehmann and James J. Sheehan, eds., *An Interrupted Past* (New York; Cambridge University Press, 1991), pp. 11–13.
3. On the early history of the U.S. Naval Institute, see Lawrence Carroll Allin, *The United States Naval Institute Intellectual Forum of the New Navy: 1873–1889.* Ph.D. Thesis, University of Maine, Orono, 1976. (Manhattan, Kansas: Military Historian/Aerospace Historian, 1978).

See also, Benjamin L. Apt, "Mahan's Forebears: The Debate over Maritime Strategy, 1868–1883," *Naval War College Review,* L(Summer 1997), pp. 86–111.

4. See S. de Christofaro, "The Naval Lyceum," U.S. Naval Institute *Proceedings,* 78(1951), pp. 868–873.

5. See the biographical sketch, A[lan] W[estcott], "Soley, James Russell (Oct. 1, 1850—Sept. 11, 1911)" in Dumas Malone, ed., *Dictionary of American Biography,* (New York: Charles Scribner's Sons, 1935), volume XVII, p. 392, and references in Mark Shulman, *Navalism and the Emergence of American Sea Power, 1882–1893.* (Annapolis: Naval Institute Press, 1995).

6. Kenneth J. Hagan and Mark R. Shulman, "Putting Naval Before History," *Naval History,* 9(1995), pp. 24–29.

7. Hagan and Shulman, p. 25.

8. Foxhall Parker, *Squadron Tactics Under Steam* (1864) and *Fleet Tactics Under Steam* (1870).

9. Stephen B. Luce, "Modern Navies," *Army and Navy Journal,* XIV(12 August 1876), p. 7; (19 August 1876), p. 26; (2 September 1876), p. 62; (9 September 1876), p. 71; (23 September 1876), p. 110; (7 October 1876), p. 135.

10. Stephen B. Luce, "Fleets of the World," *The Record of the U.S. Naval Institute* [later, *Proceedings*], 3(1877), p. 23.

11. Ibid.

12. The report of the judges, the prize essay, the first and the second honorable mention prize essays, and the discussion on the essays at a subsequent meeting of the Naval Institute on "Naval Education" were published together in *Proceedings,* 5(1879), pp. 304–405.

13. Ibid., p. 352.

14. Professor James Russell Soley, USN, *Report on Foreign Systems of Naval Education.* 46th Congress, 2nd Session. Senate. Executive Document 52.

15. Lieutenant Charles Belknap, "Annual Report of the Secretary, U.S. Naval Institute," VII (1881), pp. xxi.

16. Charles Belknap, "The Naval Policy of the United States," Naval Institute *Proceedings,* U.S. Naval Institute *Proceedings,* VI (1880), pp. 357–391.

17. J. Russell Soley, "The Naval Campaign of 1812," U.S. Naval Institute *Proceedings,* 7(1881), pp. 297–324. See the comment on this work in Theodore Roosevelt, *The Naval War of 1812.* (New York, 1882; reprinted Annapolis, MD: Naval Institute Press, 1987), Appendix C.

18. Ibid., p. 306.

19. Ibid., p. 304.

20. James Fenimore Cooper, *The History of the Navy of the United States.* (New York, 1839). William James, *Naval History of Great Britain, From the declaration of War by France in February 1793, to the Accession of George IV.* (London, 1826).

21. Mark Russell Shulman, "The Influence of History Upon Sea Power: The Navalist Reinterpretation of the War of 1812," *The Journal of Military History,* 56(1992), pp. 196–198.

22. Compare with A.T. Mahan, *Influence of Sea Power Upon History, 1660–1783.* (Boston, 1890), chapter 1.

23. Ensign W. G. David, "Our Merchant Marine: The causes of its decline and the means to be taken for its remedy", U.S. Naval Institute *Proceedings,* VIII (1882), pp. 151–186, quote from p. 157. William Glenn David (-1934) was appointed to the Naval Academy from New York and graduated third in the class of 1877. He resigned his commission in August 1884, but served again briefly during the Spanish-American War, May-September 1898.

24. *Report of the Secretary of the Navy, 1882.* (Washington: Government Printing Office, 1883), volume 1, p. 107; *Report of the Secretary of the Navy, 1883.* (Washington: Government Printing Office, 1884), volume 1, p. 244. See also, William James Morgan and Joye L. Leonhart, *A History of the Dudley Knox Center for Naval History.* (Washington: Dudley Knox Center for Naval History, 1981), pp. 3–5.

25. In fact, a large number were saved and many have since been published. See Raimondo Luraghi, *A History of the Confederate Navy.* (Annapolis, MD: Naval Institute Press, 1996), pp. 459–482.

26. *Annual Report of the Secretary of the Navy, 1888.* Quoted in Richard Rush and Robert H. Woods, compilers, "Introduction, *Official Records of the Union and Confederate Navies in the War of the Rebellion.* Series I, Volume 1. (Washington: Government Printing Office, 1894), p. viii.

27. James R. Soley, *The Blockade and the Cruisers.* The Navy in the Civil War, volume 1. (New York: Charles Scribner's & Sons, 1883).

28. Daniel Ammen, *The Atlantic Coast.* The Navy in the Civil War, volume 2. (New York: Charles Scribner's & Sons, 1883).

29. Alfred T. Mahan, *The Gulf and Inland Waters.* The Navy in the Civil War, volume 3. (New York: Charles Scribner's & Sons, 1883).

30. Captain S. B. Luce to Secretary of the Navy R. W. Thompson, 8 August 1877. Printed in Albert Gleaves, *The Life and Letters of Rear Admiral Stephen B. Luce: Founder of the Naval War College.* (New York: G. P. Putnam's Sons, 1925), pp. 168–170.

31. Ibid., p. 169.

32. Library of Congress, William C. Church Papers: Luce to Church, 2 November 1882. Quoted in Hattendorf, *et.al., Sailors and Scholars: The Centennial History of the Naval War College.* (Newport, RI: Naval War College Press, 1984), p. 17.

33. Luce to Secretary of the Navy, 6 November 1882. Quoted in Ibid.

34. Stephen B. Luce, "War Schools," U.S. Naval Institute *Proceedings,* IX(1883), pp. 633–657.

35. Ibid., p. 656.

36. Ibid.

37. Hattendorf, et al., *Sailors and Scholars,* pp. 17–18.

38. Robert Seager II and Doris Maguire, eds., *Letters and Papers of Alfred Thayer Mahan.* (Annapolis: Naval Institute Press, 1975), volume 1, p. 57: Mahan to Luce, 4 September 1884.

39. "The War College," *Newport Daily News,* 20 November 1886.

40. Naval War College Archives. Record Group 16, Box 1, file 2: Convocation Addresses: Daniel Ammen, 1885.

41. Stephen B. Luce, "The United States Naval War College," *The United Service,* XII(1885), 79–90.

42. Stephen B. Luce, "On the Study of Naval Warfare as a Science," Naval Institute *Proceedings,* XII(1886), pp. 527–546, and "On the Study of

Naval History (Grand Tactics),", XIII (1887), pp. 175–201. Both have been reprinted and annotated in John D. Hayes and John B. Hattendorf, eds. *The Writings of Stephen B. Luce*. (Newport, RI: Naval War College Press, 1975), pp.45–97.

43. R. Seager and D. Maguire, *Letters and Papers:* Mahan to Luce, 7 April 1886.

44. W. S. Holt, "The Idea of Scientific History in America," *Journal of the History of Ideas*, I(1940), pp. 352–362.

45. Luce quoting Müller. Reprinted in Hayes and Hattendorf, p. 56.

46. J. K. Laughton, "The Scientific Study of Naval History," *Journal of the Royal United Services Institution*. XVIII(1875), pp. 508–527. On Laughton and Luce, see Andrew Lambert *The Foundations of Naval History: John Knox Laughton, the Royal Navy and the Historical Profession*. (London: Chatham Publishers, 1998), pp. 30, 46, 69, 71, 72, 121–2, 126, 140, 231–2.

47. R. Seager and D. Maguire, *Letters and Papers,* volume 1, p. 629: 24 April 1886; volume II, p. 29: Mahan to Luce, 27 October 1890.

48. A. T. Mahan, *The Influence of Sea Power Upon the French Revolution and Empire, 1793–1812*. (Boston, 1892); *The Life of Nelson: The Embodiment of The Sea Power of Great Britain*. (Boston, 1897); *Sea Power In Its Relation to the War of 1812*. (Boston, 1905); to which one might also add, Mahan's contribution to William Laird Clowes, *The Royal Navy*. (London, 1897), volume 3, revised and reprinted as *Major Operations of the Navies in the War of American Independence*. (Boston, 1913).

49. For an examination of the navalist literature outside the Navy, see the works by Mark Russell Shulman, cited above in footnotes 4 and 18.

2

Luce's Idea of the Naval War College

A century ago, Rear Admiral Stephen B. Luce wrote a number of strong articles to explain his views on naval education and to define the purpose and character of the Naval War College. He clearly stated his ideas in a manner which was readily understood by the men of his time.[1] While Luce's ideas are acknowledged by naval historians as the basic impetus behind the War College, his expression of them may seem out of date today, immersed as we are in a quite different intellectual climate and a changed navy. Scattered through the range of his articles, Luce's ideas require interpretation and explanation in terms of modern conditions, if they are to be understood more widely and acted upon effectively.

Luce's central and basic idea about the Naval War College is his belief that a naval officer does something more than just perform a job. He carries out his work as a highly educated, trained specialist who operates within a clearly defined area, with established procedures and ethical standards; further, he uses a well-developed body of theoretical knowledge relating to his field, and has a strong feeling of group identity and shared knowledge with others who perform similar work. In short, a naval officer is a professional, who, like a doctor, a lawyer, or an educator, should have both advanced education and recognized credentials which certify his achievement toward mastering the progressive levels of understanding for his chosen career.[2]

In developing this idea, Luce was aware, as we are today, that a Navy requires many different types of expertise and many different specialists. Ordnance, astronomy, engineering, languages, oceanography, chemistry, and physics suggest the range of skills which are used. The Navy comprises a cross section of modern industry and shares these skills with the nation as a whole, while the universities and colleges of the land cater effectively for education in these shared fields.

Rear Admiral Stephen B. Luce
(*Naval War College Museum*)

The one area which was missing in the range of education and training, both necessary and available for a naval officer in Luce's time, was education in the highest elements which made the Navy a distinctive profession. There was no place where a naval officer could study a unique, specialized body of theoretical knowledge which differentiated his occupation from others.[3]

From time immemorial, naval officers had learned their profession on the quarter deck and through experience of war itself. In the eighteenth and early nineteenth centuries, naval academies were established as a means of preparing young officers to take up their first, practical duties in the sea service. These important schools laid the foundation upon which professional knowledge could be built, but since they concentrated on the basics they could, through necessity, provide only a glimpse and the occasional display of the erudition and knowledge needed for a master of the art.[4]

In the 1880s, the United States had just entered the period when rapid technological change had a continuing and direct effect on the character of its Navy. The development of steam and electrical engineering, the screw propeller, the rifled gun and the study of interior and exterior ballistics, together with the use of iron and then steel, provided a new fabric for sea power, spurring rapid and then continued change in ship design, engineering, armor and weapons.[5] These developments rapidly altered the physical character of navies while, at the same time, demanding new types of special expertise. It was the beginning of the present situation in American naval history, in which new equipment becomes obsolete almost as soon as it is put to sea.

If one can say that there is an American way of warfare, it can be found in American reliance on technology and the application of new inventions to practical ends. At the end of the twentieth century, we are only just beginning to understand the ways in which technology affects our behavior, in addition to increasing our capabilities. Yet, at these very early stages, Luce and his perceptive colleagues could see that technological developments were drawing naval officers away from studying the central purpose of the naval profession and into subservient areas of knowledge.[6] A century later, one can see even more clearly that technology has a momentum and logic of its own. When pursued only for the sake of its own development, it may not necessarily provide results which are immediately useful or even properly applicable to the naval profession.[7]

Although naval professionals have nothing to gain from restricting technological development, surely their central interest should be in technologies which have a direct usefulness to their profession. For this reason, Luce believed that the most important education a naval officer received was that which developed his understanding of the purpose, character, use, and nature of navies. Moreover, those who strive to reach the highest levels of the naval profession should make professional thought, rather than a technical or academic subject, their principal intellectual concern[8] Most important, if naval officers made the highest theoretical aspects of their own profession the object of their primary intellectual interest, they would tend to refine their practical efforts in a way which would focus their work and improve results. Luce believed that if naval officers were educated in theory which pertained to the naval profession after they had gained professional experience, but before they took up the highest naval responsibilities, then the Navy could reverse the process by which technology tends to create its own environment and its own set of conditions. The objective, as Luce saw it, is to ensure that naval officers, not their equipment, are the controlling factors in war at sea.

For Luce, the highest aspect of the naval profession was the study of the art of warfare. This, he believed, was properly divided into several branches. In descending order of importance, there were statesmanship, strategy, tactics, and logistics. The study of diplomacy, or statesmanship in its relationship to war, was so important to Luce's concept of education that he believed it needed, "to attain any degree of proficiency, such an amount of careful reading as to leave little leisure for extra professional studies."[9]

During the past one hundred years, students of naval and military affairs have emphasized that there is a key relationship between armed force and statesmanship in times of peace, as well as in war. Although the ultimate purpose of armed force is to be capable of successful operations in war, the relationship of armed force to the broadest aspects of national security cannot be ignored. Within the naval officer's concern in the area of statesmanship lies the thought of armed force as a peacetime deterrent and as an extension of national policy short of war. Moreover, such broad-gauged thinking also requires an appreciation of the limitations of armed force as well as the stresses, liabilities, and dangers which accompany it.

Below the all-important study of statesmanship and its relationship to armed force, Luce placed strategy, the comprehensive direction of power to control situations and areas to attain broad objectives; and tactics, the employment of specific forces and weapons to attain strategic objectives. These, in turn are followed by logistics, the creation and sustained support of weapons and forces to be tactically employed to attain strategic objectives.[10]

These are the fundamental areas which together comprise the elements of professional naval thought. In order for naval officers to command effectively, all these areas need to be in harmony and even to reflect broader aspects of national interests, values, and economics. This, Luce believed, can be done only when a commander has first been given an education at a college dedicated to the broadest perspectives in professional thought.

The Naval War College was Luce's answer to this need. He dedicated it to improving the quality of analysis among naval officers and to providing a sound basis for decisions in command, but its tangible product was designed to be a core of line officers who can function effectively in command and in staff management positions with a clear understanding of their profession.

When Luce first thought about a naval war college, there were neither books nor studies about the theoretical character of a navy. One of his main objectives in establishing the college was to have its faculty create the philosophical and theoretical literature which related the basic elements of warfare to the naval profession. The essence of this body of literature could then guide practical application.

In order to create the fundamental underpinning for professional thought, Luce turned to the study of naval history as a key source. He believed that from historical knowledge, officers could begin to generalize about the nature of navies and, thereby, provide the groundwork for professional thought. But, he warned, if this study is to be profitable, one has to be able to identify historical material which can be analyzed and reasoned upon with advantage. Here Luce admonished officers to think broadly and to range freely over the centuries, noting particularly that Thucydides, and other ancient writers, had much valuable insight even for our technologically advanced culture.[11]

In order to stimulate a profitable examination of naval history, Luce proposed that it be undertaken by those with an intimate knowledge of current practice and the broadest theoretical aspects of the art of warfare. Simultaneously, Luce suggested using the conclusions drawn from army history in a comparative way, as a guide to formulating naval theory. The basic ideas in military studies are often directly applicable to the art of naval warfare, Luce believed, but for them to be understood and characterized properly, they needed to be reformulated and modified after a detailed, thorough investigation of a wide ranging study of naval actions.

From a study of detailed cases in naval affairs, new naval generalization can be established through inductive thinking. After generalizations are established through inductive reasoning; that is, by proceeding from particulars to generalization, the process can then be reversed, through deductive reasoning, by applying the generalizations as a guide to the particulars in the present and the future.[12]

When Luce contemplated this method of approach, he was applying some of the advanced thinking of his own time. Today, when we read his own words, they seem out of date. Certainly, historians who were then only just establishing themselves within universities, have now altered their view of generalization. Few today would follow the thinking of Luce's time that historical generalization provided laws of human action, just as scientific investigation created laws of the physical universe. Despite this change in thinking, Luce's fundamental idea remains sound, but needs restatement in modern terms. The study of history contains many wide-ranging facets which go beyond that which directly concerns the naval profession. Yet, Luce's basic point, that the process of historical understanding is a key element in the development of naval thought, remains valid. Even today, many people still do not understand that responsible government officials, as well as naval officers, can learn more by analyzing the process of historical developments, rather than by concentrating on memorization of historical facts. Historical study fosters the ability to evaluate evidence and to formulate views based on that evidence. Its very essence is a warning against dogmatism on the one hand, and oversimplification, on the other. Luce understood that historical study trains the naval officer to apply concepts to problem areas, and that it teaches him how to evaluate a mass of facts. In this process, Luce stressed the need to develop the skills of analysis and criticism about human situations when there is no "right answer" and where one must reach conclusions based on informed judgment, in circumstances involving chance and affected by differing values and diverse understanding.

The naval officer who has studied history knows that similar events which occur in different historical settings may well lead to different results. He has had practice in careful and in-depth examinations of individual cases, followed by a comparison of them, so that he easily distinguished between unique and general aspects, while avoiding an all inclusive dogma which stands above human action. In dealing with the relationship between the unique and the general, Luce's emphasis on historical study was intended to provide naval officers with an insight into the process of human activity, illuminating its nature by underscoring the importance of multiplicity where many look for singleness of purpose, stressing the complex interrelationships which specialization tends to overlook, and not least, reminding them of the human condition.[13]

When applied to a thorough study of naval warfare, Luce wanted historical study to enlarge the area of an individual naval officer's experience by teaching him about the broad interaction between circumstances in their effect upon men, ships and fleets, as well as about the nature, character, purpose, and limitations of navies. The lessons are not straightforward, didactic precepts nor codified instructions for action, but a sound knowledge of the history of any naval situation or problem illuminates its nature and thereby assists in making present decisions. Historical knowledge solidifies our understanding of the past as well as the present, deepening our understanding for dealing with the future.[14]

Increasingly, in our time, knowledge has become specialized and fragmented. Both modern naval officers and academics suffer from the same disease that afflicts society in general. But the experience of World War II emphasized that the intellectual needs of the Navy lie across many disciplines. Certainly, the highest level of the naval profession involves the insights of an entire range of social scientists, including sociologists, international lawyers, economists, and political scientists. In addition, historical analysis of naval problems can benefit from the insights produced in these disciplines while still preserving its own characteristics in inquiring how navies work.

Historical study can be a corrective to the narrowness of specialization and, therefore, is particularly valuable in focusing professional thought in the armed forces. Its application to navies involves a complex process by which one must first create a description of what occurred, then analyze it, compare and contrast it to fundamental theoretical ideas, examine it in relation to other similar experiences, and refine the fundamental theory with the generalizations that emerge. In the end, one may use the generalizations as guidelines in operational planning, establishing planning procedures and taking action.[15]

It was this process which Luce set as the work of Alfred Thayer Mahan and the basis for creating a theoretical literature for the naval profession. Mahan's work succeeded in formulating some basic concepts.[16] Sir Julian Corbett, later, modified and refined them on the basis of his own historical research to establish the classic statement of traditional naval theory in his *Some Principles of Maritime Strategy.*[17]

Instead of continuing the process that Luce conceived, most naval writers since Mahan and Corbett have been content to be critics, rather than creators, of theory. In recent years, Mahan has become the whipping boy. He has been properly criticized for the inaccuracy of his research, the limitations of his conclusions, the narrowness of his historical focus, and his failure to understand technology.[18] The critics have made plain the cracks in Mahan's theory, but they have failed to agree on how to proceed in theoretical work. Following Luce, I believe that the Navy's most urgent intellectual need is the further development of sound theory. In the twenty-first century, there would be no more appropriate way to affirm the college's dedication to its original purpose—and to honor Luce—than to emphasize theoretical study, using modern views of historical research and generalization as tools to assist in the development of professional naval thought.

Once perceptions from actual experience have been established, then they can provide a useful basis from which to speculate on what can be possible, predict what might be probable, and judge what is desirable. The process must be a continuing one that tries to relate growing experience to improving perception; it is not a search for simple rules, but a quest for understanding.

Luce closely linked to the broad understanding of statesmanship, policy, strategy, and the broad function of navies, the need to investigate and to improve understanding in the additional elements which comprise the highest professional thought: tactics and logistics. As strategy is interwoven in the great issues of state that guide it, so an understanding of strategy is essential to and intertwined within logistics and tactics. Luce emphasized that none of the elements can be entirely separated or omitted if an officer is to be educated in his profession.[19] The concept of comprehensive control of armed force blends these areas, showing the various elements as gradients of a single concept which forms the essence of the best professional thinking in high command.

Both tactics and logistics are practical matters which involve the direct employment of equipment. Whatever its conception, any military operation is a combination of the two, tactics being the immediate employment of forces to attain strategic objects, and logistics, the provision of the physical resources for tactics to employ. Although practical in nature and dependent upon new technology, both tactics and logistics require a theoretical underpinning that provides a basic understanding upon which action can be taken. Far from being an unnecessary abstraction for practical naval officers, an understanding of theory in these areas sheds light on problems and provides guidelines for responsible executives who must attempt to make optimum decisions faced with chance, a variety of possible solutions, and limited resources.

Although theory is an important consideration that should be carefully developed at the Naval War College, Luce believed that the link between theory and practice is a key element deserving equal attention. "War," he wrote, "is no time for experimentation."[21] "That 'war is the best school of war,' is one of those dangerous and delusive sayings that contain just enough truth to secure currency: he who waits for war to learn his profession often acquired his knowledge at a frightful cost of human life."[22]

For this reason, Luce promoted naval war-gaming and encouraged the experimental use by the fleet of tactics and logistics concepts developed by the Naval War College. Peacetime is the proper time to explore and to experiment with new methods and concepts in order to be prepared when war comes.

In order to cultivate the highest aspects of the naval profession, Luce believed that the college should remain exclusively an educational institution. Its purpose should be to provide a place for extended and in-depth study. Its focus should be to prepare officers to help create policy, develop strategy, and to use tactics and logistics when in command.

After the British Naval War Course was established on the model already existing in Newport, Julian Corbett pointed out the difference between an institution that educated officers and one that was involved in creating actual policy. "The proper college will assist everyone and interfere with none." Corbett wrote, "It will be doing no more than providing a laboratory where the lost art of war can be recovered and where officers destined for high command can learn it. There, too, all that is best in naval thought will be gathered in fresh from the sea and spun into threads which the Admiralty and the Committee of Defence can handle with confidence and weave into the fabric of our policy."[24] Agreeing with Corbett, Luce emphasized his remark that "No attempt should be made to turn the war course into anything like an authoritative General Staff."[25]

The work of the Naval War College is educational, not executive. It should form no part of the working structure of the Navy Department, Luce believed, but it should supply the insights and educate the officers who command and direct it. "The college devotes itself to the study of naval history, naval strategy and tactics, the law of nations, and academic discussions of all conceivable types of naval problems of war." In short, Luce believed, "it supplies the alumni from which to select officers competent to command our fleets as well as those able to solve correctly the actual problems with which a naval general staff is bound to be confronted."[26]

The idea of the Naval War College creates the vision of an academic and educational establishment that is the home of theory, and the center of scholarship, original research, and in-depth thinking for the naval profession in the United States. The history of the college's first century demonstrates that Luce's vision cannot be realized without taking into account the factors that characterize an educational institution while at the same time recognizing the practical character of professional work in the Navy.

First, the college needs effective teachers who are highly qualified, able to apply their expertise to the naval profession and true teaching scholars who can honestly say of themselves what Loup de Ferrières wrote in the ninth century to Charles the Bald: "I desire to teach what I have learned and am daily learning."[27]

Second, it requires that the students who attend be those who have among them the future leaders and responsible officials who will hold the highest positions, and therefore, will exercise their knowledge of the highest aspects of professional thought.

Third, as a profession, the Navy must recognize the differences in character of mind between the teaching scholar and the decisive leader. Those with a deeply contemplative and reflective character of mind rarely have the decisive characteristics and immediate insights that denote the best combat leaders. The college exists, not merely to produce the reflective mind, but primarily to promote an interaction and an exchange of thought between reflective and decisive minds.

Professionals should be aware that decisive thinkers, if given a choice, might well prefer to ignore reflective thought. They ignore it at their peril, abandoning knowledge for guesswork. Therefore, the idea of the Naval War College is to provide education in the highest aspects of thinking about navies and naval warfare to the small and selected group of professionals who will one day be the decision makers in high command and confront directly naval problems in the context of national and international considerations.

NOTES

This is a revised version of an essay that first appeared in *The Naval War College Review*, XXXVII (September-October 1984), pp. 35–43.

1. A bibliography of Luce's writings, along with commentary and excerpts,

may be found in John D. Hayes and John B. Hattendorf, eds., *The Writings of Stephen B. Luce* (Newport, RI: Naval War College Press, 1975).

2. This idea is an assumption which runs throughout Luce's thought from his earliest writing (see ibid., p. 162) and it is particularly expanded upon in *ibid*, chapter III.

3. U.S. Congress. Senate. *Letter from the Secretary of the Navy . . . reporting the steps taken by him to establish an advanced course of instruction of naval officers at Coasters Harbor Island, Rhode Island*. 48th Congress, 2d Session. Senate Executive Doc. No. 68. "Report of the Board on a Post Graduate Course," pp. 2–6.

4. Remarks of Commodore Luce in *Inauguration of the Perry Statue, September 10, AD. 1885* (Newport, RI: John P. Sanborn, 1885), pp. 42–43.

5. Bernard Brodie, *Sea Power in the Machine Age* (New York: Greenwood Press Reprint, 1969), pp. 149–167.

6. S. B. Luce, "On The Study of Naval Warfare as a Science," reprinted in Hayes and Hattendorf, eds., pp. 65–66.

7. Elting E. Morison, *Men, Machines and Modern Times* (Cambridge, MA: MIT Press, 1966), p. 211.

8. S. B. Luce, "An Address . . . 1903," reprinted in Hayes and Hattendorf, eds., pp. 38–40.

9. Luce was directly following Jomini. See Luce, "United States Naval War College," *The United Service*, v. xii, no. 1, January 1885, pp. 80–81. The list is abbreviated here. Luce saw Jomini's two forms of tactics merging and the study of fortification interesting only as an object of naval attack.

10. Ibid. The modern and precise definitions of strategy, tactics and logistics are from Henry E. Eccles, *Military Concepts and Philosophy* (New Brunswick, NJ: Rutgers University Press, 1965), p. 69.

11. S.B. Luce, "Tactics and History," in Hayes and Hattendorf, pp. 74–75.

12. S. B. Luce, "On The Strategy of Naval Warfare as a Science," in Hayes and Hattendorf, p. 53.

13. E. H. Carr, *What is History*. (New York: Knopf, 1962), pp. 79–84; G. R. Elton, *The Practice of History*. (Sydney: Sydney University Press, 1967), pp. 38–39.

14. Ibid., pp. 48–49.

15. Eccles, pp. 21–28.

16. Don Schurman, "Mahan Revisited," *Kungl. Krigsvetenskapsakademiens Bihäfte-Militärhistorisk Tidskrift* (1982), pp. 29–43; reprinted in John B. Hattendorf and Robert S. Jordan, eds., *Maritime Strategy and the Balance of Power: Britain and America in the 20th Century*. (London: Macmillan, 1989), pp. 95–109.

17. On Corbett, see D. M. Schurman, *Julian S. Corbett 1854–1922; Historian of British Maritime Policy from Drake to Jellicoe*. (London: Royal Historical Society, 1981) and *The Education of a Navy: The Development of British Naval Strategic Thought, 1867–1914*. (Malabar, FL: Krieger, 1984), reprint of 1965 edition.

18. For a more detailed discussion of these points, see my "Some Concepts in American Naval Strategic Thought, 1940–1970," in Joyce Bartell, ed., *The Yankee Mariner and Sea Power* (Los Angeles: University of Southern California, 1982), pp. 93–107; and "American Thinking on Naval

Strategy, 1945–80" in Geoffrey Till, *Maritime Strategy in the Nuclear Age* (London: Macmillan, 1982), pp. 58–68. For a sound analysis and a corrective to earlier criticisms, see John T. Sumida, *Inventing Grand Strategy and Teaching Command: the Classic Works of Sea Power Reconsidered.* (Baltimore: Johns Hopkins University Press, 1997).

19. Eccles, p. 45.
20. Ibid, pp. 26–27.
21. S. B. Luce, "The U. S. Naval War College," U. S. Naval Institute *Proceedings*, v. xxxvi, no. 3, 1910, p. 685. See also Hayes and Hattendorf, pp. 230–232.
22. S. B. Luce, "An Address . . . 1903," Hayes and Hattendorf, p. 40.
23. Luce, "The U. S. Naval War College," pp. 687, 694.
24. Ibid, p. 687, Quoting Corbett, "Naval War Course II," *The Times* [London], Tuesday, 5 June 1906, p. 6.
25. Ibid.
26. S. B. Luce, "On The True Relations between the Department of the Navy and the Naval War College," U. S. Naval Institute *Proceedings*, v. xxxvii, no. 1., 1911, p. 86.
27. Quoted in Jacques Barzun, *The American University: How it Runs, Where it is Going* (New York: Harper & Row, 1968), p. 252.

3

Technology and Strategy: Professional Thought in the U.S. Navy, 1898–1917

Strategy has always accompanied war. At first, it was as primitive as man and his weapons were primitive. As social and political organization became more complex, war became more complex. Strategy became an art, necessary not only in war, but also in peace as preparedness. Developing this theme, a speaker at the 1912 summer conference at the Naval War College continued:

> The prototype of the Navy, the solitary savage in his canoe, has developed into the modern Dreadnought with its intricate machinery of offense and defense, its thousand souls of diversified specialties, all of which to assure success must be instantly obedient to the mandate of a mastermind.[1]

Although this imagery may have brought wry smiles to his audience, his remarks touched on a central issue of professional naval thought in the years between the Spanish-American War in 1898 and America's entry into World War I in 1917. The revolution in ship construction, ordnance, and engineering had begun more than half a century before, but the navy, as a profession, did not immediately come to grips with the new technology. Its impact was deeper than merely providing weapons of greater destructive force or developing new tactics for armored steamships. At the turn of the century, many naval officers began to understand that the developments in technology profoundly affected such broad areas as command and control, personnel training, leadership and morale, as well as the more obvious affairs of research and development, logistics, and tactics. Naval strategy became more than just the physical distribution of fleets. It became the art of comprehensively directing seaborne power. For those who practiced it, naval strategy more so than ever

29

Lieutenant William McCarty Little

William McCarty Little (1845 -1915) was the most important figure in refining the technique of war-gaming so that it could be used as an effective tool to examine and to apply the capabilities of rapidly changing naval technology to modern warfare. Arriving at the Naval War College shortly after its founding, he served as a volunteer member of staff for many years, before being promoted to captain by special act of Congress in recognition for his work in war-gaming. (*Naval War College Museum*) before involved an understanding of the capabilities and limitations of men as well as the machines with which they worked and lived.

Since the 1880s, the navy had advanced dramatically in technology. "The most obvious thing about a Navy," wrote Rear Admiral Bradley Fiske, "is its materiel: the ponderous battleship, the picturesque destroyers, the submarines, the intricate engines of multifarious types, the signal flags, the torpedo that costs $8,000, the gun that can sink a ship 10 miles away."[2] These were the things that had caught the public eye and had engrossed the attention of naval men. Many of the organizational, administrative, and personnel changes in this period were related to the problem of controlling and utilizing this new equipment.

The appearance of HMS *Dreadnought* in 1906 relegated all previous battleships to a secondary position. As an archetype of later battleships, the new British ship had a main battery twice as powerful as any other ship in the world. During trials the turbine engines steamed 7,000 miles at an average of 17.5 knots and sustained a maximum speed of 21.6 knots, far better than the performance of the ordinary reciprocating engines found in other navies. *Dreadnought* featured a number of epochal innovations that were soon imitated by navies around the world.[3] The battleship became the best-known and most controversial innovation in the period. In addition, both Britain and Germany developed the battle cruiser: a high speed, heavy-gunned ship, built to outrun battleships and outgun conventional cruisers. Destroyers evolved from the light torpedo boats of the 1880s and 1890s. Pioneered by the Germans, the battle cruisers maintained their original function for torpedo attacks, but other armament was added. The destroyer soon became an important part of the fleet as an adjunct to the scouting line and a protection for capital ships.

Within the United States Navy, technological events moved rapidly to keep pace with foreign developments. The nation gained the reputation in 1898 as a naval power to be reckoned with. The navy's first submarine, USS *Holland,* commissioned in 1900, was soon followed by five more, slightly larger boats. Seeing their usefulness, European nations began to order them for their own navies. By 1914 there were forty-nine submarines in the United States fleet. The gasoline engine designed for the original *Holland*-type boats was replaced with the German Diesel engine developed in 1909. At about the same time, a perfected gyrocompass made possible sustained underwater navigation and more accurate torpedoes.

Eugene Ely made successful landings and takeoffs from improvised light decks on navy ships in 1910 and 1911. Also in 1911, Glenn Curtiss developed and built the first seaplane. The following year Lieutenant T. G. Ellyson flew a plane launched from a compressed-air catapult, and Rear Admiral Fiske patented the first design for a torpedo plane. The first scouting flight by an airplane in a fleet exercise was made by Lieutenant J. H. Towers in 1913, and in 1914 aircraft were actually used by the navy for scouting and spotting in combat at Vera Cruz, Mexico.[4]

Naval guns grew from the 13-inch and 8-inch guns of *Kearsarge* and *Kentucky* to the *Maryland's* 16-inch, 45-caliber guns. Fleet target practice was initiated on the Asiatic station in 1902, and significant procedural changes were made in fire control. Armor-piercing projectiles, improved propellants, and "carbonized" armor were introduced and were widely used.[5]

Other important events occurred in the field of communications. The first official radio message from a United States naval vessel was transmitted from USS *New York* in 1900. By 1904, twenty-four navy ships had been equipped with radio, and nineteen naval radio stations were established ashore. In May 1916 the commanding officer of the *New Hampshire,* while at sea off the Virginia capes, held a two-way conversation with the Secretary of the Navy in Washington and the commandant of the Mare Island Naval Ship Yard in California by using both radio and land lines. Later in the same year, a chain of high-powered naval radio stations was completed with the commissioning of the station at Cavite, Philippine Islands.[6]

In other areas, the scope of the new naval technology ranged from water tube boilers, liquid oil fuel, electric logs, research into a cure for tuberculosis in naval hospitals, and a new compass card divided by degrees as well as points, to the feat of towing the floating dry-dock *Dewey* 13,089 miles from the East Coast to Olongapo in the Philippine Islands.

Although the development of the navy's new technology was obvious and dramatic, its ramifications were more extensive than many observers suspected. Technology continued the rapid development which had begun in the early years of the nineteenth century; the intellectual basis to control such complicated mechanisms was only beginning and it had wide implications in terms of finance to pay for it, industrial procurement to obtain it, bureaucratic organization to control it, education to develop it and to manage it, and politics to support it.

During the last three decades of the nineteenth century much thought was given to the implications of the new technology. In England, the Colomb brothers began to examine the broad issue of what a navy should be designed to do. As early as 1874, John Knox Laughton proposed a "scientific" study of naval history for these purposes.[7] In America, Rear Admiral Stephen B. Luce founded the Naval War College in 1884 for the systematic study of warfare. Luce gathered around him a small, but promising, group of officers. They included French Chadwick, Bradley Fiske, Albert Gleaves, Caspar Goodrich, William McCarty Little, Alfred Thayer Mahan, William L. Rodgers, William S. Sims, Yates Stirling, and Henry C. Taylor. In addition to naval officers, he drew the historian and lawyer J. R. Soley, the army's Tasker Bliss, and also the young Theodore Roosevelt. Those who gathered at Newport in the 1880s and 1890s were an unusual and relatively unknown group of intellectuals and visionaries, whose views were not widely shared in the naval service or in the nation.[8] Nevertheless, by the end of the Spanish-American War, one of the officers, Captain Mahan, had already achieved international renown. In a series of ten books published between 1890 and 1900, Mahan elaborated upon the concept of seapower as a basis for national policy. Using historical examples, he awakened a large audience to the general purposes and capabilities of naval power in its broadest context. Within the naval service, Luce, Mahan, and their disciples at the Naval War College took a wide view of the profession and avoided a narrow, technical outlook. Mahan focused professional thought on the basic purpose and nature of a naval force. Unlike Great Britain's Sir Julian Corbett, he did not work out a carefully structured theoretical statement of maritime strategy. Instead, Mahan emphasized the necessary intellectual focus, while helping to create a receptive audience for the men who developed and exercised strategic control of the sea.

Because he was the most prominent student of naval power in America, Mahan's work is particularly important in relation to the naval developments of his time. Today, the reader of his works is struck by the fact that, even in an age of dramatic technological change, Mahan could seemingly ignore the complex problems of ordnance, engineering, and communications, all of which absorbed his fellow officers. This was precisely the point of the matter. As he wrote in the Introductory to *The Influence of Sea Power Upon History, 1660–1783,*

It is not therefore a vain expectation, as many think, to look for useful lessons in the history of sailing ships as well as in that of galleys. Both have their points of resemblance to the modern ship; both have also points of essential difference, which make it impossible to cite their experiences or models of action as tactical *precedents* to be followed. But a precedent is different from and less valuable than a principle. The former may be originally faulty, or may cease to apply through change of circumstances; the latter has its root in the essential nature of things . . . . Conditions and weapons change; but to cope with the one or successfully wield the others, respect must be had to these constant teachings of history in the tactics of the battlefield, or in those wider operations of war which are comprised under the name of strategy.[9]

Although acknowledging that rapid developments in technology had vastly increased the scope and rapidity of naval operations, Mahan believed that, no matter what equipment was employed in fighting war at sea, certain basic principles had remained changeless over the ages. These included the function and objectives of a navy in war, the establishment of supply depots and the maintenance of communications between advanced depots and home bases. These principles included consideration of the value of commerce destruction, as well as the necessity of controlling positions through which all traffic must pass. In Mahan's mind, changing technologies in different areas canceled out one another and left only basic issues with which naval men must always deal. Warfare is more an art than a science, and the principles and abstract general maxims which Mahan developed were not mathematical formulae invariably applied as "rules of war." As an "art," the principles of warfare, no matter how sound and generally held, are always subject to qualification when applied in specific situations. Mahan commented in a lecture at the Naval War College,

> I must allude to the vast variety of motives, conditions of its age or surroundings which impel Art to its creation. For War these are found reproduced in the variety and changes of weapons from age to age, in the varying character of regions which are the scenes of war, in the temper and organization of the armies . . . .[10]

The man who developed the naval war game in the United States, Captain William McCarty Little, expressed the same concept when he bluntly, but ungrammatically, told War College students, "a principle apples when it applies and it don't apply when it don't apply."[11] Both men were underscoring the point that abstract strategic or tactical principles cannot be applied in real life. Application requires good judgment, which is based on an intuitive understanding of the spirit of the abstract understanding.

Technological knowledge was an essential requirement in the formulation and exercise of naval strategy. An understanding of the tools employed was as important to the tactician engrossed in their use as it was to the strategist concerned primarily with goals and principles. McCarty Little expressed the close relationship between tactics and strategy when he noted,

> . . . a fight without a mission, is action without purpose, muscle without brain. And this suggests what to some may seem a somewhat novel view of the difference between strategy and tactics, that is, the "inner" or fundamental distinction: strategy, war from the point of view or the one who has an object to attain, i.e., the planner; and the tactics, war from the point of view of the executor; or something like the distinction between the architect and the builder, the playwright and the actor.
>
> While the distinction between strategy and tactics is clear, yet when it comes down the line between the two, we find that they encroach somewhat upon each other's domain, each tending to overlap. This alone is sufficient to show that their movement of approach is from opposite sides. Strategy is the thought seeking its means of execution, and tactics is the means to carry out the desires of the thought.[12]

To his way of thinking, tactics was the servant of strategy. No tactical problem had meaning without a strategic setting. No strategy could develop successfully without reference to tactics.

The United States Navy was slow in creating an effective organization for implementing such ideas. Up to the 1880s, no centralized planning or coordinating activity existed, other than the Office of the Secretary of the Navy. The chiefs of bureaus under the secretary tended to quarrel rather than to cooperate. They were characteristically more interested in their specialties than in efficient, central direction during wartime. The temporary changes in organization instituted by Secretary Gideon Welles and Assistant Secretary Gustavus Fox during the Civil War were quickly abandoned at the end of the war. Not until the 1880s was a successful attempt made to coordinate the activities of the bureau chiefs. The Office of Naval Intelligence was established in 1882 under the Bureau of Navigation and charged with the mission of gathering information in peace and war. Seven years later the Bureau of Navigation was given the additional responsibility of supervising the fleet.[13]

This increasing general awareness of the need for planning and coordination coincided with the establishment of the Naval War College and Admiral Luce's desire to "raise naval warfare from the empirical stage to the dignity of a naval science."[14] Luce's own writings on naval administration and organization stressed the need for an organization which could effectively control the navy in rapidly changing wartime conditions. Captain Henry C. Taylor, while president of the Naval War College from 1893 to 1896, instituted studies of the German General Staff, whose strategic planning had brought about the defeat of France in 1870. These studies resulted in recommendations to combine the functions of intelligence gathering, war planning, and general staff duties into a single coordinating body. These recommendations found little support in Washington. Prior to the Spanish-American War, no effective coordinating body or war planning activity existed. In 1891, Mahan prepared "plans of operations in case of war with Great Britain" in conjunction with Secretary of the Navy Benjamin Tracy's "secret strategy board."[15] Five years later, Lieutenant William W. Kimball in the Office of Naval Intelligence prepared a general war plan for war against Spain. At nearly the same time, an ad hoc board appointed by the Secretary of the Navy also developed plans for war with Spain. Throughout this period, students at the Naval War College continued to deal with the problem of war with Spain in their solutions to the annual problems.[16] Although these plans reflected some of Mahan's theories on blockades, supply routes, and Kimball's plan even foreshadowed Admiral Dewey's victory at Manila, none of them were backed by a comprehensive doctrine and supported by an administrative organization which would allow effective implementation. Nevertheless, these plans are interesting examples of the growing trend to see warfare on a broader scale. They are the earliest attempts to apply theory to practice.

Secretary of the Navy John D. Long established the General Board of the Navy on 13 March 1900. Conceived by Rear Admiral Henry C. Taylor as an organization which would eventually evolve into a general staff of the German type, the board consisted of the Admiral of the Navy, who acted as president, the chief of the Bureau of Navigation, the chief intelligence officer and his principal assistant, the President of the Naval War College and his principal assistant, and three other officers above the grade of lieutenant commander. The board's purpose was to "ensure the efficient preparation of the fleet in case of war and for the naval defense of the coast."[17] Specifically, Secretary Long wrote Admiral of the Navy George Dewey, the General Board was to devise plans that would employ United States naval forces to the best advantage, to organize in peace a proper defense for the coast, including the effective use of the naval reserve and merchant marine, and to develop an effective cooperation with the army. The development of detailed war plans, the selection of these sites, and the observation of foreign naval activities in relation to American planning and capabilities were among the important functions of the new board.[18] Throughout this period the General Board continued to provide guidance in war plans and recommendations for the growth of the American fleet. With the assistance of the Naval War College, the General Board was capable of broad reflection on the purposes, capabilities, and disposition of the United States Navy.[19]

Following the initial impetus of men such as Luce and Henry C. Taylor, committees such as the Moody Board and the Swift Board advised the Secretary of the Navy to reorganize the service. A tentative staff organization was established in 1909. It was strengthened in 1915 with the creation of the Office of the Chief of Naval Operations. With a centralized organization directly related to the General Board, the Secretary of the Navy, backed by responsible professional advisors, could ensure a continuity of policy, while still maintaining firm civilian control.[20]

Significant patterns developed at the Naval War College which paralleled the developments in naval organization in the Navy Department. In addition to the better-known reforming leadership taken by Admirals Luce and Taylor, which complemented the publicist and theoretical writings of Alfred Thayer Mahan, there were two additional factors: war-gaming and the development of a philosophy for the military planning process.

A medically disabled naval lieutenant, William McCarty Little, had long been associated with Luce. Living in Newport, Rhode Island, he lectured at the Naval War College on a volunteer basis, advocating the implementation of Sir Philip Colomb's concept of a naval war game which had been introduced into the Royal Navy in 1878. Neither Colomb nor McCarty Little were originators of the naval war-gaming concept. As long as 1790, the Scottish merchant and etcher, John Clerk of Eldin, had publicly issued his famous work *An Essay on Naval Tactics.* In developing what became the standard text for tacticians in both the United States and Great Britain, Clerk used small ship models that he constantly carried in his pocket, "every table furnishing searoom" for his experiments. War games had been used much more extensively in the army and called the "applicatory system." In this, both the British and American armies had been influenced by the German *Kriegspiel,* when used in conjunction with "rides." In such military exercises, the troops were imaginary, but by using the physical contours of the land around them, students learned the relationship between the map and the terrain, planning tools and an environment.[22]

The applicatory system consisted of three major parts: the estimate of the situation, the writing of orders, and the evaluation of the plan through war-gaming or exercises. The "estimate" concept provided a structure to analyze a strategic problem. First, the participants considered the mission of an operation with the position and strength of both sides. Then, they developed the concept for a plan of action. The second step was writing orders to carry out the plan of action. It led to the establishment of a doctrine by which orders could be effectively passed from one level of command to another. This doctrine permitted the elimination of nonessential details from the orders of higher level officers to more junior officers. The result was maximum tactical initiative. In effect, this approach challenged the traditional demand for complete and absolute obedience from subordinates. It recognized the impracticality and inefficiency of attempting to control large and complex forces directly from headquarters. This doctrine increased the responsibility of subordinate officers, by relying upon them as rational and capable men to further the known intentions of their superiors.[23] As Colonel G. F. R. Henderson put it in his 1905 work, *The Science of War:*

> . . . no order was to be blindly obeyed unless the superior who issued it was actually present, and therefore cognizant of the situation at the time that it was received. If this was not the case, the recipient was to use his own judgment, and act as he believed his superior would have directed him to do had he been aware of how matters stood . . . [24]

The basic ideas of the applicatory system came directly from the German General Staff. In the United States, the U.S. Army was the first to study them in detail. In 1906, Major Eban Swift published his *Field Orders, Messages and Reports,* and in the same year, Major C. H. Barth published his translation of General Griepenkerl's *Letters on Applied Tactics.* Following these pioneering works, Captain Roger S. Fitch wrote *Estimating Tactical Situations and Composing Orders* in 1908.[25] These three works had a great influence at the Naval War College, where they were often cited as sources in lectures and studies by naval officers.

When Captain William L. Rodgers became president of the Naval War College, the course of study was reformed to include these new ideas derived from the army. The "estimate of the situation, the order form," and war-gaming all intermeshed in a new direction for the navy. As one contemporary noted, "a great white light broke on the service, especially in 1912 when the War College first laid emphasis upon the importance of doctrine."[26]

Shortly after the innovation of these new concepts at the Naval War College, a dramatic change was seen in the war plans produced by the General Board. Previously war plans had consisted of charts and collected data on specific areas of strategic importance. In 1904 Army Chief of Staff Lieutenant General A. R. Chaffee proposed to the Joint Board that the army's General Staff and the navy's General Board prepare a series of war plans for joint use. The "Color Plans" developed from this proposal: *Blue* indicated the United States, while *Orange* meant Japan; *Black,* Germany; *Green,* Mexico; *Red,* Great Britain; *Indigo,* occupation of Iceland; *Tan,* intervention in Cuba; *Violet,* intervention in China; *Gray,* occupation of the Azores; *Brown,* maintenance of internal security in the Philippines, et cetera.

For the most part these plans were little more than abstract exercises and had little relation to international affairs and actual events.[27] Even so, both the Orange plan for war with Japan and the Black plan for war with Germany were frequently revised and kept current with the international scene. By 1913, the basic principles of this type of planning were being used in both the army and navy. The revised versions of the Orange and Black plans increasingly reflected the concepts of the "estimate of the situation," and the "order form." At both war colleges, war-gaming had become more important as a testing device for these national strategic plans, as well as remaining an educational tool for officers. By these means, the services were developing broader conceptions of military and naval power. At the same time, they were creating methods by which these conceptions could be used to establish flexible control of military and naval forces. The use of the applicatory system and the naval war game, together with a growing understanding of the political and economic implications of warfare, helped officers to grasp the intellectual concepts pertaining to their profession.

Understanding a problem within its own context in the relation to other influences affecting it is not a concept unique to the systems analysts of today. It is an old idea in military and naval affairs. In 1916 Bradley Fiske wrote that

> . . . a machine is in its essence an aggregation of many parts, so related to each other and to some external influence, that the parts can be made to operate together to attain some desired end or object. From this point of view, which the author believes to be correct, a baseball team is a machine, so is a political party, so is any organization.[28]

Strategy is concerned with all-encompassing direction. Its work is threefold: to design the "machine," to prepare it for war, and to direct its operations in battle. At the very outset, strategy must take account of all relevant aspects.[29]

Fiske described it this way:

> . . . we must admit that as surely as the mind and brain and nerves and the material elements of man must be designed and made to work in harmony together; obedient to the controlling mind, and sympathetically indoctrinated with the wish and the will to do as that mind desires.[30]

Such a notion was not unique to Fiske. McCarty Little in 1913 had even used the same imagery when he discussed the philosophy of the order form before the summer conference at the Naval War College. "We have noted that the order form was a complete plan of action. The different agencies are the different parts of a machine, and for the machine to work satisfactorily, every piece must do its part. Solidarity is the essential quality."[31]

Inevitably differences of approach developed. One approach was to emphasize the objective and then to tailor the means to fit it. The other approach sought to tailor the objective to the means available.[32] These two approaches to war planning were reflected in a criticism of the Black plan made by a staff officer in the Navy Department. In an undated memorandum signed only "McK." the officer protested that "this is not a Plan but an Estimate of the Situation upon which a Plan would be based. A preliminary study leading to a decision but not a Plan to carry out a decision."[33]

This divergence between those who claimed precedence for the overall concept and those who stressed the technical capabilities of the available resources was recognized early by Commander Vogelgesang in the earliest exposition of the "estimate of the situation" in its naval context. He warned that the two points of view were complementary, not opposing. "Knowing the Art is common ground for us all," he wrote, "knowing our tools is our especial science; but each with his own tools may become better able to apply them to the tasks cooperatively, if each is well grounded in this knowledge of the Art."[34]

The blending of "art" and "science" in war planning can be seen in a variety of ways. The work of historians such as Mahan and Corbett had its own special place. The impact of their theoretical writings was more than esoteric, for they had a direct, if limited, influence. The 1911 Orange plan, for example, contains a discussion of the possibility of a Japanese invasion of the American mainland. To support their contention that such an invasion would obviously be doomed to failure, the strategists cited "an established military maxim, that it is the weaker form of war to project the campaign into the theater where your enemy is strongest." A full understanding of military power "would seem to brand the conception (of invasion) as too fantastic to be seriously contemplated by Orange." The writers of the Orange plan felt that it was the historian, Sir Julian Corbett, who, in his *England and the Seven Years War,* had stated the principle most adequately. It was to him that they turned as an authority on this point.[35]

The degree to which the strategist was also believed to be a technician is difficult to gauge. As many naval leaders pointed out, the typical naval officer, totally involved in the technical details of his profession, failed to see the broader issues.[36] The opposite was also true: the strategists could not forget the tools which would be used. In lectures at the Naval War College, Mahan noted:

> War is a tremendous game of skill and chance combined. The artist, to recur to my definition, may form the noblest conception, his skill may be of the highest order, and the refractory and uncertain character of his materials may defy all his efforts, a chance slip of his instrument may destroy the work of months.[37]
>
> The painter and the sculptor, likewise in realizing their conceptions, must submit to the conditions-imposed by the materials with which they work. These are the same for the veriest dauber as they are for a Raphael; they are stamped and branded by that stolid immutability of which Science boasts in the realm of Nature.[38]

The technical considerations with which strategists became concerned involved nearly every aspect of naval life. At the establishment of the General Board in 1900, Henry Taylor had carefully pointed out to Secretary Long and Admiral Dewey the dangers of becoming too engrossed in technical problems.[39] Yet, as other commentators have noted, technical considerations were necessary for the success of the broadest strategic outlook.

Dewey protested in 1909 to the secretary that a balance between designers and users had not been achieved. "The General Board believes it to be its duty," he wrote, "to invite the Department's attention to the fact that there is not . . . anything that insures reference of the details of military features as they are developed in the elaboration of the designs and in the building of the ships to seagoing officers for their comment and recommendations." In order to ensure that all fleet ships were well built, Dewey recommended that details affecting the military nature and operational capability of the navy ship be submitted to a board of experienced men for review. Dewey was especially concerned with the development of ordnance, fire control, armor, torpedo installations, ammunition stowage, and anything else which affected the command and control of the ship such as steering gear, compartmentation, accesses, interior communication, coaling plans, ash handling, and small boat stowage.[40]

With any growing technology the problem of invention, research, and development naturally arises as a related function. However, in an international situation in which technology is an object of competition, the development of new machines becomes an area of prime concern. Admiral Sir John Fisher, while commander in chief of the British Mediterranean fleet in 1901, noted that the design of fighting ships *"must follow the mode of fighting instead of fighting being subsidiary to and dependent on the design of the ship."*[41] In other words, Fisher believed that the technology of ship design must be attuned to and directed by military requirements. The United States Navy, however, was not yet organized adequately to handle this sort of fundamental direction. The General Board recommended as late as 1909 that the details of ship design be submitted to a board of officers for precisely the reason Fisher gave. Research and development related to strategic concepts began rather slowly. For example, in 1903 the General Board discovered that no satisfactory method had been devised for mountings in undeveloped areas. The board's only recourse was to request that the Bureau of Ordnance be "invited" to investigate the problem and have the marine battalion in Annapolis make a practical test of prototype equipment.[42] A few months later the General Board reviewed the problem of obtaining proper optical glass for telescopic gunsights. Dewey lamented to the secretary:

> One of the serious difficulties in this matter is the lack of expert knowledge on the part of instrument makers in this country; the best of them being very hazy as to the actual power of telescopes which they supply. Quite recently a large contractor in buying a lot of telescopes for special purposes received one of them having a power of 4 1/2 diameters when the contract called for 8, and the maker, one of our best opticians, seemed entirely unable to understand the criticism or to locate the cause of failure. It seems a fact that we must go to Berlin for expert opinions about this topic.[43]

The result of this organizational deficiency was that the United States did not have a research and development program which would be guided by the necessities of warfare. In 1908 for example, Commander A. L. Key, a former naval aide to President Theodore

Roosevelt, reviewed the construction progress of the battleship *North Dakota* in the Fore River Shipbuilding Company at Quincy, Massachusetts. Horrified by the design defects, he wrote the Secretary of the Navy, pointing out the flaws he observed and recommended specific changes. At the instigation of the President's naval aide, Commander William S. Sims, President Roosevelt directed the Secretary of the Navy to convene an investigating committee composed of the General Board and the students and staff of the Naval War College to consider Commander Key's remarks. The final report of the "Battleship Conference" covered many problems. Two of the subcommittees specifically noted in their deliberations that American designs should never be allowed to fall behind the progress of other nations.[44] Only the president of the Naval War College, Rear Admiral Caspar Goodrich, expressed disappointment in the United States Navy's record in making an original contribution to battleship design:

> The evidences are unmistakable of the manner in which this design was reached. Its object is as plain as a pike-staff-to be just a little better than some particular foreign design—to see John Bull, for example, and go him one better. . . They preferred to ignore the plain teachings of naval history, they built along narrow and preconceived lines, they failed to deal with their task in a broad and enlightened manner.[45]

In 1907, Bradley Fiske charged that the Navy's "ultraconservatism" retarded the adoption of new mechanisms. Although much of his discontent arose from the fact that many of his own inventions had not been accepted by the service, it was not unique. William S. Sims had experienced much of the same difficulty in the United States Navy as had Sir Percy Scott in the Royal Navy in his efforts to improve naval gunnery. Fiske's remedy was to establish an "experimental department" which would have the duty of improving old appliances, inventing new ones, and examining the schemes of others. He pointed out that such an organization had been used successfully by large business corporations. Such a department, as Fiske conceived it, would be a function of a general staff that directed the Navy as a whole and guided the various components of the service.[46] As the Secretary of the Navy's Aid for Operations, Fiske several times urged establishment of a board of invention and development.

Shortly after Fiske left this post, Secretary of the Navy Josephus Daniels established the Naval Consulting Board.[47] Daniels wrote to Thomas Edison on July 7, 1915, to ask him to head the new board, the first duty of which would be to consider countermeasures for that "new and terrible engine of warfare," the submarine. "One of the imperative needs of the Navy in my judgment," Daniels wrote.

> is machinery and facilities for utilizing the natural inventive genius of Americans to meet the new conditions of warfare as shown abroad . . . . With a department composed of the keenest and most inventive minds that we can gather together, and with your own wonderful brain to aid us, the United States will be able to meet this new danger with new devices that will assure peace to their country by their effectiveness.[48]

To an enthusiast such as Fiske, the application of new mechanisms was the Navy's greatest glory. Writing in retirement at the Naval War College in 1916, Fiske exulted, "The Navy more than any other thing, will give opportunity for mechanisms and to mechanism. Far beyond any possible imagination of today, it will become the highest expression of the Genius of Mechanism and the embodiment of its spirit."[49]

Not all naval thinkers were willing wholeheartedly to accept Fiske's implicit assumption that technology per se was the ultimate measure of a navy. A controversial individual to begin with, Fiske's penetrating and often unorthodox observations were not always accepted. However, as Aid for Operations (1913–16) and president of the United States Naval Institute (1911–1923), his ideas were widely circulated and debated.

Some members of the General Board believed that naval technology should not be measured in absolute terms, but rather in terms relative to other nations. The executive committee of the General Board concluded in a confidential memorandum on 6 August 1915 that "the phenomenal and unprecedented progress in naval development made by other powers, therefore, subordinates consideration of the ultimate strength of the United States fleet as recommended by the General Board to that of relative strength." The committee felt that this conclusion was clearly illustrated by the fact that Germany's great merchant marine and powerful navy had been driven from the seas because it was "inadequate" to cope with the navy of Great Britain.[50] Only the German submarine had demonstrated the potential to operate effectively, which meant the technology of the British opponent was less capable of meeting that particular challenge. The point of relativity of naval technology was dramatically underlined in May of 1916 when a numerically superior British force faced a highly efficient German battle fleet at Jutland and fought to a draw.[51] There was little difference in the technological development of the two fleets. Neither side had an advantage. If the balance were tipped either way, it would be because of other factors. Professional thinkers of the day began to realize that when opposing technologies had similar capabilities, the difference between victory and defeat lay with men, not machinery. Success would rest on the coordinated ability to manage an enterprise, to control specific weapons, and to develop a strategy.

Recognizing the importance of management and logistics in this problem, one officer detected in 1916 a change in the relative importance of the factors involved in war, a change not entirely realized by those vitally concerned with the problem. Before, it had seemed a question of generalship, and numbers of men that determined victory, but "now surely it is no disparagement to the skill of the strategist, to the vigilance of the tactician, or to the valor of the soldier in the ranks, to say that victory will rest with that side which can maintain the combat more vigorously and for the longest time."[52] Although this option might not have met with total professional agreement among those who advocated moral courage as the determining factor in war, few would deny that the problem of logistics was crucial to the issue.

Commander Vogelgesang attempted to impress upon his lecture audience at the Naval War College the practical importance of this aspect of warfare. Logistics, he noted, had no direct relationship to tactics, but it is the dynamic force behind strategy. He felt that it was somewhat trite even to point out that "Materiel is soulless; it cannot be pushed to an endurance beyond that which the mind of man designs for it." Yet, Vogelgesang really wondered if naval men fully realized the obvious. Is the navy "prepared to say that the *being able to* is harmonized with the wishing . . .?[53] The most artful strategy, supported by the highest order of valor and courage, but lacking a sound logistic understanding, "is only a phantom that lures *disaster, defeat,* and *disgrace.*"[54]

Others noted that modern warfare had developed into a national and an industrial undertaking rather than an undertaking of a specialized group of military experts. Warfare in this new era involved the organization of every detail and drew upon every resource in the nation.[55] Much of this organization would be in the realm of logistics and preparedness. Preparedness for war, the ability to mobilize military forces and equipment quickly and then to support them, is crucial to survival. The nation which has used peacetime to equip her fleet and to ensure its readiness as an offensive weapon at the outbreak of war has added materially to its chances for success, particularly if the enemy has been negligent.

Building a carefully balanced fleet demanded understanding a potential enemy's fleet and its capabilities. While navalists and their associates directed their attention to the international battleship-building rivalry, the strategists who planned for war knew very well the need for a strong and balanced naval force. Paymaster General T. J. Cowie noted that

> . . . the auxiliaries of a fleet can truly be said to be as necessary to the battleship and cruisers, as Logistics is essential to Strategy. Embracing as they do, the colliers, fuel ships, transports, despatch boats, scouts, aeroplanes, etc. they represent the arteries that furnish and renew the speed an battling power of the fighting ship.[56]

Admiral Dewey wrote the Secretary of the Navy in 1910 that America's international commitments, her obligation to uphold the policies of the Monroe Doctrine, the Open Door, and the neutrality of the Panama Canal required an efficient and balanced fighting fleet with "fighting adjuncts" as well as auxiliaries. "The battleship fleet without its destroyers, repair ships, scouts, transports, supply ships, colliers, hospital ships, etc. is not complete, for it cannot keep to the sea continuously unless it carries its base with it and is accompanied by the train necessary for this purpose."[57] In the eyes of the General Board, strategists needed to understand the use and function of each type of ship and how these complemented one another. They needed to visualize the actual operational requirements of each type and to comprehend the technical basis of employment and support.

As naval officers dealt with the problem of coordinating technologies and bringing them into a complementary balance, they discovered that technology had intruded into the very execution of command. Communication by electromagnetic means threatened the efficiency of the command structure and the relations between men. In a letter to William McCarty Little, Captain William L. Rodgers noted that "modern improvements in communications, typewriter, telegraph, telephones and radio all tend to centralization. We cannot dispense with any of them and yet . . . both responsibility and unity of control and plan tend to disappear."[58] Rodgers went on to note that the Secretary of the Navy *thinks* he is in control since he is continually signing orders, but real control remained in the hands of an unknown clerk or junior officer who prepared the correspondence. With the delegation of this function to unrelated subordinates, each dealing with his own specialty, there appeared a loss of overall planning and a disorganized product. "No one is in charge of putting a given task through as a whole; and so we have the familiar order, counter order, disorder."[59] Rodgers was not alone in detecting the dangers of centralization and the detrimental aspects of long-range communication. Secretary of the Navy Daniels himself noted that

> . . . on proposal there is another gesture about a system of communications which is capable of such large expansion, and that is that the temptation will be ever present to rely on such a system for momentary communication or orders instead of the development of doctrine and the reduction of the need for any system to a minimum.[60]

There were times, of course, when direct communication was useful and effective. Admiral Dewey remarked that "there is a psychological effect of direct personal communication between responsible officers which it is desirable to have the facilities for carrying out in terms of great emergency."[61] Few observers recognized the paradox of rapid, long-distance communication weakening the command structure. The novelty and advantages of direct communication with the Navy Department and high-level commanders overshadowed a serious threat to efficiency. The vision of concentrating all decision-making power in a single person or office foreshadowed a faltering, inefficient executive and an uncontrollable bureaucracy. The unregulated centralization of command would withhold initiative from subordinates, thus denying the full exercise of judgment, expertise, foresight, and response in every echelon. Although not designed specifically to handle the problem of modern communications, the concept of the "order form" could be easily adapted to maintain a decentralized organization and still take advantage of the rapid exchange of information.

The Tampico incident illustrated another aspect of the problem in command relations. At that time in 1914 Tampico, Mexico, was in the throes of a revolution. On 9 April a whaleboat with an officer and eight sailors was sent ashore from the USS *Dolphin* to purchase gasoline for Rear Admiral Henry T. Mayo's barge. While at the wharf, local guardsmen seized these uniformed men. When the local military commander learned of the arrest of American sailors, he immediately released them and sent a personal apology to Admiral Mayo on board the *Dolphin*. Admiral Mayo, however, considered that the seizure be punished, and that the American flag be raised prominently and saluted with twenty-one guns. In addition, the Mexicans' reply was to be received and the salute fired within twenty-four hours. In Washington, President Wilson seized upon the admiral's ultimatum as an affair of national honor. The failure of the Mexicans to comply led Wilson to ask Congress for authority to use armed force against the Mexican forces under General Huerta. A minor incident had become a *casus belli*.[62] President Wilson and his cabinet completely supported

Admiral Mayo's initiative. Although there was no question of improper conduct on Mayo's part, such incidents clearly raised the question of the level at which a particular type of decision should be made. Mayo had assumed responsibility for an area of policy making that properly lay at the highest level of government. As a result of this incident and because modern communications were available, Secretary of the Navy Daniels changed article 1648 of Naval Regulations on 15 September 1916 to require a commander to communicate first with the Navy Department before issuing an ultimatum, "except in extreme cases where such action is necessary to save life."[63]

The dangers of overcentralization were matched by the other extreme of ineffectiveness resulting from fragmented control. "From all this we are rescued," wrote Captain William L. Rodgers, "if we appreciate the methods of problem solving, estimate of the situation and order writing."[64] In other words, to avoid the extremes which the new communications technology thrust upon the Navy, it was necessary to understand the kinds of decisions which should be made at each level of command and to issue orders and commands on that basis. For the system to be effective, each level of command must display both an obedience to the direction it received and, at the same time, be able to exercise initiative within its own realm of responsibility. Good organization required a clear apprehension of a subordinate's area of discretion and the superior's sphere of action. As William McCarty Little put it,

> the expert is probably superior to the employer in ability to exercise the expert's art; but the employer does not feel in any way humiliated by employing him to exercise his skill . . . therefore there should be no squeamishness in giving to a subordinate all the latitude in execution which his capacity and the requirements of the problem permit.[65]

The problem arising from technology could be controlled through human leadership and discretion. It was a problem of men, not of machines.

The importance of men over machines was emphasized when Professor Hugo Munsterberg lambasted "the world of newspaper readers" who were hypnotized by the naval machinery of the day. He told the students of the Naval War College in 1912,

> . . . in the midst of this unquestioning enthusiasm for the material development of the physical progress of the battleship, you stand for the conviction that it is after all the man, man's thought, and man's emotion, and man's will which is of decisive importance. You do not submit to the pop-

ular prejudice which expects success only from the marvels learned of steel and power and electricity. You have learned too well the great lesson of history which demonstrates that throughout four thousand years the victory has been with the ships who were fit to win. It is not true that fate has been with heavy guns; it has been with great minds. The knowledge of the ships and the armament becomes a living power only if it is embedded in the understanding of strategies and grand tactics, and they would be empty if the psyche of man were not acknowledged as their centre.[66]

Recognizing that even in a highly technological era it is human understanding that links together all the elements of a navy, professionals went further to ask what kind of individual man was required for this work. They dealt with the issues of proper training and the type of knowledge naval men should have.

In a highly technical society it seems natural that there would be a tendency for specialization among individuals. Even so, the General Board and other officers in the Navy continually rejected recommendations for further specialization. It was evident to the General Board in 1909 that the Navy would continue to need a large number of officers who were thoroughly trained and highly specialized in engineering to perform the duties of inspection and design. They agreed that the operation and care of machinery is different from its design and construction. Such tasks might be successfully performed by men not qualified as designers. The military advantage of having all the duties involving the management and control of the ships and their preparation for battle performed by one body of officers, the board felt, was so great that it should be regarded as fundamental and thus, should not be changed.[67] The General Board strongly believed that the determination of naval policy, fleet composition, and the strategic and tactical qualities of ships should always lie in the hands of the "military seagoing man." Control of the military features in warships could never be achieved if the seagoing man simply accepted what shore-based experts supplied him. Additionally, the board strongly believed that shipboard engineer officers should not be specialists in the single field of engineering. The advantage of discipline, military efficiency, and professional development was far greater if well-rounded officers of the line fulfilled this function.

Characteristically, Bradley Fiske wrote,

. . . he who sails the sea and braves its tempests, must be in heart and character a sailor—and yet he who fights the scientific war-craft of the present day cannot be merely a sailor like him of the olden kind, but must be what the New York Times, a few years ago, laughingly declared to be a combination quite unthinkable, "a scientific person and a sailor."[68]

W. B. Norris, an instructor at the United States Naval Academy, explored Fiske's argument. In his mind a naval leader should know more than just drills, parades, and cruises. He should be master of his calling. He should be at home with seamanship, electricity, engineering, and ordnance. Most important, "he should be able to put into operation and practical use all the principles of these subjects. In him the mastery of the sea which we associate with the old time seaman is joined with a professional attainment and a scientific attitude of mind that have hitherto flourished only ashore."[69] Although the naval officer may not be able to perform every task done on board ship, he should have a practical acquaintance with everything an understand its relation to the efficiency of the fleet. Such a goal was difficult to achieve because the entire atmosphere of shipboard life was permeated by mechanism. "Life on ship board is almost like spending one's days and nights in an iron foundry," Norris admitted. The constant and overpowering presence of machinery tended to harden the mind and give everything a mechanical turn. In that kind of environment the concept of men acting as if they were machines grew stronger. "Personality then drops into the background and the necessity of man's being a source of inspiration to those he commands is forgotten."[70] Still, the knowledge of engine rooms and guns was important to the navy. After all, as Admiral Luce pointed out, ". . . every naval officer must be something of a marine engineer; and the better the engineer he is the better for the Navy. The point is: Why should his education stop there?"[71]

Education and training were the keys. Because wars are relatively rare situations, a man cannot learn about warfare on a day-to-day basis as he might learn about steam engines or seamanship. No one can comprehend one subject by concentrating on another. As one officer remarked, "no one ever learned to handle an oar by swinging dumbbells."[72] The art and science of naval warfare can be learned only through continuous training operations at sea and extensive study of the principles in warfare. Fleet maneuvers and ship tactics are essential to this goal, and they can be augmented by war gaming. By employing "the applicatory system," students learned from actual practice the principles of their art that could not be gleaned from a textbook. On the game boards at the Naval War College, model ships moved over measured areas at a rate compatible with existing equipment. American ships were opposed by forces whose guns and capabilities conformed to the latest intelligence, thus testing American forces and strategies in a simulated crucible of war. When mock battles were played in this manner, the results were not always happy. One group of officers in 1903 reported that,

> ... the game has been played to solve the problems of what should be the proper tactics to be followed by our fleet in order to get the best results against the fleet of the enemy in the problem of the year. The game has been played as if making use of the means at hand. The result has been that we lose. In one game we tied and in every other we lost.[73]

Such work not only improved methods, but officer-students acquired skill in their profession by solving the kind of strategic and tactical problems that the use of their equipment involved. Politics, geography, and weather; logistics, engineering, and ordnance; command and control, planning, and decision making—all joined on the game board to simulate actual situations. As McCarty Little expressed it, "the game offers the players the whole world as a theatre, and puts no limit to the forces either in numbers or kinds, any type of ship may be had for the asking, the only requirement being to state its qualities so they may be expressed in game convention."[74] The common purpose of war-gaming and fleet maneuvers was to make the object so closely associated with the method that one suggested the other. Through continuous practice and repetition, art in naval warfare had to become instinctive.[75] The most perceptive students understood that when war did come, military and naval officers must rapidly respond to unknown forces. In the final analysis, they could not place their faith in machines alone: soldiers and sailors had only their own ability for reasoning and their own intuition and perception to fall back upon.

The brief span of years between the Spanish-American War and the American entry into World War I witnessed rapid changes in naval technology. Instead of engulfing professional naval men in the chaos between innovation and obsolence, naval strategists and their articulate seagoing associates concentrated their efforts on developing the means by which men could logically control and direct this expanding technology for the purposes which they devised. Situations were avoided in which technology became its own object. Awakened by the teachings of Luce, Mahan, and the naval reformers of the late nineteenth century, the professional men of the early twentieth century were able to devise administrative structures, methods of operation, training procedures, and doctrine which contributed to a broadly based direction of naval power. The naval professional

learned that a balance must be struck between the goals and principles of warfare and the realities, limitations, and characteristics of
available technology. Neither the professional of the day nor the historian of the era can deny that an understanding of naval power derives from a clear vision of its vast scope, for it takes into account
international politics, human nature, war principles, technology,
strategy and tactics, and the national wealth and will, all at the same
moment. The professional understanding which developed in the
first decade and a half of the new century provided the background
for naval operations in both World War I and World War II. It was in
these years after the turn of the century that naval men learned to
control the new technological environment which they, themselves,
had created.

NOTES

This is a revised version of an essay that first appeared in the *Naval War
College Review,* XXIV (November 1971), pp. 25–48, and was also printed
in B. Mitchell Simpson, III, ed., *War, Strategy and Maritime Power.* (New
Brunswick, NJ: Rutgers University Press, 1977), pp. 111–138.

1. Surgeon A. W. Dunbar, "The Medical Department in Warfare,: typescript in the Naval War College Lecture Collection, Naval Historical
   Collection, Naval War College, Newport, RI, p. 1. (Henceforth abbreviated: NWC Lectures, NHC.)
2. Bradley A. Fiske, *The Navy is a Fighting Machine.* (New York: Scribners, 1916). p. 129.
3. Richard Hough, *Dreadnought.* (New York: Macmillan, 1964), pp. 15–23.
4. For some of the best recent studies on the growth of British naval
   technology and its broader implications in this period, see Jon Tetsuro
   Sumida, *In Defence of Naval Supremacy: Finance, Technology and
   British Naval Policy, 1889–1914.* (Boston: Allen & Unwin, 1989);
   Nicholas A. Lambert, "The Influence of the Submarine upon Naval
   Strategy, 1898–1914, unpublished D.Phil. thesis, Oxford University,
   1992, and *Sir John Fisher's Naval Revolution.* (Columbia: University of
   South Carolina Press, 1999); Nicholas A. Lambert, "Admiral Sir John
   Fisher and the Concept of Flotilla Defence, 1904–1909," *Journal of Mil-
   itary History,* 59 (October 1995), pp. 639–630; Nicholas A. Lambert,
   "'Our Bloody Ships' or 'Our Bloody Policy'? Jutland and the Loss of the
   Baltic Cruisers, 1916," *Journal of Military History,* 62 (January 1998),
   pp. 29–55; Stephen D. Chiabotti, ed., *Tooling for War: Military Trans-
   formation in the Industrial Age.* (Chicago: Imprint Publications, 1995).
   Also Brian Ranft, ed., *Technical Change and British Naval Policy,
   1860–1939.* (London: Hodder & Stoughton, 1977). An example of the
   older and outdated view can be found in Elmber B. Potter and Chester
   W. Nimitz, eds. *Sea Power: A Naval History.* (Englewood Cliffs, NJ:
   Prentice Hall, 190), pp. 388–393.

5. Wilbur R. Van Auken, *Notes on a Half Century of United States Naval Ordnance.* (Washington, DC; Banta, 1939), pp. 13–24.
6. Linwood S. Howeth, *History of Communications-Electronics in the United States Navy.* (Washington, DC: U.S. Govt. Print. Off., 1963), p. 518–527.
7. A study of the contributions of these men may be found in Donald M. Schurman, *The Education of a Navy* (Chicago: University of Chicago Press, 1965).
8. John B. Hattendorf. et al., *Sailors and Scholars: The Centennial History of the Naval War College.* (Newport: Naval War College Press, 1984), chapter 2. See also, R. H. Spector, *Professors of War: The Naval War College and Development of the Naval Profession.* Ph.D. dissertation, Yale University, New Haven, CT: 1967, (Newport, RI: Naval War College Press, 1977).
9. Alfred T. Mahan, *The Influence of Sea Power Upon History, 1660–1783.* (London: University Paperbacks, 1967), p. 7.
10. Alfred T. Mahan, "Lectures on Military Strategy," unpublished manuscript and typescript in NWC Lectures, NHC pp. 11–77. Believed to have been originally written about 1889, these lectures were often repeated and later used as assigned reading at the Naval War College in the first decade of the twentieth century.
11. William McCarty Little, quoted in Frank Schofield, "Estimate of the Situation," lecture before the summer conference, June 1912, Solution to the Problem 1912, Naval War College Archives, NHC, pt. H, pp. 29–30.
12. William McCarty Little, "The Strategic Naval War Game or Chart Maneuver," lecture, Naval War College, Newport, RI, 10 June 1911. Naval War College Archives, NHC
13. This brief review is based on an excellent summary of the beginning of U.S. naval war planning which may be found in D. J. Costello, "Planning for War: a History of the General Board of the U.S. Navy, 1900–1914," unpublished Ph.D. dissertation, the Fletcher School of Law and Diplomacy, Medford, MA, 1968, pp. 1–22.
14. Luce to Mahan, 15 July 1907; original carbon typescript copy in Naval War College Archives, Ms. # 184, NHC. Italics are Luce's. See Luce's articles "Our Naval Policy," *The United Service,* 6 (May 1882), pp. 501–21; "Annual Address, 1888," United States Naval Institute *Proceedings,* 14 (1888), pp. 1–8; "Naval Administration," United States Naval Institute *Proceedings,* 14 (1888), pp. 561–581; "Naval Warfare under Modern Conditions," *North American Review,* 162 (January 1896), pp. 70–77.
15. William R. Braisted, *The United States Navy in the Pacific, 1897–1909* (Austin: University of Texas Press, 1956), pp. 21–22. The original plan may be found in the National Archives, RG 42, Records of the North Atlantic Station. A photocopy has been included in War Plans files, Records of the General Board, Naval History Division, Washington, DC See David F. Trask, *The War With Spain in 1898.* (New York: Macmillan, 1981).
16. Kenneth Bourne and Carl Boyd, "Captain Mahan's'War' with Great Britain," United States Naval Institute *Proceedings,* July 1968, pp. 71–78. Also, John A. S. Grenville and George B. Young, *Politics, Strategy, and American Diplomacy: Studies in Foreign Policy* (New Haven, CT: Yale University Press, 1966), pp. 93, 171–172; Walter R. Herrick,

54 NAVAL HISTORY AND MARITIME STRATEGY

Jr., *The American Naval Revolution* (Baton Rouge: Louisiana State University Press, 1966), pp. 78, 126, 140; Ronald Spector, "Who Planned the Attack on Manila Bay?" *Mid-America,* Vol. 53, No. 2, April 1971, pp. 94–102. Mahan's Plan is published in Robert Seager II and Doris Maguire, eds., *Letters and Papers of Alfred Thayer Mahan.* (Annapolis: Naval Institute Press, 1975), volume III, pp. 559–576.

17. Navy Department General Order 544, 13 March 1900, quoted in Costello, p. 25.
18. Long to Dewey, 30 March 1900, quoted in Costello, pp. 25–26.
19. Damon E. Cummings, *Admiral Richard Wainwright and the United States Fleet* (Washington, DC: U.S. Govt. Print. Off., 1962), pp. 213–217; Mark A. deWolfe Howe, *George von Lengerke Meyer: His Life and Public Services* (New York: Dodd, Mead, 1920), pp. 466–469; Henry P. Beers, "Development of the Office of the Chief of Naval Operations," *Military Affairs,* Spring 1946, pt. 11, pp. 60–64.
20. Costello, pp. 2–3.
21. For an outline history of naval war gaming, see Francis J. McHugh, *Fundamentals of War Gaming,* 3rd ed. (Newport, RI: 1966); Spector, chap. VI.
22. George P. Ahern, A Chronicle of the Army War College, 1899–1919, processed Washington, DC, 24 July 1919, No. 21 of 32 copies, NHC, NWC, pp. 81–82. W. P. Cronan, "The Greatest Need of the United States Navy: Proper Organization for the Successful Conduct of War, An Estimate of the Situation," United Sates Naval Institute *Proceedings,* July-August 1916, p. 1153.
23. Charles W. Cullen, "From Kriegsacademie to the Naval War College: The Military Planning Process," *Naval War College Review,* January 1970, pp. 10–15.
24. Cullen, p. 11. Quote from George F. R. Henderson, *The Science of War* (London: Longmans, Green, 1905), p. 5.
25. Cullen, pp. 14–15.
26. Cronan, p. 1153.
27. Louis Morton, "War Plan Orange, Evolution of a Strategy," *World Politics,* January 1959, p. 227. For the most complete study of Plan Orange, see Edward S. Miller, *War Plan Orange: The U.S. Strategy to Defeat Japan, 1897–1945.* (Annapolis: Naval Institute Press, 1991). On Plan Black, see Holger H. Herwig, *Politics of Frustration: The United States in German Naval Planning, 1889–1941.* (Boston: Little Brown, 1975) and Ivo Nikolai Lambi, *The Navy and German Power Politics, 1862–1914.* (Boston: Allen & Unwin, 1984), ch. 12.
28. Bradley A. Fiske, *The Navy as a Fighting Machine,* p. 406.
29. Ibid., p. 193.
30. Ibid., p. 228.
31. William McCarty Little, "Philosophy of the Order Form," Lecture, Naval War College, Newport, RI: 12–13 August 1913, NWC Lecture, NHC, p. 14.
32. W. R. Shoemaker, "Strategy of the Pacific: an Exposition of the Orange War Plan," Lecture, Naval War College, Newport, RI, 23 August 1914, NWC Lecture, NHC.
33. Typescript, "Notes and Comments on G. B. Plan Blue vs. Black, undated, signed "McK.," laid in Black Plan War Portfolio No. 1, Reference

No. 5–4, Germany War Plan, Copy No. 1 General Board copy. Records of the General Board, Naval History Division, Washington, D.C. This writer believes "McK." to be Capt. Josiah Slutts McKean, USN.

A Naval War College graduate and former staff member, McKean served as assistant for material in the Office of CNO from 1915 to 1919. He remained on duty in the Navy Department for several years. During World War I he was promoted to rear admiral and, later, admiral. As assistant CNO he served as the acting chief of naval operations when Admiral Benson was naval adviser to the U.S. delegation of Versailles, 5 January to 20 June 1919 and from 5 September to 1 November 1919, between the retirement of Admiral Benson and the appointment of Admiral R. E. Coontz as CNO.

34. Carl T. Vogelgesang, "Estimate of the Situation," Report of the Conference 1911, pt. II, p. 2, NWC Archives, NHC.
35. Orange Plan, P. 7, War Plans File, Records of the General Board, Naval History Division, Washington, DC (Henceforth abbreviated: GB Records, NHD.)
36. See for example, A. T. Mahan to W. L. Rodgers, 17 May 1910 quoted in Spector, p. 250.
37. Mahan, "Lectures on Military Strategy," p. 42–43.
38. Ibid., p. 8.
39. Costello, p. 26–27.
40. George Dewey to SecNav, 16 June 1909, General Board Letters, vol. VI, p. 0093, GB Records, NHD.
41. Quoted in A. J. Marder, *The Anatomy of British Sea Power* (New York: Knopf, 1940), p. 525. See also, references throughout Sumida, *In Defence of Naval Supremacy,* and Nicholas A. Lambert, "Admiral Sir John Fisher."
42. Dewey to SecNav, 28 February 1903, General Board Letters, vol. II, p. 0210, GB Records, NHD.
43. Dewey to SecNav, 16 May 1903, General Board Letters, vol. II, p. 0261, GB Records, NHD.
44. "Report of the Board to Consider CDR A. Key's Comments on the Design of the Battleship *North Dakota,* July 1908," Report of Committee B, p. 4, and Report of Committee Z, NWC Archives, NHC. This controversy is discussed at length in Elting E. Morison, *Admiral Sims and the Modern American Navy* (Boston: Houghton, Mifflin, 1942), pp. 201–15.
45. Key Board, "Appendix H. Paper Read by Admiral Goodrich"
46. Bradley A. Fiske, "The Naval Profession," United States Naval Institute *Proceedings,* June 1907, pp. 570–573; Bradley A. Fiske, *Midshipman to Rear Admiral* (New York: Century, 1919), pp. 397–39; and Sir Percy Scott, *Fifty Years in the Royal Navy* (New York: Doran, 1919). See also the comparable controversy over fire-control in Sumida, *In Defence of Naval Supremacy;* Sumida, ed. *The Pollen Papers: The Privately Circulated Printed Works of Arthur Hungerford Pollen, 1901–1916.* Publications of the Navy Records Society, vol. 124. (London: Allen & Unwin, 1984) and Anthony Pollen, *The Great Gunnery Scandal.* (London: Collins, 1980).
47. Fiske, *Midshipman to Rear Admiral,* pp. 580, 591–92. Fiske gives the impression in his autobiography that the Naval Consulting Board was seriously considered only after the newspaper announcement on 5 July

1915 that Sir John Fisher had been appointed head of a similar board in the Royal Navy. There is evidence in E. David Cronon, ed., *The Cabinet Diaries of Josephus Daniels 1913–1921* (Lincoln: University of Nebraska Press, 1963), p. 102, that the 7 July 1915 letter to Edison was being drafted as early as 30 June 1915. See also Josephus Daniels, *The Wilson Era* (Chapel Hill: University of North Carolina Press; 1944), chap. 52, pp. 490–500. *The New York Times* interview with Edison which inspired Daniels to enlist the inventor's support appeared on 30 May 1915, pt. V, "Magazine Section," pp. 6–7, not in "early July" as stated by Daniels in his autobiography.

48. Daniels to Edison, 7 July 1915, quoted in Lloyd N. Scott, *Naval Consulting Board of the United States.* (Washington: U.S. Govt. Print. Off., 1920), pp. 286–287.
49. Fiske, *Fighting Machine,* p. 63–64.
50. "Confidential Memorandum Adopted by the Executive Committee, 6 August 1915," General Board Study 420–422, 30 July 1915. (GB Records, NHD.
51. See H. H. Frost, *The Battle of Jutland* (Annapolis: U.S. Naval Institute, 1936), pp. 505–518, and Arthur Marder, *From Dreadnought to Scapa Flow,*Volume 3: *Jutland and After.* (London: Oxford University Press, 1966, revised and enlarged 1978); Paul G. Halpern, *A Naval History of World War I.* (Annapolis: Naval Institute, 1994, pp. 310–328; Andrew Gordon, *The Rules of the Game: Jutland and British Naval Command.* (London: John Murray, 1996) for an evaluation of the battle.
52. R. D. Gatewood, "The Industrial in Modern War," United States Naval Institute *Proceedings,* (May-June 1916), p. 757.
53. Carl T. Vogelgesang, "Logistics-Its Bearing upon the Art of War," lecture before the summer conference of 1911, NWC Lectures, NHC, pp. 6–8.
54. Carl T. Vogelgesang quoted in J. S. McKean, Naval Logistics: A Lecture Delivered . . . at the Naval War College Extension, Washington, D.C., 10 March 1913 (Washington, DC: U.S. Govt. Print. Off., 1915), p. 7.
55. Gatewood, pp. 757–759.
56. T. J. Cowie, "Logistics," Lecture, Naval War College, Newport, RI: 13 May 1915, NWC Lectures, NHC, p. 20.
57. Dewey to SecNav, 28 September 1910, General Board Letters, vol. VII, p. 0058, GB Records, NHD. Earlier letters on the same topic contain similar reasoning; see Dewey to SecNav, 9 February 1903, General Board Letters, vol. II, p. 0177 and 26 January 1904, vol. III, p. 0006.
58. William L. Rodgers To W. McCarty Little, 10 May 1914, pp. 3–4, manuscript letter in NWC Archives, Research file, "Little," NHC.
59. Ibid.
60. Josephus Daniels, SecNav, to W. H. Bullard, Superintendent, Naval Radio Service, 3 March 1916; letter (Second Endorsement) from Superintendent, Radio Service, 7 December 1915, GB Records, NHD.
61. Dewey to SecNav, Serial 467 of 19 January 1916, File 419, GB Records, NHD.
62. For a detailed account of the Dolphin incident, see Jack Sweetman, *The Landing at Vera Cruz: 1914* (Annapolis: U.S. Naval Institute, 1968), pp. 30–40.
63. Josephus Daniels, *The Wilson Era.* p. 191. Daniels indicates that the

1916 order was delayed for more than two years so that it would not be construed as a rebuke to Admiral Mayo.

64. Rodgers to Little, 10 May 1914, p. 4.
65. William McCarty Little, "Philosophy of the Order Form," Lecture, U.S. Naval War College, Newport, RI: 1913.
66. Hugo Munsterberg, "The Psychology of the Navy," Lecture Naval War College, Newport, RI: 4 June 1912, NWC Lectures, NHC, p. 2.
67. Letter (Fourth Endorsement) on W. T. Culverinus's letter, 15 February 1909. Comments on the condition of the commissioned personnel, 23 December 1908, General Board Letters, v. V, p. 0433, GB Records, NHD.
68. Fiske, *Fighting Machine,* pp. 196–97.
69. W. B. Norris, "Leadership and Freedom," United States Naval Institute *Proceedings,* January-February, 1916, p. 51.
70. Ibid., p. 61.
71. Stephen B. Luce, "On the Relations between the U.S. Naval War College and Line Officers of the U.S. Navy," United States Naval Institute *Proceedings,* September 1911, p. 788.
72. H. G. Bergen, "The Principles of Training," Lecture, Naval War College, Newport, RI: 1909, NWC Lectures, NHC, p. 10.
73. "Solution to the Problem of 1903, Conclusions Deducted from the Use of the Game Board," p. 65, NWC Archives, NHC.
74. William McCarty Little, "The Strategic Naval War Game."
75. William McCarty Little, "Genesis of the Masterpiece of a Genius," unpublished typescript and notes for study of Napoleon's strategy, c. 1902, NWC Archives, Research File "Little," NHC.

4

Alfred Thayer Mahan
and American Naval Theory:
The Range and Limitations
of Mahan's Thought

Theory is not practice; history is not strategy. Yet, there can be important connections between such differing spheres, even though they may be neither sustained nor continuous. Too often, modern writers have jumped to the conclusion that Alfred Thayer Mahan's ideas were identical with the naval strategy of the United States. Mahan was a writer and a historian, and although he was a naval officer, never held a position in which he had even a remote chance of directing national, naval strategy. It is true that Mahan was well known and he did have influence in some quarters. Nevertheless, the process of directing national power in the United States was so complex, even in his day, that the ideas of a single writer could not possibly outweigh the complex interplay of national and international politics, finance, industrial production, developing technology and bureaucratic decision making that lies behind the exercise of naval power. Just as theory describes a pattern of action, without being the motive force behind it, so Mahan was trying to provide intellectual models that, through historical analogies, gave meaning and understanding to some of the events that were occurring around him. In doing this, he made connections with military theory, identifying a few broad principles that were applicable to navies and developed a few more general ideas about the role of navies.

In a letter to John Knox Laughton in 1896, Mahan wrote, "Our nation [the U.S.A.] is in Egyptian darkness, from my point of view, as regards its place and mission in the world."[1] Certainly, Mahan wrote to bring a light to this darkness, but this was not his only objective. At the same time, the U.S. Navy did not accept his ideas fully nor did

Rear Admiral Alfred Thayer Mahan
(*Naval War College Museum*)

it implement them fully into any policy or strategy. On the other hand, his books and his ideas were widely read within the Navy and create a kind of intellectual currency for discussions about the broad aspects of naval power.

The distinction here is important. Naval strategy is a practical issue and has to do with the comprehensive direction of ships and weapons to achieve specific practical ends through forceful control. It is a rare situation in which abstract ideas would or even could drive it. We might attribute this either to fundamental differences or, alternatively, only to the common paradox between ideals and actual behavior. But, it is important to understand that theory exists to shed light for our reflections, allowing us to understand the purpose, inner calculus and related elements within a broad theme. Practitioners can use it only as a very vague guide to action, putting the long-glass of theory to a blind eye as quickly as current reality presents new factors. In any real-life situation, a competent practitioner must know how to compromise between conflicting optimum solutions and know when one theoretical consideration outweighs another. This is the judgment of experience, in the light of theoretical understanding. Historians should never let their appreciation for successful books and good ideas lead them into assuming that abstract ideas drive navies. This is particularly true in trying to understand the United States Navy. If there is such a thing as American national character, no one has ever attributed a deep and abiding interest in theory as part of that character. Americans like to think of themselves as practical people, not abstract thinkers. As an American admiral exclaimed a century after Mahan in the 1990s, "Don't give me some abstract explanation; I am a meat and potatoes man."

MAHAN IN CONTEXT

To understand Mahan and what he was saying, one must understand him in just that context. He was providing abstract explanations to an audience that, by and large, was not very interested and fundamentally doubted their value. That situation changed somewhat later, in the Progressive Era in American history, when scholars began to be accepted as experts.[2] This was a result of a tremendous change in American attitudes, but it is one that, even today, is not fully shared in large areas of society.

Certainly, Mahan wrote before that change was completed and the Navy was no fertile ground for its growth. In 1861, Stephen Luce had complained, "Compared to the Army with their wealth of professional literature, we [in the Navy] may be likened to the nomadic tribes of the East who are content with the vague traditions of the past."[3]

A dozen years later, that situation was slowly beginning to change. By 1873, there were enough officers interested in professional writing to support the establishment of the U.S. Naval Institute. At least some American naval officers were aware of professional thought and events in France and in Britain, reading such periodicals as *Revue Maritime, The Journal of the Royal United Services Institution* as well as their own *Army and Navy Journal,* The Naval Institute's *Proceedings* and the short-lived, *United Service.* By 1890, the drive toward professionalization in the armed forces had included a large professional literature. Much of it, however, was scientific, practical, and technical. Relatively few were interested in questions of history and policy, although there were a few who wrote in that area. Mahan was not alone.

Mahan's work is a reaction to the overwhelming dominance of technology in the Navy. While in command of the USS *Chicago* in 1894, he had complained, "The infinite and infinitely small details of a modern ship consume time while yielding small results."[4] At that moment, he was deep into writing his biography of Nelson and irritated by shipboard distractions, but his irritation reflected a larger and deeper issue.

In 1884, Admiral Stephen Luce had founded the Naval War College in Newport, Rhode Island, with the express purpose of counteracting the overwhelming dominance of technological imperatives in the Navy. At a time when many felt that rapidly developing technology had swept away the old wisdom and demanded a completely new basis, Luce and his colleagues looked in other directions,

- to international law and diplomacy as a means to control and to guide warfare;
- to the use of war games as a means of logically controlling, evaluating and directing technological developments; and
- to history as a means of revealing important and continuing patterns of thought and guides to behavior.

Each of these areas has its own history of individual development, although Luce had linked them. Obviously, Mahan is most clearly connected to the third of these categories, but he is also part of the whole school of thought that the Naval War College, as an institution, represented, and over which he twice presided in 1886–89 and 1892–93.

The debate continues between those who argue that technology has made the past irrelevant to modern and future military affairs and those who see history as something of continuing value in its midst. Mahan played a role in this debate, in the second of its several phases, while Admiral Luce had been involved at a very early stage, and was influential in setting the agenda of the debate. In this, Mahan made clear his debt to the Naval War College, when he wrote in his preface to the *Influence of Sea Power Upon the French Revolution and Empire.*

> . . . in the race for material and mechanical development, sea officers as a class have allowed their attention to be unduly diverted from the systematic study of the Conduct of War, which is their peculiar and main concern . . . That the author has done so is due, wholly and exclusively to the Naval War College, which was instituted to promote such studies.[5]

Seen in this context, Mahan's work was clearly an attempt to fill a gap in a key area of professional thought, not to provide an overarching explanation of the way in which navies function. Because of this, Mahan's work bypasses the important issue that historians wrestle with today: how the presence of constant technological innovation affects navies.

In laying out the ground on which Mahan was to begin his work, Admiral Luce clearly identified his preference to use history and to relate naval history to military theory. In concluding a lecture during the first session of the Naval War College in 1885, Luce wrote,

> Inspired by the example of the warlike Greeks, and knowing ourselves to be on the road that leads to the establishment of the science of naval warfare under steam, let us confidently look for that master mind who will lay the foundations of that science, and do for it what Jomini did for the military science.[6]

Some twenty years later, Luce recalled this very comment and noted, "He is here; his name is Mahan."[7] Mahan's advent, however, was no bolt from the blue. It is very clearly part of a long-term development in which he had both predecessors and successors.

In attempting to put Mahan's work into perspective, we must look at it through a number of overlapping view points. As already mentioned, we must see him in terms of the growth of professional literature, but more particularly, we must see him

- as part of the development of the subdiscipline of naval history, linking international politics to naval action;
- as part of the development of military and naval theory, with an

early application of Jomini's ideas and other thinkers to maritime
problems;

- as part of the growth of political commentary, using geopolitical
  ideas and historical examples;
- as part of a growing, but rudimentary sophistication in general
  historical studies, at this point somewhat reluctantly accepting
  the importance of original research;
- as a reflection of the social and intellectual values of his times, in
  terms of understanding the armed forces, international rivalry,
  economic competition, imperial power, and religious belief.

When we see Mahan, thus in depth, in breadth, and in context, we
see him as part of a broad progression. We see others, before him,
working in related fields. In this, we can see relationships in the
early work being done in the Royal Navy by the two Colomb brothers, John and Philip, and Sir John Knox Laughton. We can see Mahan's debt to Jomini and to Clausewitz as well as to his own father's
work in that area, to historians in Britain and France. We see Mahan acquire, use, and interpret and develop those ideas further. After him, we find another set of writers and thinkers, like Sir Julian
Corbett and Sir Herbert Richmond, who recast and reinterpreted his
ideas in the light of new insights, new information and more varied
experiences. Beyond that, we can find a whole range of writers, historians and commentators who have applied his ideas, sometimes
distorting and changing them in the process, and creating a "Ma-
hanian doctrine" and attributing to him ideas that are somewhat at
variance with what Mahan, himself, wrote. With that in mind, let us
not continue to see Mahan as doctrine, as a lens by which we should
interpret naval power, but let us see him as a man with some ideas,
in the context of his own time, at a particular stage of development
in the progression and refinement of naval thought.

As a keen observer of international events in the late nineteenth
century, Mahan saw clear historical parallels to it in the structure of
European international relations between 1660 and 1815. He saw
some similarities in terms of imperial responsibility, the competition
of empires, naval rivalry, the role of maritime trade and the relationship of naval battles to the general conduct of wars. He seems to have
seen his own world as one in a kind of neomercantilist period. This
kind of world structure in international relations a world so very different than what we see about us in the 1990s provided the striking
parallels he wanted to use to excite the minds of his fellow countrymen
and his fellow officers. For us today, the seventeenth and the eigh-

teenth centuries are, indeed, "a world we have lost." The historian looking at that period today needs to bridge a large gap with historical imagination and faces an even wider gap in trying to understand the elements in it that attracted a late nineteenth century naval officer.

Mahan was not alone in his interest in the Napoleonic War period. For his generation, it was, after all, the "last great war." In terms of both relative distance in time and popular interest, the Napoleonic wars had an attraction that could be roughly likened to that which the world wars of this century continue to exert on us. As the centenary approached, popular interest rose and much professional writing touched on the same period as well. Army officers consistently turned to Henri Jomini's writings, even as they slowly began to find an interest in works by Carl von Clausewitz.[8] Regardless of quality, there was a host of books and writers on the subject, even in the naval area. Among his exact contemporaries in Britain, John Knox Laughton and Philip Colomb had each, independently of Mahan, chosen the same period to examine for professional purposes. Given Mahan's own purposes as well as the wide interest in the period, it is not surprising or unusual that he turned to it.

CATEGORIES OF MAHAN'S WRITINGS.

Moving beyond the general context, it is worthwhile to see the pattern of Mahan's works. Most of his twenty volumes remain in print today, nearly a century after they were written, yet many commentators have lumped them together as a single opus.[9] However, one can distinguish between several different categories of his work, noting, at the same time, the various links between them.

Mahan is remembered today largely for his series of books on *The Influence of Sea Power*, yet the common idea of his views on naval strategy come from another series of works. There are five distinct categories:

1. the broad role of sea power in international relations;
2. the basic principles of naval operations;
3. commentaries on general contemporary events;
4. thoughts on the role of the United States in international affairs;
5. personal memoirs and religious beliefs.

The last category, touching on personal religious beliefs, has been often ignored as irrelevant to the others.[10] Today, with our recent experience in international relations, one can more readily appreciate the interplay between religious conviction and military force. For Mahan, this connection was certainly present. His view of international relations is clearly consistent with one of his favorite Biblical passages, *St. Paul's Epistle to the Romans,* 14:4. A ruler, St. Paul wrote, "is the minister of God, a revenger to execute wrath upon him that doeth evil." Not only was the use of military and naval force just and righteous, in his view, but Western international relations were closely tied to a commitment to spread Christian values and to promote Christian evangelism in the areas under Western control and influence. Such fundamental beliefs underlie Mahan's thought on naval affairs and his understanding of history.

Mahan's broadest understanding of history is laid out in his *Sea Power* series which consisted of four titles: His most famous book, *The Influence of Sea Power Upon History,* followed by his study, with a similar title, on *The French Revolution and Empire.* This was followed by *Sea Power in Its Relation to the War of 1812* and his biography of Nelson. Today, one often forgets the fact that this biography is part of the same series and that he subtitled it *The Embodiment of the Sea Power of Great Britain.* In his correspondence, he repeatedly declared as he was writing *Nelson,* "If I succeed in bringing the work up to the mark at which I aim, it will stand as the work of my life I so intend it."[11] In dealing with Nelson, the man, Mahan was "disengaging the figure of the hero from the glory that cloaks it.[12] At the same time, as he was dealing with the external part of Nelson's career, "the same aim is kept in view of showing clearly, not only what he did, but the principles which dominated his military thought, and guided his military actions, throughout his life."[13] Thus, from a literary and conceptual point of view, Mahan was trying to bring together, in his study of a single man, the concepts he had laid out in his earlier volumes through the abstract terms of international relations. "Wars may cease," Mahan wrote, "but the need for heroism shall not depart from the earth, while man remains man and evil needs to be redressed."[14]

In his first *Sea Power* book, Mahan had laid out his basic elements of sea power, emphasizing that

the first and most obvious light in which the sea presents itself from a political and social point of view is that of a great highway; or better, perhaps, of a wide common, over which men may pass in all directions, but on which some well-worn paths show that controlling reasons have led them to choose certain lines of travel rather than others. . . . called trade routes.[15]

Thus, in his view, commercial trade was the essence of maritime activity and the fundamental reason for navies. For much of the history Mahan reviewed, he found three key factors supporting commercial trade:

1. production, with the need to exchange goods;
2. shipping, by which the exchange is carried on; and
3. colonies, which enlarge shipping operations and provide additional points of safety for shipping.

For a nation to be successful in such commercial, maritime endeavor, Mahan laid out his six fundamental factors underlying it: geographical position, physical characteristics of its harbors, climate and production, extent of territory, number of population, character of the people and their aptitude for commercial trade, the character of the government and the national institutions supporting commerce and trade.

Often one finds students stopping at this point, thinking they have grasped Mahan's views, when in fact one must move further on, through his other volumes, to see the full range of his ideas. The volumes on the *War of 1812,* in particular, deal with his ideas on the war against trade. "To attack the commerce of the enemy is therefore to cripple him, in the measure of success achieved, in the particular factor which is vital to the maintenance of war . . . ," Mahan wrote." Money, credit, is the life of war; lessen it, and vigor flags; destroy it, and resistance dies."[16]

While fully recognizing its great importance in dealing with a fundamental factor in any war, Mahan found in historical examples some reasons to look beyond commerce destruction as a general aim in naval warfare. He saw that the relative value of commerce warfare varied with the situation. It was a type of warfare to which countries that had no large naval establishment could resort. Even countries with a large naval force could easily engage in this type of warfare, without much preparation. Stressing it did not help the argument he wanted to make, promoting the building of a larger navy in the United States.

Mahan noted that one of the most effective tools a major naval power had was using warships to impose a commercial blockade. A weaker nation's natural response to commercial blockade was to at-

tack the enemy's trade on the high seas. Thus, Mahan found it difficult to generalize on this subject, since it was largely dependant on
the relative position of the nation employing commerce destruction.
In order to clarify the issue, Mahan tried to cast it in different terms:

> It is not the taking of individual ships or convoys, be they few or many,
> that strikes down the money power of a nation; it is the possession of that
> overbearing power on the sea which drives the enemy's flag from it, or al-
> lows it to appear only as a fugitive; and which, by controlling the great
> common, closes the highways by which commerce moves to and from the
> enemy's shores.[17]

The importance that Mahan placed on trade led him to take a
strong position in the contemporary controversy over the immunity
of private property at sea. Although some people sought to protect
private property from capture of injury during war at sea, Mahan opposed the idea of immunity, arguing that capture of an enemy's commerce "is a means of importance to the ends of war."[18] As he explained in *The War of 1812,* relinquishing the rights of a belligerent
to forbid the free use of the sea to an enemy's merchant ships, aban-
dons control of the sea in so far as it is useful in warfare.[19] Later, he
elaborated on this point:

> Which will most promote, and maintain, a steady aversion to war? . . . .
> Depend on it, the interest of humanity demands that war is not to be a
> mere question of champions, land or sea, but that the whole people should
> be made to feel, individually, that the war will find its way to them, in
> purse as well as in sorrow.[20]

In the *Sea Power* series, Mahan outlined his broad ideas on the
role of sea power in history, but he reserved a detailed study of the
basic principles of naval operations for his book *Naval Strategy.*
This was a volume of his War College lectures that he had been re-
luctant to publish, obviously designed for the professional officer
and not the general public.[21] While Mahan could confess that he had
"never been so sick of anything" he had written,[22] nevertheless, it
remains, perhaps, the most important statement of his ideas on
naval theory.

In fact, Mahan was uncomfortable with the assignment that Admiral Luce had given him to apply military theory to naval operations. While finding a few principles that he could appropriately link,
he stressed the need to look at an ever widening range of applications
in terms of particular cases, rather than to a strict recitation of the

abstract principles themselves. "Extensive study of cases," he wrote, "gives firmer grasp, deeper understanding, wider views, increased aptitude and quickness to apprehend the critical features. . . . "[23]

Here Mahan reiterated the importance of trade to navies, noting that naval strategy has for its end, in peace and in war, the support and increase of a nation's sea power. In contrast to military operations, navies operate on a relatively large geographical scale. This factor dictates the need for concentrating naval force in advance, rather than distributing it widely, using the navy's mobility as a key to maintaining its usefulness in strength. This was a key factor which differentiated navies from armies. While the possession of key strategic positions is an essential point in military theory, Mahan emphasized that, in naval affairs, there could be too many ports, leading to dispersal of force rather than concentration. Mobility allowed the Navy to balance this situation. In the face of opposition, naval forces could not expect to hold the whole field, but it is essential to hold the key points that allow them to control the greater and most important parts of it. Thus, a major factor in naval affairs was the possession of key, advance positions, ranging from being able to maintain a blockade off an enemy port to holding a distant harbor.

The importance of forward positions lay at the heart of Mahan's theory. Mahan identified two basic factors for consideration in exercising naval strategy: strategic position and strategic lines. When examining strategic position, Mahan saw three principle conditions that determined its value: position, strength, and resources.

The first and most important condition for strategic position is its relation to the major trade routes at sea. To be valuable, it must lie within the limits of strategic effect. Thus, among the best positions are the intersections of two or more sea routes, the narrow channels or highways through which trade must necessarily pass in order to gain wide distribution.

The second condition which determines the value of a strategic position is its military strength, both offensive and defensive. In terms of seaports, one must consider both the landward and seaward components of this. In Mahan's view, ports are best defended by land defenses, not naval resources. The Navy's true role, he felt, was in the offensive. In this dimension, ports held offensive capability if a large military force of both warships and transports could assemble there, if such force could easily and safely launch itself into open water from that position and if the port could continue to support the force until the end of the campaign.

For Mahan, the final condition for determining the value of a position was the availability of natural and man-made resources. The most important of these was dry docks which, when close to the scene of action, could effect rapid repairs and supply, returning ships to the fleet quickly.

In parallel with strategic position, Mahan emphasized the importance of strategic lines. "The strategic points on a given theater of war are not to be looked upon merely separately and as disconnected," Mahan wrote.

> After determining their individual values by the test of position, military strength, and resources, it will remain to consider their mutual relations of bearing, distance, and the best routes from one to the other.[25]

Taking his cue from Jomini, Mahan noted that one could give a variety of names to these routes, depending on the use one put them to; line of operation, line of retreat, line of communication, etc. The most important of them at sea, however, are the lines of communication over which the essential supplies pass. Mahan believed that these strategic lines were controlled at sea through the mobility of organized naval force, i.e., a battle fleet. Thus, the fleet was the heart of an enemy's strength. If an enemy's fleet could be decisively defeated or dislocated, preventing it from controlling the sea, the object of naval strategy was achieved. This, to Mahan, was the determining factor in naval warfare. Both the decisive defeat of the enemy fleet, or rendering it completely inferior, resulted in dislocation of the enemy's lines of communication.

In Mahan's mind, the key to success at sea lay in having an adequate, efficient and numerically superior fleet at sea. Superiority was identical with holding the decisive position at sea, for it prevented an enemy from concentrating a rival force to challenge it. At the same time, naval preponderance at sea meant secure communications. The single most important point in Mahan's view was the need to be superior to the enemy at the decisive point, whatever the relative strength of the two opposing parties as a whole. In cases when superiority was unclear, then one needed to fight a battle. The results of that battle determines which fleet controls the strategic position and the lines of communication.

When the fleet has won the key to the strategic position, the fleet passes from an offensive role to a defensive one. In joint operations, the navy moves to deal with communications, its natural element, while the army assumes the offensive and continues the campaign ashore.

These were the main points of Mahan's theory, as he worked them out in his study of history. Yet, Mahan was not solely concerned with history. A large proportion of his writing was devoted to it, but, to a degree, he was dissatisfied with historical study. In his 1896 letter to Laughton, Mahan had written,

> . . . it seems to me we are approaching an age in which events of great political interest will occur before your and my generation goes under the sod. I feel the impulse more and more strong to turn my attention to the future, from the point of view of Sea Power, and to address the public through magazines.[26]

In doing this, Mahan used many of the principles he worked out from history. He saw very clearly that, in historical study, a careful observer could trace and formulate the causes of events, showing the various interactions which produced the result. But the situation was different in trying to analyze present situations, and even more difficult in trying to predict the future. In his preface to *The Problem of Asia,* Mahan wrote,

> Past history contains indeed lessons which, well digested, are most valuable for future guidance; but when the attempt is made to utilize their teachings, contemporary conditions are found to differ so much from those preceding them that application becomes a matter of no slight difficulty, requiring judgement and conjecture rather than imparting certainty. Positiveness in such matters, indeed, is the doubtful privilege of the *doctrinaire,* and commonly unfortunate in the result. The instruction derived from the past must be supplemented by particularized study of the indications of the future.[27]

Within a decade of the time he wrote his first *Sea Power* book, Mahan was clearly aware that historical examples and doctrinaire theory could not forecast the future, but he continued to believe that one could gain through the study of history. One could, at least, use history to help to determine the essential factors and the range of key relationships involved in situations. "Even so much is gain," he concluded.[28]

As Mahan was writing, the historical profession was only just beginning to emphasize the need for constant attention to documents and to detail. The German approach to documentary research had not yet fully taken over, although the first graduate schools in history were already beginning to point toward the future path. In England, Laughton had been the pioneer and among the very first to use the Admiralty archives for research. In this context, it is interesting to see Mahan's reaction to Laughton's suggestion that Mahan might profit from a look at some newly available private papers for his study of *Nelson*. No, thank you, Mahan replied. "I have practically given up in many cases, accepting ignorance of details as not material to the broad lines I wish to draw."[29]

THE RANGE AND LIMITATIONS OF MAHAN'S THEORIES

The range of Mahan's theory was both broad and limited. He looked at European history over a period of 150 years, focusing on both the British and French navies. But much of what he said was not necessarily applicable to other periods, other countries or other types of naval power. He wrote with an eye toward educating his own countrymen, particularly his colleagues in uniform, and to promoting the development of the U.S. Navy. Clearly, some of historical conclusions reflected that bias.

In terms of his time, much of what Mahan wrote was a revelation. Mahan's approach to applying selected aspects of Jomini's thought along with other aspects of military theory to navies was brilliant, and Mahan had done a sound job of working abstract ideas into historical narrative. His work opened up a wide, new range of thought for contemporaries. Like any such intellectual construct, it served its purpose, but it was also limited. Mahan's own hesitancy to stress the abstract principles, preferring instead to study the details in case after case, was indicative of the fundamental problem. The principles were a useful, if limited, guide in the mind of a man who had broad knowledge and could compare and contrast, seeing the variations and vagaries involved. Jomini's principles, however, have always caused difficulty. They left a great opportunity for readers to seize upon such clearly and simply worded statements, forcing them into formulae, as if they were circuit boards rather than abstract impressions. Mahan saw the problem. He dealt with it indirectly and reticently, at first, and explicitly later, but many readers missed the point.

Mahan made some remarkable contributions to historical understanding, but his approach to history was already waning as he wrote. His disregard for documentary and detailed research may seem deplorable today, although he did more than many in his time. Nevertheless, many of his historical explanations no longer stand.[30] His histories are as dated as his contemporary analysis, but his works were important steps in the history of naval theory on its way to modern development. Their role and their limitations represent part of the intellectual heritage of navies.

American naval theory has evolved considerably since the days when Mahan wrote, but its evolution is largely the result of influences from writers in other countries, academics and civilian analysts working outside the navy, as well as from a much wider and deeper range of historical research and naval experience. Yet, theoretical interests are no more attractive to the U.S. Navy, today, than they were when Mahan wrote. It is rare to find anyone working in the area. One can count on the fingers of a single hand, the number of Americans who have made any serious contribution to this field. In the eighty years since Mahan's death, among those who have been career officers in the U.S. Navy, there are only two that stand out: Rear Admiral Henry E. Eccles (1898–1986) who wrote *Military Concepts and Philosophy*[31] and a series of important conceptual papers on naval logistics and Rear Admiral J. C. Wylie (1911–1993) who wrote *Military Strategy: A General Theory of Power Control.*[32] The last, in particular, had a discernable, conceptual influence on American naval planning in the 1980s.[33]

Although theory is not practice and history is not strategy, Mahan was the most influential and prolific writer in the United States to show that there can be important connections between such differing spheres. Today, his conceptualizations lie in the far distant historical background. Since his time, officers of the United States Navy have neither made a sustained nor a continuous effort to develop those connections into any new theoretical formulation and show no inclination to do so. Yet, the cultivation of broad connections between theory and practice, history and strategy remain an important part of the work of the Naval War College and of the academic work of the officers who attend its courses. Today, it is not enough to read Mahan's work and cite his principles, or alternatively to turn to any other abstract formulae. Today, modern naval officers must deal with a broader understanding of the historical process as a guide to critical analysis in thinking about what navies can and can not do.[34] With a thorough understanding of the past, the modern naval officer must be his own Mahan.

NOTES

This is a revised version of an essay first published in Keith Neilson and Jane Errington, eds., *Navies and Global Defense: Theory and Strategy.* (Westport, CT; Praeger Publishing, an imprint of Greenwood Publishing Group, Inc., 1995), pp. 51–67.

1. National Maritime Museum, Greenwich: MS 79/067: Mahan to Laughton, 20 March 1986.
2. Richard Hofstadter, *Anti-Intellectualism in American Life* (New York: Random House, 1964), chapter 8.
3. Library of Congress, Luce papers: Luce to Commandant of Midshipmen, U.S. Naval Academy, 26 February 1861.
4. NMM, MS 79/067: Mahan to Laughton, 31 January 1894.
5. Mahan, *The Influence of Sea Power Upon The French Revolution and Empire.* (Boston: Little Brown, 1892), vol. 1, pp. v–vi.
6. S. B. Luce, "On the Study of Naval Warfare as a Science, U.S. Naval Institute *Proceedings*, XII (1886), pp. 527–46, reprinted in Hayes and Hattendorf, eds., *The Writings of Stephen B. Luce* (Newport, RI: Naval War College Press, 1975), chapter III.
7. Ibid., p. 68, fn. 71.
8. Christopher Bassford, *Clausewitz in English.* (New York and Oxford: Oxford University Press, 1994), see chapters 1–2.
9. For a list of his works, see John B. Hattendorf and Lynn C. Hattendorf, compilers, *A Bibliography of the Works of Alfred Thayer Mahan* (Newport: Naval War College Press, 1986). For the best general analysis of Mahan's ideas, showing how they changed and developed over his lifetime, see Jon T. Sumida, *Inventing Ground Strategy and Teaching Command.* (Baltimore, MD: Johns Hopkins University Press, 1997).
10. On this subject, see Leo N. Leslie, Jr., "Christianity and the Evangelist of Sea Power: The Religion of Alfred Thayer Mahan," in Hattendorf, ed., *The Influence of History Upon Mahan.* (Newport, RI: Naval War College Press, 1991), pp. 127–139.
11. NMM, Mahan to Laughton, 31 January 1894; See also, Robert Seager II and Doris D. Maguire, eds., *The Letters and Papers of Alfred Thayer Mahan.* Naval Letters Series (Annapolis, MD: Naval Institute Press, 1975), vol. II, pp. 229, 470, 509.
12. Mahan, *Nelson: The Embodiment of the Sea Power of Great Britain.* (London: Marston Low, 1897), vol. I, p. vi.
13. Ibid., p. vii.
14. Ibid., vol. II, p. 397.
15. Mahan, *The Influence of Sea Power Upon History, 1660–1783.* (Boston: Little, Brown, 1890), pp. 25–59.
16. Mahan, *Sea Power in its Relations to the War of 1812.* (Boston: Little, Brown, 1905), pp. 284–290.
17. Mahan, *The Influence of Sea Power Upon History*, p. 138.
18. Mahan, "The Hague Conference: The Question of Immunity for Belligerent Merchant Shipping," National Review (June 1907) reprinted in *Some Neglected Aspects of War.* (Boston: Little, Brown, 1907), pp. 190–191.
19. Mahan, *Sea Power in its Relations to the War of 1812.* (Boston: Little, Brown, 1905), vol I., pp. 144–148.
20. Mahan, "Comments on the Seizure of Private Property at Sea" in Seager and Maguire, *Letters and Papers,* vol. III., pp. 623–626.
21. Mahan, *Naval Strategy Compared and Contrasted with the Principles and Practice of Military Operations on Land: Lectures delivered at the U.S. Naval War College, Newport, R.I., Between the Years 1887 and 1911* (Boston: Little, Brown, 1911).

22. Seager and Maguire, Letters and Papers, vol. III, p. 440: Mahan to T. Roosevelt, 23 December 1911.
23. Mahan, *Naval Strategy,* chapter 6, reprinted in Hattendorf, ed., *Mahan on Naval Strategy* (Annapolis, MD: Naval Institute Press, 1991), p. 99.
24. Ibid., p. 107.
25. Ibid, chapter VIII, p. 142.
26. NMM, MS 79/067: Mahan to Laughton, 20 March 1896. The quote in note 1 directly follows this one.
27. Mahan, *The Problem of Asia: and Its Effect upon International Policies* (Boston: Little, Brown, 1900), pp. vi-vii.
28. Ibid.
29. NMM, MS 79/067: Mahan to Laughton, 21 March 1893.
30. See, in particular, D. M. Schurman, "Mahan Revisited," in Hattendorf and Robert S. Jordan, *Maritime Strategy and the Balance of Power: Britain and America in the Twentieth Century* (London: Macmillan, 1989), pp. 95–109. See also the important, revisionist work by Jon Tetsuro Sumida, *Inventing Grand Strategy and Teaching Command: The Classic Works of Alfred Thayer Mahan Reconsidered.* (Baltimore and Washington: Johns Hopkins University Press, 1997).
31. Henry E. Eccles, *Military Concepts and Philosophy* (New Brunswick, N.J.: Rutgers University Press, 1965) and *Military Power in a Free Society* (Newport, RI: Naval War College Press, 1985). Eccles's extensive collection of papers and correspondence are in the Naval Historical Collection, Naval War College, Newport, Rhode Island. See Evelyn Cherpak, compiler, *Register of the Henry E. Eccles Papers.* 2nd Edition (Newport, RI: Naval Historical Collection, 1988).
32. J. C. Wylie, *Military Strategy: A General Theory of Power Control* (New Brunswick, NJ: Rutgers University Press, 1967). Reprinted with an introduction by John B. Hattendorf, a selection of his other key writings and with a postscript by J. C. Wylie in the Classics of Sea Power series (Annapolis, MD: Naval Institute Press, 1989).
33. See chapter 9, below, p.
34. See George W. Baer, "Conference Summary: Corbett and Richmond . . . Mahan and Us," in James Goldrick and Hattendorf, *Mahan is Not Enough: The Proceedings of a Conference on the Works of Sir Julian Corbett and Admiral Sir Herbert Richmond* (Newport: Naval War College Press, 1993), pp. 287–294.

5

Sir Julian Corbett on the Significance of Naval History

On 13 February 1917, *The Times* of London announced, 'His Majesty has been pleased to confer the honour of knighthood upon:—

JULIAN CORBETT, Esq.
Secretary of the Historical Section of the Committee of Imperial Defence. He practised at the Bar until 1882, and was special correspondent of the *Pall Mall Gazette* in the Dongola Expedition, 1896, Ford Lecturer in English History, Oxford University, in 1903, and for many years Lecturer in History at Naval War college. In 1914 was awarded the Chesney Gold Medal. Is engaged on the official naval history of the war.[1]

For decades following his death in 1922, Corbett's work was virtually ignored among navies and naval historians. His importance to thinking in the late twentieth century was made apparent entirely through the devoted effort of Professor Donald M. Schurman, working in Canada.[2]

Born in 1854, Corbett, like his slightly older American contemporary Rear Admiral Alfred T. Mahan, was greatly influenced by the naval biographer and editor, Sir John Knox Laughton. Again, like Mahan, Corbett did not turn to serious historical work until he was in his forties. Educated at Cambridge, he unenthusiastically practiced law for a number of years, then turned to travel, and finally, to writing. In 1886, Corbett published the first of his novels, the beginning of a published record that clearly reflects a growing and maturing perception of history and its practical relationships to current affairs. In his personal life, for a quarter century between graduation from Cambridge in 1875 and the publication of his second major historical study, *The Successors of Drake* in 1900, there seems to have been a sense of conflict and unsettled purpose in Corbett's mind. His legal practice, desire for travel and adventure, participa-

Sir Julian Corbett
(*courtesy of D.M. Schurman*)

tion in the Dongola Expedition, and fiction writing all provided contrasts within his life. Jasper Festing, the hero in his second novel, *For God and Gold* revealed what may well have been Corbett's own belief when he declared:

> The great struggle of my life had begun, though I knew it not; the strife for mastery of me between the inward man-made life of scholarship and vain hurry after God, and the strong, pure out-o' door life of England that God Himself had given me for my birthday present.[3]

Earlier, in the same work, he had philosophized:

> . . . Now must not a scholar be content with the light that comes softened and tender hued through a library window if he would pass for wise among men. Now must he plunge out into the day and seek for the new wisdom amongst the haunts of thronging men, where the sun light beats fierce and bright upon the world to show to him who fears not all its beauty, and all its baseness, too.[4]

It would be wrong to place too much emphasis on these early novels in relation to Corbett's mature philosophy. However, one is struck by the attempt to bring action and scholarship together within one person. Although not unique to Corbett, it is certainly a thread which is carried throughout his life. He seems to have accepted fully the advice given to his hero Jasper when the tutor counseled, "Moreover, you need not lay aside scholarship, but must labor thereat, even as I have done, to make of it a weapon wherewith at last you shall hew Agag in pieces before the Lord."[5]

For God and Gold was followed two years later by another novel, *Kophetua the Thirteenth.* In the same year, his first historical work was also published, a brief biography for Macmillan's 'English Men of Action Series' on George Monk, Duke of Albermarle, one of the 'Generals at Sea' in the Second Dutch War. Corbett's biography of Sir Francis Drake, which appeared the next year in the same series, was a logical extension of his interest in the era which had been the setting in *For God and Gold.* After completing his biographical studies, Corbett turned to travel and to more adventurous pursuits. He published his last novel, *A Business in Great Waters* in 1895 and then obtained an assignment as special correspondent to cover the Dongola Expedition in the Anglo-Egyptian Sudan. Corbett's war experience during this period seem to have crystallized his ideas and probably led him to determine that the scholarly study of war could have practical applications. Returning to England, he began to work again in the area of his old interest, the history of *Drake and the Tudor Navy.*

Completed in 1898, Corbett's careful and balanced scholarship has stood the test of time. For Garrett Mattingly and G. R. Elton it remained the classic study of the subject.

While doing the research for his study of Drake, Corbett came into contact with Sir John Knox Laughton, founder of the Navy Records Society. At the latter's request, Corbett edited *Papers Relating to the Navy During the Spanish War 1585–87*. This was the beginning of a long association with the Society, during which Corbett would edit six documentary publications.

Corbett's marriage in 1899 seems to have marked a turning point in his career. Then, at the age of forty-five, he devoted himself exclusively to the study of naval history. In 1900, he published a sequel to his volume on the tudor Navy entitled *The Successors of Drake*. These two books demonstrate the basic approach which Corbett would employ throughout the rest of his career.

Corbett's approach to naval history was a new one. He broke with the tradition of such men as William James who had concentrated solely on a narrative of battles and isolated naval actions. He broke, too, with the tradition carried on by his friend Laughton who concentrated so heavily in the field of biography. Corbett took a broader view and focused on the wide scope of national and international events. His product was designed to be more than antiquarian; it was to have a practical application in the events of Corbett's own day and to provide a guide for the present and the future. Influenced by Mahan in his view of placing naval history within a broad context, Corbett profited by the American's popularity and showed, though a study of strategy, the power that navies exerted by their intelligent disposition.[6]

Although writing for a British audience, Corbett was not interested in promoting any specific concept of naval strategy nor in making a patriotic appeal to bolster a particular group. Rather he tried to be objective about history. His attitude can be clearly seen in an incident during World War I. At the height of a controversy over removing a statue of England's King William III presented to Britain some years earlier by Kaiser Wilhelm, Corbett wrote the editor of *The Times* that the statue was "an historical landmark representing a characteristic phase of our foreign relations. It is not our way," he said, "to destroy historical landmarks when history takes a new direction. We have better methods of marking our disapproval of William II [the Kaiser]. So why not let us enjoy the irony of his gift for the statue he presented is that of the man who first showed us how to bring an arch-disturber of the peace of the world to his knees."[7]

Often seeking principles within history, rather than constructing a philosophy and drawing on history for his "proof," Corbett believed that strategy, in its highest sense, was the most significant aspect of any naval study. In he preface to *England in the Seven Years' War,* he wrote:

> In endeavoring to recover the principles of the art which were so real and familiar to its old masters in those days, it has been found unavoidable to introduce a certain amount of strategical exposition. For this some apology is due to civilian readers. A less technical and more epic treatment of the great contest for maritime empire would doubtless have received a kindlier welcome. Yet in mitigation of the literary transgression it may be urged, even for those who read history for its romance, for its drama and its poetry, that surely the deepest notes of what they seek can only be heard when we watch great men of action struggling, as in some old Greek tragedy, with the inexorable laws of strategy, or riding on them in mastery to the inevitable catastrophe.[8]

As a civilian studying a topic which had previously been the province of professional naval officers, Corbett was somewhat uneasy. He realized that the technical and professional knowledge of sailors was largely acquired by long service afloat. This he knew was his major handicap and in spite of detailed study, he could never gain the insight from practical experience. Lacking this expertise he developed a close association with leading naval officers to remedy it and gratefully commented, "those of us who have dared to walk upon the waters know well the need of their helping hands."[9] Corbett recognized that his scholarly approach provided a view which was uncommon among naval officers. For this reason he warned against both the civilian historian who was isolated from naval men, and the naval officer who was uneducated in the historical discipline. The perfect solution, he felt was the scholar who was associated as closely as possible with the Navy. In this context, it is interesting to note that Corbett's most prominent disciple was the officer-historian Admiral Sir Herbert Richmond. In his campaign to encourage the establishment of an historical office in the Admiralty, Corbett wrote:

> It has indeed been suggested that a Professorship of Naval History at a University might supply the need. But however such a chair might succeed for Military History or for forming a sound national opinion, for the practical needs of the Service it seems foredoomed to failure. What is of the sea must breathe the breath of the sea. Without it it will pine in academical speculation. In salt water the old naval tradition was born, and by salt water alone can it be nourished. sever the work of [the] revival [of

naval history] from the Admiralty and you sever it from the well-spring of
that intangible spirit which is our peculiar asset. . . . The most perfect organization, the most scholarly research, the most elaborate technical science, cannot supply its place. . . . The atmosphere they have engendered
is the soul of the matter, and nowhere out of intimate touch with the fleet
can its can its inspiration be assured.[10]

In contrast to his broad approach to naval history, Corbett's
method emphasized the minute, while at the same time serving a
larger purpose. His edition of *The Spencer Papers* provides an interesting example. Here with documentary evidence, we have the lowest common denominator of all historical sources: the letters and papers of a single man. Corbett, however, did not merely transfer one
man's chaos from manuscript to print. He organized his material into
groupings of similar subject matter which he felt provided a valuable
service in illuminating naval warfare. Typically, in his introduction
to one section,[11] Corbett noted four major points of lasting interest:
(1) the precariousness of moving troops over the sea when an active
fleet is able to strike at any time, (2) the danger of keeping admirals
at sea in ignorance of the general war plan, (3) how successful combined operations may employ diversion to achieve surprise, and (4)
how the concentration of fleets tends to throw open the sea to the enemy's counterattack on trade. As editor and historian, Corbett was
striving to understand men in the midst of a situation. The general
flow of events in the battles was recorded, but what had not been previously understood was the way in which responsible men had reacted and demonstrated the lessons of patience, confidence, and as-
surance of victory.

Corbett's *Campaign of Trafalgar* illustrates another characteristic
which places him at variance with contemporary naval writers such
as W. L. Clowes. Instead of approaching the battle in the blood-and-
guts tradition, detailing the gore as it ran from the scuppers or concentrating on individual ship movements, Corbett showed the battle
in the light of international policy. Viewing his work as a "staff history" similar to the type of work he believed a naval staff should prepare in the Admiralty, he covered diplomacy, national politics, and
personalities as well as fleet operations. His final evaluation was not
an evaluation of the tactics employed, but rather a study of the influence which a naval victory had on the outcome of a war. It is surprising to some readers to discover that Corbett found in Trafalgar,
not the glory of a mighty navy, but an example of the limitations of
sea power in determining the outcome of a war.

Again in a review of Charles de la Roncière's *Histoire de la Marine*

Française, Corbett revealed much of his own balanced method when he noted:

> Facts it is true are lavished upon us with a profusion that tells of infinite labor and an unsurpassed enthusiasm for research. But facts and research alone will not make a naval history. Rather for the bulk of readers do they tend by themselves to deepen the obscurity that hangs around an obscure subject. Without some sustained attempt to correlate the apparently disconnected events, to deduce from them some kind of principles, to explain their bearing on the development of naval science, and their general place in the broad progression of war, such a work sinks to the position of a chronicle. It can not be called a history. . . . The antiquaries lack of interest in the living professional aspect of the subject is not doubt in some measure to blame.[12]

Corbett did not allow his concern for the present and the professional value of his work to form anachronisms in his history. His great concern for primary source material and for detailed, original research helped him to avoid this pitfall. One of the greatest challenges for the historian, he felt, was the task of placing himself in the exact state of mind of the men about whom he was writing. Great care must be taken to shut one's eyes to all that the person in history would not know.

An understanding of sea power was vital to Corbett's concept of history. Although he was a naval historian, he saw his field on such a wide scope that it is probably more accurate to consider him as a student of war specializing in the naval aspects. He saw the force that could be projected from the sea as one which had a threefold capability: (1) it could support or obstruct diplomatic effort, (2) it could project or destroy commerce, and (3) it could further or hinder military operations.[13] In order to fulfill these objectives, Corbett believed that the basic problem in naval history was the reconciliation of ships' endurance at sea with the free movement of ships.[14] In other words, the command of the sea and the ability to project one's power at sea was basically a problem in the control of maritime communications.[15] That consideration was the means to an end, and in Corbett's mind, it could never be an end in itself.[16] When he reviewed the Battle of Trafalgar, he noted that the battle *did* rescue the British Isles from invasion, French naval power was destroyed, and bases were gained in the Mediterranean and in the East which firmly secured the British overseas empire. Yet the war raged on for ten years; Napoleon was not defeated.[17] The Battle of Trafalgar had not been a naval pressure combined with a military pressure. This key connection was missing, and so the limitation of sea power was defined in Corbett's mind. As he pointed out in both *The Successors of Drake* and *England in the Seven Years' War,* sea power was impotent, in anything other than a defensive war, in deciding the final outcome of a war against great continental states.[18] To be effective, a well organized and highly trained navy must be complemented by a well organized and highly trained diplomatic and military establishment. In reaching this conclusion, Corbett was not attempting to destroy the arguments in favor of naval power; on the contrary, he was demonstrating very precisely that the navy could not operate in a vacuum. He showed effectively the strength of position given by command of the sea and the resulting power of offense. Beyond the clash of battles, he perceived, too, that the silent pressure of a naval presence was the most potent force of the navy.[19] "For it is not successful battles that bring peace," Corbett wrote, "but the fear or experience of what these battles give the victor power to do."[20] Often reiterating the point that naval and military history should never be separated, he saw that the question for the Army was "What can the Navy enable us to do?" while for the Navy the question was "What does the Army want to do?"[21]

Turning to the more far-reaching aspect of naval history as a scholarly pursuit, Corbett sought to give the subject its rightful place as part of general history. He felt, quite rightly, that the original sources of naval history had never been properly worked, particularly in the broader relationship between naval, military, and political events. Often, he noted, the general historian ignored the events on the sea having missed the "striking and comprehensive new outlook which is almost always to be obtained from the sea."[22] Carrying his concept one step further, he proclaimed that,

> . . . Naval History is the main binding link that unifies world history. The general historian, then, cannot afford to neglect it, and he is the poorer for that link never having been fully forged for him. Most of us, I think, who have made Naval History our study could name many trite criticisms which pass from historian to historian, but which will not stand a breath of salt wind.[23]

In any discussion of Corbett, one inevitably thinks of his work on the official history of the Royal Navy during World War I. The three volumes which were produced under his name were the product of a staff working under him, therefore, they are considerably different from his other works. Corbett fully realized the difficulty of writing contemporary history. Frankness was not always possible, not only because of security considerations; but also because many of the participants who were still living tended to modify criticism and objective treatment. Time alone could provide the remedy. In spite of this problem, he believed that such studies were not valueless. They "are not quite histories, but rather they are-like collections of documents-materials for history."[24] Although valid criticism can be made of his writings on World War I, it cannot be denied that as period pieces they are key documents in understanding the era. Corbett, personally, had access to the highest levels of military and naval command throughout the course of the war. His use of the information he obtained from these sources provides valuable insights to the scholar.

His mature concept of naval history appeared when he published his "Revival of Naval History" in *The Contemporary Review* (December 1916) and his book *Some Principles of Maritime Strategy* (1911). By this time, Corbett had determined that the highest aim of naval history was to open more widely the rich treasures of the Royal Navy's experience to the Navy itself. He believed that the great naval heroes were the great masters from whom the modern day naval leaders could learn, and he felt that it was the specialist in naval history who could successfully bring them together.[25]

In attaining this goal, however, there was a peculiar problem. The events in which naval officers take part often seem so tremendous and so different from anything which had gone before, that those who participate are inclined to shrug off the value of historical study, particularly in an era of technological change. Corbett consoled those who felt overwhelmed by the present and those who saw the past as something insignificant for study by men of action:

> Let us remember that great wars always had this effect at the time. While we are close to the stupendous event, it seems like a flood that has gathered up and swept everything on which the old lore rested. But it is not so. As time gives us distance we see the flood as only as one more pool in the river as it flows down to eternity, and that the phenomena of that pool, however great it may be, cannot be understood unless we know the whole course of the river and the nature of all the tributary streams that have gone to make its volume. No, a great war does not kill the past, it gives it new life.[26]

In his documentary volumes on tactics, *Fighting Instructions 1530–1816* (1905) and *Signals and Instructions 1776–1794* (1908), Corbett clearly addressed himself to the men of action. He pointed out that the problems in these volumes applied to the age of sail, but that the validity of studying them was not destroyed by a change in the methods of modern propulsion or a change in weapons or the material with which ships were constructed. The principles of tactics did not change, he contended, only the method of applying them. What was important was the thought processes which the old masters had used to arrive at their conclusions. Bearing this in mind, Corbett was able to see recurring attitudes which led to the atrophy of essentially good tactical principles, and others which allowed the revision of weak principles and the development of new ones.[27]

In viewing the education of naval officers, Corbett saw the fundamental purpose as one to make "a man" and "a seaman" of the future naval officer, while at the same time teaching him a mass of technical knowledge. In the scope of this knowledge, naval history was the key to the highest perception of naval problems.[28] Through history it was possible to determine the "normal" and to see that certain lines of conduct normally produce certain effects. Since he believed that wars tend to take specific forms which are related to the object of the war, certain types of combat operations are inappropriate to certain forms of warfare. In clarifying his point, Corbett used an analogy which would be understood by sailors:

> The laws of storms and tides, of winds and currents, and the whole of meteorology are subject to infinite and incalculable deflections, and yet who will deny nowadays that by the theoretical study of such things the seaman's art has gained in coherence and strength? Such a study will not by itself make a seaman or navigator, but without it no seaman or navigator can nowadays pretend to the name. Because storms do not always behave in the same way, because currents are erratic, will the most practical seaman deny that the study of the normal conditions are useless to him in his practical decisions.[29]

In evaluating Sir Julian Corbett's significance as an historian, one appreciates the fact that he combined a breadth of vision with an unusual grasp of detail. In this respect, he was a rarity in his field. He, himself, was part of a growing self-awareness that turn-of-the-century Britain was experiencing. In this historic role, Corbett played a key part in the development of strategic principles. As one historian has pointed out, it is arguable whether he overplayed his hand in the deduction of principles from history, "but the fact that he invented the game is not" arguable.[30] Perhaps, Corbett's significance in historiography is best seen in relation to Mahan. Both were contemporaries and both influenced and respected the other, although their methods were quite different. Mahan's philosophy was built upon wide reading from secondary sources, while Corbett's was built on deductions from primary sources. It is significant that Mahan's first major work, *The Influence of Seapower upon History, 1660–1783* was a broad survey, while Corbett's was a detailed examination of the Tudor Navy. To the end of his career, Mahan resisted making an abstract, analytical summary of naval affairs, while Corbett produced *Some Principles of Maritime Strategy* as the result of a career of research. Corbett, himself, wrote that Mahan had based his theories on unproven ground and that his generalizations covered large areas that had not been carefully studied. Paying tribute to the value of the American's ideas, Corbett could marvel, "the wonder is that Mahan could build as well as he did on a foundation so insecure."[31]

Corbett's great effort was to bring the scholar and the man of action together where they could mutually achieve the concrete goal of a better Navy. Although Corbett is still hardly as well known as Mahan, his work in systematically considering British naval history in the period 1585 to 1763, expanded the work of Mahan and gave it depth as well as breadth. From this vantage point alone, readers could evaluate Mahan's ideas more accurately. In the realm of practical politics, no less a figure than Winston Churchill was greatly affected by his thought, [32] showing that there was efficacy in his scholarly achievement.

For the naval historian in the late twentieth century, Corbett's work provides a successful example of careful scholarship usefully employed. Although more than half a century has elapsed since his death, naval history has not yet been fully accepted within the scope of general history. The aids to historical navigation which Corbett left behind remain in position and provide valuable points from which new work may be guided. Most significant was his example of impartial study. His historical works disguise neither a bias in favor of imperial expansion nor a political argument for building more naval ships. He could study the failure of sea power as closely as he could scrutinize its brilliant achievements. When he took sides in an argument, he clearly demonstrated what was fact and what was interpretation in his exposition. Like any historian's work, Corbett's writing did not always meet the high standard which he had set for himself, but his intention was clear and laudable: to employ historical scholarship as the most effective means for the professional understanding of the value, limitations, and capabilities of seaborne power.

NOTES

This is a revised version of an essay that was the author's first published piece. It originally appeared in *The American Neptune,* XXXI (1971), pp. 275–285.

1. The Times [London], 13 February 1917, p. 9e.
2. When this essay was first published, the only works on Corbett available were P. M. Stanford, "The Work of Sir Julian Corbett in the Dreadnought Era," U. S. Naval Institute *Proceedings,* LXXVII (1951), 61–71 and D. M. Schurman's influential study, *The Education of a Navy; The Development of British Naval Strategic Thought, 1867–1914* (Chicago: University of Chicago Press, 1965), chapter 7. Since that time, many of Corbett's works have been reprinted and Schurman published his biography, *Julian S. Corbett (1854–1922): Historian of British Maritime Policy from Drake to Jellicoe.* Royal Historical Society Studies in History Series, volume 26. (London: Royal Historical Society, 1981). In 1992, a Naval War College Conference produced, James Goldrick and John B. Hattendorf, eds., *Mahan is Not Enough: The Proceedings of a Conference on the Works of Sir Julian Corbett and Admiral Sir Herbert Richmond.* (Newport, RI: Naval War College Press, 1993), which includes as appendices bibliographies of works by Corbett and Richmond as well as essays on many aspects of their work. For a commentary on aspects of Corbett's later thought, see Hattendorf and Schurman, "Introduction" to Julian S. Corbett, *Maritime Operations in the Russo-Japanese War, 1904–1905.* (Annapolis: Naval Institute Press, 1994).
3. Julian S. Corbett, *For God and Gold.* (London: Macmillan, 1887), p. 88.
4. Ibid., p. 41.
5. Ibid., p. 60. (Here the biblical allusion is to I Samuel 15:33.)
6. Schurman, *Education of a Navy,* p. 163.
7. *The Times,* 23 May 1918, p. 87.
8. Julian S.Corbett, *England in the Seven Years' War.* (London: Longmans, Green., 1907), I, v-vi.
9. Julian S. Corbett, "Staff Histories" in J. S. Corbett and H. J. Edwards, eds., *Naval and Military Essays.* (Cambridge: University Press, 1914), p. 31.
10. Julian S. Corbett, *The Campaign of Trafalgar.* (London: Longmans, Green., 1910), p. xii.
11. Julian S. Corbett, ed., *The Spencer Papers, 1794–1801.* (London: Navy Records Society, 1913), I, 69–70. Corbett's emphasis on the 'guerre de course' in his fourth point places him in opposition to Mahan.
12. Julian S. Corbett, Review of Charles de la Roncière, *Histoire de la Marine Française,* in *The American Historical Review,* VI (1901), pp. 546–47.
13. Julian S. Corbett, *England in the Seven Years' War.* (London: Longmans, Green, 1997), I, 6.
14. Julian S. Corbett, *Drake and the Tudor Navy.* (London: Longmans, Green, 1898), I, 3.
15. Corbett, *Seven Years' War,* II, 308.
16. Ibid., I, 6.

17. Julian S. Corbett, *The Campaign of Trafalgar.* (London: Longmans, Green, 1910), p. 424.
18. Julian S. Corbett, *The Successors of Drake.* (London: Longmans, Green, 1900), pp. vii, 407–410; Corbett, Seven Years' War, I, 5.
19. Julian S. Corbett, *England in the Mediterranean.* (London: Longmans, Green, 1904), p. 4.
20. Julian S. Corbett, *The League of Peace and a Free Sea.* (New York: G. H. Doran, 1917).
21. *The Times,* 8 January 1916, p. 8e.
22. Julian S. Corbett, 'The Revival of Naval History,' *The Contemporary Review,* cx (1916), 739.
23. Ibid.
24. Corbett, "Staff Histories," p. 28.
25. Corbett, "Revival," p. 739.
26. Ibid., p. 740.
27. Julian S. Corbett, *Fighting Instructions, 1530–1816.* (London: Navy Records Society), pp. ix-x.
28. Julian S. Corbett, "Education in the Navy I", *Monthly Review,* VI (1902), 38.
29. Julian S. Corbett, *Some Principles of Maritime Strategy* (London: Longmans, Green, 1911), pp. 7–8.
30. Schurman, *Education,* p. 152.
31. Corbett, "Revival," pp. 734–735. For comments on Mahan as an historian, see W. E. Livezey, *Mahan on Seapower.* (Norman: University of Oklahoma Press, 1947), pp. 23–35; and W. D. Puleston, *Mahan* (New Haven, CT: Yale University Press, 1934), pp. 97–98, 326–36, Robert Seager II, *Alfred Thayer Mahan: The Man and His Letters* (Annapolis, MD: Naval Institute Press, 1977) and "A Biography of a Biographer: Alfred Thayer Mahan, " in Robert S. Love, *Changing Interpretations and New Sources in Naval History.* (New York: Garland, 1980), pp. 278–292. For the most recent study, see Sumida, *Inventing Grand Strategy.*
32. Schurman, *Education,* pp. 189–190.

6

Purpose and Contribution in Editing Naval Documents: A General Appreciation

There is no question that the standards and reputation of naval history, as a field of academic enquiry, need improvement. One important way to do this is to improve the available source material and to point the way toward critical appreciation of naval documents. Well-edited volumes of naval papers can do this. They can smooth the way for general readers and for beginning students; they can improve the available source materials for popular writers; and they can provide a selection of key source materials which constitute the basis of new interpretations. Documentary publications are particularly important for naval history, a field which depends equally upon personal insights from private papers as well as on the release and interpretative analysis of official, government documents.

The editing and publication of historical documents has been a widespread feature in many countries and in many languages, but the publication of naval documents has become largely an Anglo-American tradition. Historians working in French, Dutch, and Spanish language materials have made important contributions, but their effort has not been sustained over so long a period or so large a body of published documents. Despite the common interest among English-speaking historians, however, the attitude, approach, and history of naval documents publications in Britain and the Untied States differ considerably.

In the United States, government archives have traditionally been open to scholars and to the public, although problems in the release of classified documents have created difficulties in the 1980s and 1990s. In the early nineteenth century, both the state and federal governments placed greater emphasis on the publication of documents as the principal means of their preservation than on the care and arrangement of the original papers. As early as 1823, John Brannan published the *Official Letters of the Military and Naval Officers of the United States during the War with great Britain in the Years 1812, 1813, 1814, and 1815.* His claim that they were copied from or compared with the originals in the War and Navy Departments reflected an open-door policy at the archives, even if his work lacked more modern editorial standards.

His work was followed by the government sponsored collection of *American State Papers* published during the period 1834–1861 by Seaton and Gale which included three large volumes on naval affairs covering the first forty years of the republic's history.[1]

In 1884 Congress appropriated funds to begin work on the publication of *The Official Records of the Union and Confederate Navies in the War of the Rebellion,* following the path already established by an Army series. The first of the thirty-one naval volumes appeared in 1894, beginning a continuing process of government publication that has included documents on American naval operations in the Spanish-American War, the Quasi-War with France, the Barbary War, the War of 1812, and the American Revolution.[2]

This emphasis on publishing these older documents received great emphasis with the personal interest of President Franklin Roosevelt. In 1913, as Assistant Secretary of the Navy, he had "discovered" the Navy's oldest records under the eaves of the old State-War-Navy building and personally supported the proper housing of the office of Naval Records. In 1934, he even requested Congress to establish a special fund to print naval documents.[3] Through its documentary publishing programs, the U.S. Navy's Naval Historical Center and its predecessor offices have made their most substantial and enduring contribution.

Despite this large-scale program by the U.S. Navy, the publication of documents by scholarly societies, university, and other presses has been intermittent at best. The Naval History Society, which was formed for the purpose of publishing documents relating to American naval history, published only eleven volumes in its twenty-year life span. The U.S. Naval Institute published only four titles in the "Naval Letters Series" it began in 1964, before that idea withered away. Other presses have published the occasional volume of naval documents, but more often than not they are items from associated libraries and archives and not a sustained effort toward the study of naval history.

In England, the situation has been quite different. The Admiralty archives were completely closed until 1879 when John Knox Laughton was given personal permission to consult naval records up to 1815. In 1885, the records up to 1805 were opened to the public for the first time, and two years later, the documents up to 1815 were added.[4] Beyond the documents presented to Parliament and published over the years in its journals and in Command Papers, the Admiralty has never undertaken a sustained effort to edit or publish historical documents relating to the Royal Navy. Faced with this situation, Rear Admiral Sir Cyprian Bridge and Sir John Knox Laughton formed the idea in 1892 to publish naval manuscripts through a private society.[5] On 13 June 1893, the Navy Records Society was formed to publish material for subscribing members. Interestingly enough, the only American founder-member was Captain Caspar Goodrich, USN,[6] who in 1911 founded the Naval History Society in New York for a similar purpose.

The British government began to publish some fundamental historical manuscripts as early as 1767 with the *Rotuli Parliamentorum* and the *Domesday Book* in 1783. In 1800, the Record Commission was established, followed by the Senate Paper Commission in 1825. The publication of *The Rolls* series began in 1858. In Britain, as in America, official publication of historical documents predated private initiative. In Britain, however, there was an additional development.

Since the 1830s and 40s, scholars and antiquarians had established a number of societies to print "historical books which no publisher would risk."[7] Among them were the Surtees Society, The Camden Society, The Percy Society, The Hakluyt Society, and later the English History Text Society and the Roxburgh Club. The Navy Records Society took as its models the Camden Society and the Hakluyt Society,[8] both of which had already published items of interest to potential members of the Navy Records Society.

The Navy Records Society's first volume appeared in 1894. Edited by Laughton, it documented the defeat of the Spanish Armada. After making these documents available in print for the first time, Laughton declared "it will henceforth be impossible for anyone wishing to pose as an historical writer, to repeat the transparent fictions which had grown up round the memory of our victory."[9]

For more than a century, the Navy Records Society has been the most important organization in the scholarly study of British naval history. In the more than 140 volumes the Society has published in that span of time, include documents from the thirteenth century through World War II, including official reports and personal papers that provide information on a wide range of topics. As a body of ma-

terial, it is interesting to compare and contrast the Navy Records Society volumes with the material produced by the U.S. Navy's historical office in exactly the same period. The means of publication and
the method of finance have had an obvious effect on the emphasis
and approach to the topic. The U.S. Navy's focus has been largely on
the record of naval operations and battle. Through sustained work
over many years, a full record of documents has been produced by
government-paid historians. The Secretary of the Navy declared, as
early as 1885, that "the ultimate object of publication was to place
the navy's Civil War record in a permanent and accessible form
where it can be referred to by the naval service, by the executive and
legislative departments of the government in their efforts to insure
the highest efficiency in the Navy. . . . "[10] Over the years, the Navy
has continued to note the professional and current relevance of its
historical work for those in active service.[11] That very same purpose
for naval history was always at the center in Laughton's mind: "To
know what the men of old did, and why and how they did it, to know
that they failed in doing, and why and how they failed, is the best of
all guides for achieving success or avoiding failure."[12]

Laughton's younger disciples, Julian Corbett and Herbert Richmond, echoed these thoughts in the volumes which they edited for the
Navy Records Society. In contrast to work in America, however, the
Navy Records Society volumes came to be edited increasingly by academics and scholars whose primary interests lay beyond the practical needs of the naval service. This difference in editorial aim combined with the fact that the scholarly work was given to the society
without remuneration produced pressure for an increasing selectiv-
ity in approach. Throughout its history, the Navy Records Society has
been a group with varied interests within the field of naval history. In
order to meet the demands of its members, the Society faces great
pressure to issue volumes on varying topics, from varying eras. Instead of long sustained series on naval operations, based on official
dispatches, the Navy Records Society has produced volumes on selected topics, particular operations, papers relating to a single individual, and themes such as administration, law, social history and
health as well as memoirs, journals, pamphlets and treatises and
other documents that fit conveniently into single volumes. In one respect, it has had no clear policy, beyond taking the best of what is offered. By contrast, official publications are free to serve scholarly and
professional interests in historical research untroubled by the sales
market. The Navy Records Society, however, is far more able to meet
the demands of changing academic interests and editorial practices

while the long-term projects supported by the government find themselves perpetuating methods and subjects chosen long ago.

The general differences in approach between naval documents published in America and those published in Britain are fundamentally created by the circumstances of publication. The student of American naval history has been better served than his British counterpart with information on general naval operations, but more poorly supplied with insights from private papers, and documents on administration, social history and other themes. Elting Morison's "Naval Administration: Selected Documents on Navy Department Organization, 1915–1940" remains unpublished in the Navy Department Library.

Some of these topics are included in various series of documents which have been published for students in other areas, for example, the Naval War College's International Law "Blue Books" include volumes of documents as well as legal studies and law situations.[13] Naval documents touching diplomatic affairs may be found in series such as *The Foreign Relations of the United States, British and Foreign State Papers,* and *Documents on British Foreign Policy.* Similarly, there is important naval material to be found in the published diplomatic papers of allied powers. By the nature of the subject, the naval historian can find much valuable material within the boundaries of other historical specialties. "If national history may be compared to a cake, the different layers which are different aspects of national life, then," as one overly quoted statement has it, "naval history is not a layer, but a slice of that cake."[14] The scope ranges from industrial history to the history of science. Indeed some of the most valuable material has been published in the papers of leaders who at one time or another held a political appointment as a naval secretary. On the American side, the presidential papers of Theodore Roosevelt and Franklin Delano Roosevelt, as well as the papers of Secretaries of the Navy John D. Long, Josephus Daniels and James Forrestal[15] offer some sidelights into naval administration while their main thrust illuminates the broader political process. For British history, the companion volumes to Martin Gilbert's biography of Winston Churchill add a similar perspective,[16] although the administrative insight is more common in British naval history.

Despite its necessary connection to other areas, naval history remains a recognizable special subject dealing with the use of armed force at sea. The published historical documents which can be identified as primarily of interest to naval historians fall into six main categories: (1) documents on general naval history; (2) documents on a specified theme; (3) documents relating to a single individual; (4) manuscripts of book length such as journals, diaries, letter books, treatises; (5) multivolume series of operational dispatches; and (6) calendars of manuscripts. There are additional categories, such as microfilm publication, but they are largely differences of form rather than content. They are important, and deserve separate consideration. On the surface, however, the approach among all these categories ranges from the greatest care in selection and interpretation to "print everything."

GENERAL NAVAL HISTORY

There have been only two volumes of *Select Naval Documents* which were designed to illuminate a long span of history, the 1922 volume by Hodges and Hughes and the 1993 volume issued to commemorate the centenary of the Navy Records Society.[17] Both are source books for the history of the Royal Navy and designed to supplement interpretive readings for students. Hodges and Hughes saw their purpose as "the provision of colour and the heightening of the personal aspect" as well as the more serious issues involved in "smoothing the approach to a highly technical subject" and giving "concrete illustrations of the limiting condition of sea warfare."[18] Seventy years later, the Navy Records Society editors saw their role in a more sophisticated light, seeing their work as providing key documents that illustrated the best current interpretations of naval history as well as a stimulus to further archival research.

Students must have a sound basis of history before they can use and appreciate the reading of historical documents. Certainly, advanced students at schools and universities should have an appreciation of documents, although this approach to teaching has been much more common in England than in America. Students without a proper foundation, however, can find themselves with too much, too soon, bewildered by the mass of details that they fail to correlate. However, the use of documents in teaching history is important, particularly in training future professionals. As one historian explained, "Reading history ready-made is to making out oneself from documents what looking on at a football match is to playing the game oneself, or what reading a detective story is to tracking out a criminal."[19] Documents are the foundation and the evidence upon which broader historical interpretations are made. Published, critical editions of them are an essential means by which they may be more widely used, be more accessible, and be more thoroughly examined and understood. Teachers must consider and plan carefully how far they can go in using documents with their students. Yet one can never forget that documents are the basis of the historical discipline. They are the elements, and as Daniel Boorstin said of his collection of documents for *An American Primer,* they are "elementary in the most sophisticated sense of the word."[20]

The most ambitious and most successful series of selected for use in teaching is *English Historical Documents,* under the general editorship of David C. Douglas. Begun just after World War II, the series was abruptly cancelled by the publisher in 1981 and the contracts for remaining volumes withdrawn. Sadly, a projected volume for naval history was among those lost.[21] The basic value of the series remains, even in its unfinished form, and a few naval items can be found within its pages. This type of document publication is one that requires the greatest amount of interpretation and editorial appreciation. Each chosen document must somehow reflect an interpretive point. Chosen from the immense accumulation of historical material, they are useful in illustrating the elements and serve as a foundation relating to the analytical interpretations built on them. Historical studies build interpretations on documents which are often not available to the readers of analytical works. Without an accessible and representative collection of sources, historical "opinion proceeds without that direct study of evidence which alone can give validity to historical judgment."[22]

THEMATIC SELECTION

A second type of publication is that which selects documents to illustrate a theme or subject. The Navy Records Society has issued a variety of volumes in this category, ranging from R. G. Marsden's *Law and Custom of the Sea,* and *The Old Scots Navy* to Daniel Baugh's *Naval Administration,* Stephen Roskill's *The Naval Air Service* and Michael Simpson's *Anglo-American Naval Relations, 1917–1919.*[23] Other than the Navy Records Society, few publishers have undertaken the thematic approach, although Edouard Desbriere's two volumes on *Trafalgar: The Naval Campaign of 1805* and the Hakluyt Society's volumes on English colonization in Newfoundland and on the early English New England Voyages come to mind. Douglas Stein's volume on *American Maritime Documents, 1776–1860: Illustrated and Described* presents a different, but equally valuable, type of thematic selection, in which the focus is on representative types of documents that a maritime and naval histo-

rian encounters rather than on specific historical events. Another
variant on the thematic approach is the publication of related charts,
paintings, and drawings, treating them as historical documents as
well as works of art. One of the most successful examples of this is
the related work of Andrew David and Rüdiger Joppien in a variety
of publications, from various presses, relating to Captain James
Cook's three Pacific voyages.[24]

PAPERS OF AN INDIVIDUAL

The third category of published naval documents are those culled
from the papers of a single individual. One or two deal with a single
theme, such as Pitcairn Jones's volume of the Edward Codrington
papers, *Piracy in the Levant 1827–28*.[25] More commonly, however,
such volumes take a more biographical approach and are devoted to
the major period of a subject's career or representative of his entire
life. Usually these volumes are devoted to great men or at least those
who have held high office at interesting times. In this category, we
encounter most of the great names of British naval history: Hawke,
Vernon, Nelson, Warren, Collingwood, Sandwich, Spencer, Jellicoe,
Fisher, Beatty, Keyes, Somerville, Cunningham, and many others.
For the American Navy, there are far fewer, with substantial selec-
tions from only the Samuel F. DuPont, Mahan, John Paul Jones, and
Gustavus Fox papers. The editors who undertake such projects have
taken differing views. Sir Nicholas Harris Nicolas devoted seven volumes to Nelson and tried to publish everything he could find. "Where
genius exists, and where no great and absorbing feeling occupies the
mind," Nicolas wrote, "the most insignificant, as well as the most
studies and important letter, bears more or less of its impress: thus,
there is scarcely a note of Nelson's that does not contain some word
or line, or sentence, indicative" of his genius.[26] In his volumes of
Fisher letters, Arthur Marder took the opposite view: "Completeness
for the sake of completeness is a pedantic ideal that I reject. I have
been 'ruthless, and remorseless' (in the best Fisher tradition) in
pruning passages and eliminating hundreds of letters of little or no
interest or importance."[27]

Both editors have had their work supplemented by the publication
of additional volumes on both Nelson and Fisher, but looking at their
work, one can readily see the difference. Nicolas has tried to let the
documents speak for themselves while Marder asks his reader to accept his own judgment and criteria; Nicolas wanted the reader to
form his own judgment, but Marder gives us only his own estimate.

I doubt that there will ever be a happy meeting ground between those two points of view. Marder can easily be convicted of over-severity in editing, while the value of Nicolas's work is lessened, in one respect, by its very completeness. Few professional naval men have taken the time to study its bulk, leaving it to the professional historian. As John Knox Laughton implied in publishing a one-volume selection from Nicolas, both approaches may be needed.

Among the editions published in Britain, the volumes of letters of a single individual, tend to be a selection of incoming and outgoing letters in an exchange of correspondence, but typically the very few editions published in America, such as the *Mahan* and the *S. F. DuPont* letters have emphasized the outgoing letters from the pen of the individual concerned.[28]

BOOK-LENGTH MANUSCRIPTS

The fourth category of documents includes manuscript books, more modern versions of what scholars of ancient and medieval history might call a codex. For our purposes in naval history, they range from journals, such as Barlow's seventeenth-century volumes which paint so vivid a picture of sea life, to treatises such as *Boteler's Dialogues* on maritime affairs, Monson's Naval Tracts. For the eighteenth century, such works include the *History of the Russian Fleet during the Reign of Peter The Great,* and Penrose's memoir of James Trevenen's active career in both American and Russian waters."[29] This is the most common form of published naval document and it contains among it one of he great pieces of English literature, *The Diary of Samuel Pepys.* The new eleven-volume edition of this extremely difficult manuscript is a model of scholarship that must serve as an inspiration to all document editors.[30] Pepys's diary opens a marvelous perspective into the administrative life of the navy in seventeenth-century London. For the pathos and humor of a sailor's life in the same period, one should not overlook *The Diary of Henry Teonge,* "one of the most human and entertaining in that golden age of diarists."[31]

One may also find letter books, sketch books, journals, autobiographies, memoirs and logbooks in this the largest category of published naval documents. In general they are the easiest of all types of documents to edit since their form and shape are already determined, yet they need transcription, elucidation, indexing and, just as important, a scholarly introduction which gives he volume its place in the literature, explaining its importance and contribution.

Procedures and the technical aspects of the craft of editing are extremely important and must be considered in evaluating published documents. These procedures are well known and must be adhered to, for they are the elements that bring quality to craftsmanship.[32] We have examples of bad craftsmanship among historical documents which discredit the use of the published documents. Among the atrocities in English naval history is Oscar Browning's faculty transcription of the *Journal of Sir George Rooke*.[33] American naval historians have had to contend with the far murkier history of *The Diary of Gideon Welles,* Secretary of the Navy under Abraham Lincoln. Fortunately, the *Diary* has been reedited and the fabrications, additions and omissions of the 1911 edition corrected by Howard K. Beale.[34] Others have suffered from such overzealous elucidation that the manuscript is lost in the annotation.[35]

In most cases naval documents have been published in strictly chronological order, but in editing the *Spencer Papers* for the Navy Records Society, Julian Corbett suggested that a thematic approach would be much more useful. "A simple chronological presentation would have been easy enough," he wrote, "but would have scarcely served the purpose for which the Society exists. If such papers are to be of real and general service in illustrating the principles of naval and maritime warfare an arrangement by subject is imperative."[36]

With the same purpose in mind, John D. Hayes presented his selection from the letters of Samuel Francis DuPont in chronological order, but hoped that their publication would draw attention to neglected naval subjects, "such as logistics, prize captures and the blockade, or to general problems suggested by career-versus-civilian contention for control of naval operations, by political influences upon the conduct of the naval war, and by early efforts at interservice cooperation."[37]

MULTIVOLUME SERIES OF OPERATIONAL DISPATCHES

In the fifth category of publications, the U.S. Navy's series on *The Official Records of the Union and Confederate Navies, The Barbary Wars.* and *The Quasi War with France* have dominated. The two most recent series, *Naval Documents of the American Revolution* and *The Naval War of 1812,* have widened the focus slightly and considered some aspects beyond the operational records of battles and engagements. *The Naval War of 1812* volumes, in particular, are much more selective in their approach as well as more thematic.[38]

There are no multivolume series of twentieth century operational documents. The vast range and quantity of such documents present a difficult problem of selection, but the fact that many of these documents were produced on a typewriter presents an opportunity. In their sixty-eight-volume series, the editors of the "War Diary of the German Naval Staff, 1939–45" have employed an innovative approach. In this case, the editors reproduced the document as a photographic facsimile, adding notes at the end of each volume.[39] Their approach could be a model for others who deal with similar types of documents that are typewritten and uniform in their layout.

THE CALENDAR

The final category is the calendar form of editing. In this form, documents are not quoted verbatim, but are abstracts with occasional extracts from individual documents. The editors of the British *Calendar of State Papers* developed a form which provided so much data that they came to be regarded as substitutes for the documents themselves. British practices in calendaring documents were adopted widely in the United States, but in recent years, they have fallen out of favor. In America, they have not been used for naval documents, although in England the London Record Society published in 1983 a calendar of *Trinity House Transactions,* some of which have great naval interest.[40]

In search for form and unity, other editors have attempted to intersperse descriptive passages and explanatory text between selected document entries. Louis Jennings employed this method in the *Croker Papers*[41] and following Martin Blumenson's successful approach to the papers of General George S. Patton, Craig Symonds used the same idea in his *Charleston Blockade.*[42] Others have taken greater liberties with documents, bringing varying types together, piecing together extracts from letters, diaries and reports, into an arrangement that attempts to make a unified and more readable narrative than if the documents were published separately and in full.[43]

TRANSCRIPTS, PHOTOCOPIES, AND MICROFILM

The issue of spelling and form of transcription is a matter which raises the strongest passion among document editors. We only need to remember the "Great Spelling Controversy of 1867" which nearly destroyed the Camden Society to realize the depth of such passions.[44] Here too lies an issue upon which no compromise will be found among the contenders. With acid in his pen, Michael Oppenheim wrote in 1896: "A Fifteenth Century manuscript dressed up in modern English has a painfully artificial appearance, and, when thus masquerading, bears much the same resemblance to its source as does a translation to its original."[45]

In her recent edition of the fifteenth-century account books of William Soper, Susan Rose took the opposite view, and in a single sentence embraced all the sins that Oppenheim had fulminated against. "In this translation," she wrote, "the aim has been to provide a text which is clearly understandable and is as close to the original as is consistent with that aim."[46] One must add, however, that the Navy Records Society has generally published its works using the form of transcription which modernizes spelling and expands abbreviations. On the other hand, the U.S. Navy and the Hakluyt Society have used a form of transcription that attempts to reproduce more exactly the look of the manuscript. In the case of Norman Thrower's Hakluyt Society edition of Captain Edmond Halley's Journals,[47] this has meant the use of a variety of symbols and unusual characters. The purpose of this approach is undoubtedly "to preserve as fully as possible the flavor and character of . . . [a] manuscript by retaining . . . peculiarities of spelling and punctuation."[48]

The publication of documents through microfilm, microfiche and other inexpensive, miniaturizing procedures has revolutionized modern research methods. Documents and collections have been made available, which would otherwise have remained closed to everyone except researchers able to travel the world seeking their quarry. The cost to the researcher has been drastically reduced, while at the same time wear and tear on fragile original documents has been reduced by preserving or replacing them with microfilm publications. Yet microfilm remains difficult and unpleasant to use.[49] It still requires a specialist to interpret handwriting and abbreviations, identify and clarify references. Although immeasurably valuable to the researcher, microfilm publication must have the same scholarly assistance as that already described for selecting and editing letterpress editions. Simple reproduction of documents is not the purpose of historical editing, but thoughtful selection, interpretation, and clarification are the important matters.

Electronic media present another new approach for publishing documents and we are just beginning to make some use of them. As government offices and international organizations come increasingly to use Internet Web sites and to post current documents, one can envisage placement of these materials in some type of electronic archive that grows over time, allowing available electronic search and retrieval of documents.

In choosing among methods as in developing an approach, form and character of a volume, a good editor must carefully weigh the nature of the material in the light of the range of people who should use it and how it can best be presented for the most appropriate audience. In this day that means also an eye toward production costs. Peculiarities of spelling and punctuation are important to philologists, a joy to antiquarians, routine to the average historian and repulsive to both typesetters and ordinary readers. Whatever the choice, someone will be displeased; it is a matter of choosing friends and conserving enemies.

To look at published naval documents from another angle, let us take a general look at the overall body of material that has appeared. The bulk of it is found in the over 140 Navy Records Society volumes and the fifty-eight volumes published by the U.S. Navy. Beyond that, the material is scattered. At the present time, none of the naval bibliographies provides an accurate means to identify the full range of documentary sources in print. The most difficult of all to find are the stray items published in journals, tagged on as appendices to other works, included in document collections relating to different specialties or lost in the morass of government publications. A perceptive naval bibliographer could do a great service by compiling a thoroughly researched and carefully organized list of published documents. So much bad naval history has been written that we would all be well served if we could quickly and easily find references to the accessible foundation stones that are already in print. Reference to good sources is the best means in improving the standards of naval history and in raising naval history to an academically respectable level. A greater body of published naval documents is necessary to do it; documents are the essential foundation of historical scholarship.

In an overall view of published naval documents in America and in England, the five categories I have talked about and the long series of operational dispatches published by the U.S. Navy show the same general patterns. First, we can see that the seventeenth and eighteenth centuries up to 1815 dominate the scene. Much less has been done for the earlier period, and work on the nineteenth and twentieth centuries is spotty. We have no volume of select documents in either British or American naval history, which effectively gives an accessible and representative collection of sources for the general student to use. The disparate and varied sources which have been published have clear cut and valuable purposes behind them. One can point to a variety of volumes that contain insights into the naval profession which have deep significance and enduring value in understanding the formulation of naval strategy and tactics. We have at our fingertips the basis for understanding the function, purpose, limitations and contribution of navies; yet the synthesis remains to be done.

All of us who put our hand to editing documents have a deep responsibility to observe the highest scholarly standards making them as useful as possible to those who read and study naval history. We must show clearly that our choice of documents for publication is not merely serendipitous or random, but the product of careful thought and deep understanding in relation to the contribution which the material makes to our general field of study. Too often, editors of naval documents have produced a volume which stands authoritatively on the shelf but is never read or understood. Our purpose is clear, but the contribution intended has not yet been achieved. There is much to be done if the insights and interpretations offered by carefully edited volumes are to be fully accepted as part of the historical literature, not merely sources for experts. The fault lies with document editors who fail to explain their purpose and the meaning of their contribution as well as with those readers who limit their understanding by assuming too quickly that an analytical or narrative work is the only means by which the development of historical opinion can proceed. Perhaps we would be wise to remember Samuel Pepys's reflection on the issue as he contemplated his own projected history of the Royal Navy. Documents and memoirs, he wrote,

> are true and useful stars, whilst studied histories are those stars joined in constellations, according to the fancy of the poet.[50]

Editors of historical documents cannot look successfully at these stars without understanding the nature of the galaxy in which they lie. They must rationally explain to readers their order of magnitude and judge their place in the heavens beyond.

NOTES

This is a revised and up-dated version of an essay that originally appeared in *Editing Naval Documents: Selected Papers from the Sixth*

Naval History Symposium, U.S. Naval Academy, Annapolis, Maryland, 29 September 1983. (Washington, DC: Naval Historical Center, 1984).

1. G. Philip Bauer, "Public Archives in the United States," *In Support of Clio: Essays in Memory of Herbert A. Keelar,* ed. William B. Hesseltine and Donald R. McNeil (Madison, 1958), pp. 57, 62.

2. An outline history of the office responsible for most of these publications appears in William James Morgan and Joye L. Leonhart, *A History of the Dudley Knox Center for Naval History* (Washington, 1981). See also the unpublished study by John McElroy, "Office of Naval Records and Library, 1882–1946," in the Navy Department Library, Washington, D.C.
   The Naval Historical Center and its predecessors published all the volumes, except the volume on the Spanish-American War: Bureau of Navigation, U.S. Navy Department, *Naval Operations of the War with Spain: Appendix to the Report of the Chief of the Bureau of Navigation* (Washington, 1898); *Official Records of the Union and Confederate Navies in the War of Rebellion* (Washington, 1894–1927); *Naval Documents Related to the Quasi-War Between the United States and France,* 7 vols. (Washington, 1935–38); *Naval Documents Related to the United States Wars with the Barbary Powers,* 7 vols. (Washington, 1939–44); *Naval Documents of the American Revolution,* 9 vols. to date (Washington, 1964-); *The Naval War of 1812: A Documentary History* 2 volumes to date. (Washington, DC, 1985-).

3. *Naval Documents Related to the Quasi War . . . ,* I: iii, The foreword was signed by Franklin D. Roosevelt.

4. John Knox Laughton, "The Study of Naval History," *Journal of the Royal United Services Institution,* XL, pt. II (1896): 801.

5. Ibid., p. 808.

6. National Maritime Museum, Greenwich: MSS, NRS/I: Minutes of Council, List of Members, p. 2.

7. Charles Johnson, "The Camden Society," Appendix I in R. A. Humphreys, *The Royal Historical Society 1868–1968.* (London, 1969), p. 53.

8. Laughton, "The Study of Naval History," p. 808. See also, A. N. Sainsbury, *History of the Navy Records Society* (London, 1993) and R. C. Bridges and P. E. H. Hair, eds., *Compassing the Vaste Globe of the Earth: Studies in the History of the Hakluyt Society, 1846–1996.* Publications of the Hakluyt Society, series II, volume 183. (London, 1996), p. 15, fn.3, 45 fn.2.

9. Ibid., p. 809.

10. "Annual Report of the Secretary of the Navy for 1888," in *Official Records of the Union and Confederate Navies in the War of the Rebellion,* Series 1, I: viii.

11. See for example Franklin D. Roosevelt's forewords to the *Quasi-War* and *Barbary War* series and the various forewords and the introductions to *Naval Documents of the American Revolution* volumes.

12. Laughton, "The Study of Naval History," p. 795.

13. The series, begun in 1901, published documents for the years 1914–25, 1940–54 and 1979.

14. One excellent example of British naval information in Dutch diplomatic papers for the period of the War of the Spanish Succession 1702–14 is

A. J. Veenendaal, ed., *De Briefwisseling van Antonie Heinsius, 1702–1720.* (The Hague, 1976-). For a detailed description of the edition, see Hattendorf, "A Dutch Door to Europe, 1702–1720" *Documentary Editing,* 19 (September 1997), pp. 57–61.

The quotation is from John Ehrman, *The Navy in the War of William II., 1689–1697* (Cambridge, 1953), p. xxii.

15. Theodore Roosevelt, *The Letters of Theodore Roosevelt,* ed. Elting E. Morison, John M. Blum and John J. Buckley, 8 vols. (Cambridge MA, 1951–54). Vols. 1–2 contain naval material; Franklin D. Roosevelt, *FDR: His Personal Letters,* ed. Elliott Roosevelt, 4 vols. (New York, 1947–50), vol. 2; John D. Long, *America of Yesterday as reflected in the Journal of John D. Long,* ed. Gardiner Allen (Boston, 1939); Josephus Daniels, *The Cabinet Diaries of Josephus Daniels 1913–1921,* ed. E. David Cronan (Lincoln, NE, 1963); James Forrestal, *The Forrestal Diaries,* ed. Walter Millis (New York, 1951).

16. See in particular the years as First Sea Lord in Martin Gilbert, *Winston S. Churchill: Companion Volume III,* 2 parts (London, 1973), part 1 (July 1914–April 1915).

17. H. W. Hodges an E. A. Hughes, eds., *Select Naval Documents* (Cambridge, 1922). Compare with later editions for changing emphasis in teaching British naval history.

18. Ibid., p. v.

19. Quoted in T. C. Mendenhall, B. D. Henning, A. S. Foord, eds., *Ideas and Institutions in European History, 800–1715: Select Problems in Historical Interpretation.* (New York, 1948), p. iv.

20. Daniel J. Boorstin, ed., *An American Primer.* (Chicago:University Chicago Press, 1966), p. xiii.

21. The naval volume was to have been edited by John B. Hattendorf and R. J. B. Knight. More than decade later, the concept for it, with the editorial advice and assistance of a wide variety of other scholars, became the basis for the Navy Records Society centenary volume of documents, *British Naval Documents, 1203–1960.*

22. David C. Douglas, ed., *English Historical Documents.* (London, 1953–81), I:iii.

23. R. G. Marsden, ed., *Documents Relating to the Law and Custom of the Sea,* Navy Records Society, vols. 49–50 (London, 1915–16); James Grant, ed., *The Old Scots Navy from 1689 to 1710,* Navy Records Society, vol. 44 (London, 1914); D. A. Baugh, *Naval Administration, 1715–1750,* Navy Records Society, vol. 120 (London, 1977); S. W. Roskill *Documents Relating to the Naval Air Service,* Navy Records Society, vol. 113 (London, 1969); Michael Simpson, ed. *Anglo-American Naval Relations, 1917–1919.* Navy Records Society, vol. 130. (London, 1991).

24. Edouard Desbriere, ed., *Trafalgar: The Naval Campaign of 1805.* (Oxford, 1933). Gillian T. Cell, *Newfoundland Discovered: English Attempts at Colonization, 1610–1630.* Publications of the Hakluyt Society, Series II, volume 160. (London, 1982) and David B. Quinn and Alison M. Quinn, *The English New England Voyages, 1602–1608.* Publications of the Hakluyt Society, series II, volume 161. (London, 1983). Douglas L. Stein, compiler. *American Maritime Documents, 1776–1860: Illustrated and Described.* (Mystic, CT: Mystic Seaport Museum, 1992); Andrew

David, Rüdiger Joppien, and Bernard Smith, eds. *The Charts & Coastal Views of Captain Cooks Voyages.* Publications of the Hakluyt Society, Extra Series, volumes 43, 45, 46. (London, 1988–1997). Rüdiger Joppien, *The Art of Captain Cook's Voyages* . . . *with a descriptive catalogue of all known original drawings of people, places, artifacts and events and the original engravings associated.*Three volumes. (New Haven, CT: Yale University Press, 1985–88).
25. Sir Edward Codrington, *Piracy in the Levant 1827–8. Selected from the papers of Admiral Sir Edward Codrington,* ed. C. G. Pitcairn Jones, Navy Records Society, vol. 72 (London, 1934).
26. Horatio Nelson, *Dispatches and Letters of Vice Admiral Lord Viscount Nelson,* ed. Sir Nicholas Harris Nicolas, 2nd ed. with add. letters, 7 vols. (London, 1845–46).
27. John Arbuthnot Fisher, *Fear God and Dread Nought: The Correspondence of Admiral of the Fleet Lord Fisher of Kilverstone,* ed. Arthur J. Marder, 3 vols. (London, 1953–59), I:11.
28. Horatio Nelson, *Letters and Dispatches of Horatio, Viscount Nelson, KB,* ed. John Knox Laughton (London, 1886), p. vii.
29. Cyprian A. G. Bridge, ed., *History of the Russian Fleet During the Reign of Peter the Great by a Contemporary Englishman,* Navy Records Society, vol. 15 (London, 1899); Edward Barlow, *Barlow's Journal of His Life At Sea in King's Ships, East and West Indiamen and Other Merchantmen from 1659 to 1703,* ed. Alfred Basil Lubbock (London, 1934); Nathaniel Butler, *Boteler's Dialogues: A Dialogical Discourse Concerning Maritime Affairs Between The High Admiral and a Captain at Sea,* ed. W. G. Perrin, Navy Records Society, vol. 65 (London, 1929); Sir William Monson, *The Naval Tracts of Sir William Monson,* ed. M. Oppenheim, Navy Records Society, vols. 22, 23, 43, 45, 47 (London, 1902–14); James Trevenen, *A Memoir of James Trevenen,* by C. V. Penrose, ed. Christopher Lloyd and R. C. Anderson, Navy Records Society, vol. 101 (London, 1959).
30. Samuel Pepys, *Diary of Samuel Pepys,* ed. Robert Latham and William Matthews, 11 vols. (London: G. Bell and Sons, 1970–1983).
31. Henry Teonge, *The Diary of Henry Teonge, Chaplain on board His Majesty's ships Assistance, Bristol and Royal Oak, anno 1675–1679,* ed. Sir E. Denison Ross and Eileen Power (1825; reprint ed., London, 1927), p. 26.
32. For rules and procedures, see "Report on Editing Historical Documents," *Bulletin of the Institute of Historical Research,* vol. 1 (1923): 6–25 and vol. 2 (1925): 13–26, and the section entitled "Editing and Printing," in *Harvard Guide to American History,* ed. Frank Freidel, 2 vols. (Cambridge, MA, 1974), I:27–36.
33. Sir George Rooke, *The Journal of Sir George Rooke,* ed. Oscar Browning, Navy Records Society, vol. 9 (London, 1897).
34. Gideon Welles, *Diary of Gideon Welles, Secretary of the Navy Under Lincoln and Johnson,* ed. Howard K. Beale, 3 vols. (New York, 1960). See pp. xxii-xxiv for an examination of the 1911 version.
35. See for example, George T. Fullam, *The Journal of George Tounley Fullam: Boarding Officer of the Confederate Sea Raider Alabama,* ed. Charles G. Summersell (Mobile, AL, 1973).
36. George John Spencer, *Private Papers of George, Second Earl Spencer,* ed.

Julian S. Corbett, Navy Records Society, vol. 46, 48, 58, 59 (London, 1913–24), 46:x.

The same approach was also used in Gustavus Vasa Fox, *Confidential Correspondence of Gustavus Vasa Fox, Assistant Secretary of the Navy 1861–1865,* ed. R. M. Thompson and Richard Wainwright, Naval History Society, vols. 9–10 (New York, 1918–19), pp. xiii-xiv. These two volumes were published without an index, but this fault was repaired by a stenciled index compiled in 1934 by Louis H. Bolander and distributed to several naval libraries.

37. Samuel Francis DuPont, *Samuel Francis DuPont A selection from His Civil War Letters,* ed. John D. Hayes, 3 vols. (Ithaca, NY, 1969), I: cviii.

38. For a detailed discussion of these volumes, see Hattendorf, "We Have Met the Enemy and They Are Ours': The Naval War of 1812," *Documentary Editing,* 15 (September 1993), pp. 57–60.

39. For a detailed description of this series, see Hattendorf, 'The War Diary of the German Naval Staff, 1939–1945, " *Documentary Editing,* 18 (September 1996), pp. 58–62. [A review article on Werner Rahn, et al., eds., *Kriegstagebuch der Seekriegsleitung, 1939–1945.* (Hereford: Verlag E. S. Mittler & Sohn, 1988–1997)].

40. G. G. Harris, ed., *Trinity House of Deptford, Transactions, 1609–35,* London Record Society, vol. 19 (London, 1983).

41. John Wilson Croker, *The Croker Papers . . . Secretary to the Admiralty from 1809 to 1830,* ed. Louis J. Jennings, 3 vols. (New York, 1884).

42. John B. Marchand, *Charleston Blockade: The Journal of John B. Marchand, U.S. Navy, 1861–62,* ed. Craig L. Symonds. (Newport, RI, 1975).

43. See, for example, my own experiment with this in Joseph H. Wellings, *On His Majesty's Service: Observations of the British Home Fleet from the Diary, Reports and Letters of Joseph H. Wellings, Assistant U.S. Naval Attache, London, 1940–41,* ed. John B. Hattendorf. (Newport, RI, 1983).

44. Johnson, "The Camden Society," p. 64.

45. M. Oppenheim, ed., *Naval Accounts and Inventories of the Reign of Henry VII,* Navy Records Society, vol. 8 (London, 1896).

46. Susan Rose, ed., *The Navy of the Lancastrian Kings,* Navy Records Society vol. 123 (Winchester, MA, 1982), p. 56.

47. Edmond Halley, *The Three Voyages of Edmond Halley in the Paramore 1698–1701,* ed. N. J. W. Thrower, Hakluyt Society, 2nd series, no. 156–57 (London, 1981).

48. Joseph T. Downey, *The Cruise of the Portsmouth 1845–1847: A Sailor's View of the Naval Conquest of California by Joseph T. Downey, Ordinary Seaman,* ed. Howard Lamar (New Haven, CT, 1958), p. xviii.

49. Bernard J. S. Williams, "Microforms, pro and contra," *The Times of London Literary Supplement,* 14 October 1983, p. 1139.

50. Samuel Pepys, *Samuel Pepys' Naval Minutes,* ed. J. R. Tanner, Navy Records Society, vol. 60. (London, 1926), p. 69.

7

The Anglo-American Way in Maritime Strategy

Over the centuries, nations have used maritime strategies in a variety of ways for a variety of purposes. That statement, simple though it is, runs counter to general wisdom in this country. Far too often one finds in the English language literature on maritime history the assumptions that all nations have shared the same concept of maritime strategy and that particular nations have always had the same maritime strategy. However, a careful look will show that we in the United States have changed our conceptions during our own history, as have the British within the course of theirs.

The maritime strategies of major sea powers have been different one from another. The ancient Greeks and Romans, the Venetians, the Portuguese, the Spanish, the Dutch, the French, the Germans, the Japanese, the Soviets-each has acted with varying ideas in mind. Yet at the same time, there are relationships among these strategies. To find both the differences and the similarities, one needs to look carefully at patterns of thought and at the nature of the circumstances involved in each case. The issues in such an examination revolve around each nation's role within the international politics of its day, the nature of the objectives each sought to achieve, the differing role that each navy served in carrying out national policy and the relative importance of seaborne commerce in each national economy.

Among the various types of maritime strategies, the Anglo-American strand is the dominant one and tends to obscure the others. As a body of theory, Alfred Thayer Mahan and Sir Julian Corbett based it primarily on an interpretation of British naval history in the seventeenth and eighteenth centuries as linked to the events of the period when they were writing (in the years just before the First World War). Mahan was the first prominent writer to show sea power as a basis for national policy, while Corbett made the most effective abstract statement of the theory.

In this Anglo-American strand, maritime strategy is twofold: first, the establishment of a nation's control of shipping at sea, and second, the use of that control in order to affect events on land. Scholars today have a tendency to divide the naval from the merchant marine, the public from the private, and the civilian from the military. Although there is a reasonable basis for doing that, the tradition of Anglo-American maritime strategy runs counter to this trend. It is an overarching idea that seeks to link national policy to both commercial and naval use of the sea, setting them among the wider aspects of relations with nations. In order to understand the concept, we need to identify its elements while sowing its relationship to particular ideas, historical situations and national institutions.

The Anglo-American theory is a description of the global international relations of the dominant maritime power and of balance of power politics. In British history, this concept had its first major application in the period beginning in 1688, when King William III brought England into a European coalition against France. From this time forward, the concept can be followed throughout Britain's role as a great power. It entered American thinking through aspirations for great power status about 1890, and became a full feature of American policy when the United States took over Britain's role as the dominant maritime power after the Second World War.

The relationship between British and American maritime power and thought is one of sequential development. There was not a direct collision, as one might have expected from previous historical examples, between the expanding maritime power of the United States and the already established power of Britain. There were crises, certainly, and even contingency plans in the case of war between the two countries, but after 1815 neither power was willing to use force directly against the other. Until the end of the nineteenth century, Britain's naval power, although usable against America's principal coastal cities, was stalemated by America's ability to deploy force against Canada.

During this period America's priorities were regional while Britain's were global. Now, a century later, the roles have been reversed: America's priorities are global and Britain's are regional. The key events of this role reversal can be traced as follows: the Naval and Shipping Acts of 1916, which resulted in a huge expansion of American merchant and naval shipping; the Washington Naval Treaty of 1922, which established naval parity between the two countries; the arrangement by which American destroyers were traded to Britain in 1940 for a ninety-nine-year American lease on British land for bases in the West Indies; the American domination of the war in the Pacific overshadowing the British contribution; and finally, the establishment of NATO and other security arrangements in the postwar period by which the United States assumed the traditional British role in a global balance of power.

As a great maritime power in the late twentieth century, the United States has taken on many of the characteristics that marked British power in earlier periods. The conceptual basis on which America has exerted her maritime power in the twentieth century derives from earlier British conceptions of international order and the use of force at sea. Both British and American conceptions of maritime strategy share an interest in maintaining a balance of power, but this interest was not and is not an abstract one. Historically, it is an attempt to preserve and expand worldwide patterns of trade and commerce as well as to promote progressive notions of social and political development. These have been the national policy goals, and in this sense, a balance of power is a means to these ends, and not an end in itself.

In examining the Anglo-American tradition of maritime strategy in the twentieth century, one finds three dominant subareas for investigation: first, the institutions of government that formulate maritime strategy; second, the development of theory about maritime strategy; and third, the practice of maritime strategy in both peacetime planning and the actual conduct of war.

THE MACHINERY OF GOVERNMENT FOR STRATEGIC DECISION MAKING

The machinery for twentieth century coalition warfare has its roots in the British cabinet system of government, as developed through the Committee of Imperial Defence. This is the model for the major international command and organizational structures developed in the twentieth century, including the League of Nations, the allied Combined Chiefs of Staff during the Second World War, the United Nations, and NATO, as well as the U.S. Joint Chiefs of Staff and the National Security Council.

In contrast to the authoritarian system of decision making practiced by the Prussian General Staff, Britain developed during the last twenty years of the nineteenth century a system for interdepartmental cooperation and advice in defense matters. These arrangements became a permanent feature of the British government in December 1902 with the establishment of the Committee of Imperial

Defence. This new committee, with flexible membership and direct access to the highest officials, held direct responsibility for defense planning, giving it continuity while coordinating the relations of departments and preventing any one department from prevailing without full consideration of the whole range of national issues. Along with it came a permanent and professional staff to work with the ministerial members of the committee, under the chairmanship of the prime minister.

British experience with the committee system of decision making in the first half of this century showed, as Professor Norman Gibbs has suggested, that the velvet glove of advice works better than the whip of orders.[1] In addition, the system demonstrated that the most effective action came when those who plan are also those who execute the plan. When top officials and admirals do not have time to think in-depth about issues, it merely compounds the problem to separate planning and execution.

Although the system has good effects in restraining the intemperate use of force by balancing military solutions with further consideration of diplomatic, political, economic and moral judgments, it does create problems in how to distribute funds among rival organizations. Indeed, as defense budgets rose in the years after the Second World War, both Britain and the United States tended to centralize power and authority in higher defense matters as a means to control budgets and rationalize defense requirements.

Despite this trend, the committee system remains the basis for international decision making. As practiced by the United Nations and NATO, the system's variety of national objectives, capabilities and strategies provides a means to give careful attention to the full range of national interests while also coordinating deterrent strength. It serves as a means for international planning in the conduct of war and in collective efforts for peace. At the same time, it provides rational restraint to the use of force.

The British model provides a structure for the thorough consideration of all aspects of maritime strategy, preventing the dominance of any one facet or the isolation of any other. As Sir William Blackstone noted about the English governmental system in the eighteenth century, the varied elements "impel the machinery of government in a direction different from what either acting by themselves would have done; but at the same time in a direction partaking of each and formed out of all."[2] This system blunts the natural tendency to isolate thoughts and activities in different compartments, and it reinforces the Anglo-American tradition in maritime strategy of linking the commercial and naval use of the sea through the broad understanding of national interests.

ANGLO-AMERICAN MARITIME THEORY

Theory provides the intellectual framework from which practical activity is planned and understood. As an intellectual study, Anglo-American maritime theory derives from the work of Alfred Thayer Mahan, who studied the period between 1660 and 1815 in European history, deriving lessons from the relationship of British imperial and foreign policy to naval operations in the eighteenth century. Mahan identified sea power with the broad commercial interests of a nation in using the sea; and at one time he even went to so far as to say that without a merchant marine, there was no function for a navy.

Mahan's famous description of the British navy in the Napoleonic wars epitomized his general view of naval strategy: "Those far distant, storm-beaten ships, upon which the Grand Army never looked, stood between it and the dominion of the world."[3] Behind this image lay Mahan's view that sea power was a decisive factor in history, that a great maritime power's navy must be the superior force at sea, and that it was properly employed near an enemy's coast where it could control, at the source, a threat to its own "command of the sea" (a phrase coined by Mahan). Mahan saw that much of the work of sea power was in "the noiseless, steady, exhausting pressure with which sea power acts, cutting off the resources of the enemy while maintaining its own supporting war in scenes where it does not appear itself, or appears only in the background, and striking open blows only at rare intervals. . . . "[4] At the same time, he stressed the importance of large, decisive battles between opposing fleets. In making this point, and suggesting that Horatio Nelson and the Battle of Trafalgar embodied the essence of sea power, Mahan contributed to a continuing myth in the Anglo-American tradition. Less appreciated, perhaps, were his complementary points on the role of bases in maintaining control of the sea lanes, the importance of concentration of force, and the relation of strength to geographic position. The key to Mahan's thought is his emphasis on the principle "of being superior to the enemy at the decisive point, whatever the strength of the two parties on the whole."[5] Through this principle, he promoted the offensive and concentrated use of naval force to achieve command of the sea.

Mahan's work was part of the developing rationale for a new American navy that would come to challenge British power and domination. Although he provided the initial impetus for an abstract understanding of naval strategy, he never gathered his ideas together into a coherent, analytical statement of a complete theory. Sir Julian Corbett took up that task in his book *Some Principles of Maritime Strategy,* first published in 1911.

Corbett's work deserves far greater appreciation than it has received in America, for it is the most complete and careful summary of the Anglo-American tradition in maritime strategy. In writing it, Corbett had the advantage of following Mahan and could build on his initial work, bringing new insights as well as a deeper knowledge of British naval history.

Corbett argued that maritime strategy should focus on the use of the sea for communications and passage. A navy's role is to guard the communications of its own country and to seize or disrupt those of its enemy. In his mind, the naval function is inextricably tied to the commercial and civilian realm. That, the coordination and control of armed force at sea is more properly called maritime strategy than naval strategy, since it is an overarching concept that links the ultimate purpose of the navy to the more extensive and varied scope of general activity at sea.

In discussing the role of navies, Corbett created three general categories: first, methods of securing command; second, methods of disputing command; and third, methods of exercising command.

In examining methods of securing command, he noted that the normal condition of the sea is an uncommanded one—command of the sea exists only in wartime, and in peacetime one can only discuss the potential for command of the sea in wartime. To achieve it in wartime, a navy had two basic options. It could seek a battle which would destroy the ability of the enemy to challenge its commerce on the sea or, alternatively, it could blockade the enemy so that the enemy's ships stayed in port or on the defensive in its own coastal waters.

A nation which concedes mastery to the enemy but still seeks to oppose the enemy at sea may create a "fleet-in-being." By its very existence such a defensive fleet establishes a potential threat, and it may conduct minor counterattacks, carefully choosing time, place and target to achieve maximum effect.

Finally, Corbett turned to the ways in which a nation exercises command of the sea once it has secured it. Here he considered such functions as defense against attack on one's own country, the support of overseas military expeditions, and attacks on enemy commerce as well as defense of one's own.

Experience has modified both Corbett's and Mahan's theories. These modifications have come in several areas and have often been associated with changes in naval technology. One of the areas affected by technological innovation was commerce warfare, in which submarines and aircraft came to play a significant role in the protection and destruction of commerce. So effective did the submarine become in its ability to attack commerce that it moved commerce warfare from a secondary function, limited in theory to minor counterattack to one with the potential for major and decisive consequences. Most important, however, Anglo-American maritime theory has been modified by consideration of the peacetime and political uses of armed force. Corbett and Mahan examined the use of navies in wartime, not in peacetime. They omitted gunboat diplomacy as an important factor, although it had long played a major role in British imperial history. In the years since the Second World War, the appearance of nuclear weapons and the attention given to deterrence led to detailed consideration of the political role of navies in peacetime. The use of navies for political purposes, linked as it is to special weapons and capabilities as well as high governmental policies, quickly becomes a specialist's subject. But such a use requires free passage on the sea. Through this requirement it makes a link with maritime commerce and connects with the traditional view in Anglo-American strategy by which the superior naval power, be it Britain or America, refuses to allow any nation or law to restrict its freedom in using the sea for its own purposes.

Anglo-American maritime theory has changed, as it should, with new developments and new events. A good theory sheds light and understanding on the issues which it concerns, but it must constantly be reevaluated and modified in the light of new conditions and new insights. This point brings us to the third major area of consideration in analyzing the Anglo-American tradition of maritime strategy: the relationship, or lack of relationship between prewar planning of maritime strategy and the actual conduct of strategy in the course of a war.

PREWAR STRATEGIC PLANNING AND MARITIME STRATEGY

Prewar strategic planning is not strategy; it is only preparation for it. Strategy itself is the actual use of force. As a function of grand strategy, maritime strategy is the comprehensive direction of power at sea to control a situation. Commonly, the situation is not one isolated at sea, but involves the interrelationship of affairs at sea with those ashore, including the extension of power from the sea to control events on land.

The very idea of planning for a future naval war was new at the beginning of this century. In examining the relationship between prewar strategic planning for the navy in the years between 1898 and 1914 in contrast to the conduct of war in 1914–1918, Paul Kennedy has shown that prewar planning was largely irrelevant. Much of prewar thinking assumed that a future war would be a limited conflict, much like the Spanish-American or Russo-Japanese wars. The war that came in 1914 was nothing like them. The British planners based their thinking on a rigid expectation that future naval war would be centered around offensive battleship actions on the open sea or in enemy waters. Kennedy sees the First World War as chiefly a land war in which navies played an indirect, although important, supportive and essentially negative role. As he concluded, "to put it crudely, if the German submarines had been able to interdict the Allied lines of communication in the Atlantic and the Mediterranean, they would in all probability have won the land war as well; because they did not block those sea lanes, they lost the overall conflict."[6]

On reflection, the fixation with decisive battleship actions was simpleminded and distracted strategists from seriously examining alternative uses of sea power that were appropriate to the geographical and strategic circumstances of the situation they faced. However, the officers in charge had neither the mental preparation for such flexible thinking nor had they equipped the fleet for such alternative uses.

The Washington Naval Conference of 1921–22 laid the basis for peacetime strategic planning in the wake of the First World War. It combined two major elements: reflection on the experience of the war, and planning for what might happen in the future. It resulted in the elimination of international competition in building battleships (a factor seen by some as a destabilizing element in the years leading up to the war), but it left loopholes for the development of submarines, cruisers, and aircraft carriers. The treaty also marked Britain's agreement to America's rise to naval parity with her, although the United States harbored ambitions for a "navy second to none."

In the subsequent planning, there was a strong element which led to preparations for fighting a future war that would have actions similar to that of Jutland in 1916. At the same time, however, the in-

terwar years saw consideration of new concepts and rapid developments in the use of naval aviation, submarines and amphibious warfare. As Malcolm Murfett has commented, "It is doubtful whether
any nation that is neither initiating nor seeking war is ever entirely
prepared for it until it happens."[7] Throughout the interwar period,
both Britain and the United States adopted a defensive approach in
their strategic planning, and each took a different and inherently fal-
lible approach to predicting the future. These mixed approaches
made for some success in prewar planning. Among the many ideas
and plans that were considered, certainly even the belated and re-
luctant thought given to preparation for the protection of merchant
shipping proved its use for both Britain and America during the Second World War. Many later wished it had been explored more thoroughly. The failure of Japan to examine the implications of the First
World War on this point proved to be a fatal mistake. If only War Plan
Orange (among the numerous American color plans) proved useful
in the actual conduct of war, it was still evidence that improvisation
and flexibility of thought remained a paramount aspect of maritime
strategy. Experience shows that any nation needs more than one
strategy and more than one way of looking at contingency issues.

Careful historical study of the contrast between the preparation
for war and the actual conduct of war reveals not only the limitations
of planners' abilities to predict the future, it also shows the restraints
on them. The peacetime mix of international affairs, national finance, and domestic politics appropriately restrains the creation of
an armed force that is capable of meeting the full range of wartime
threats. In peacetime it is not only very difficult to foresee the future,
it is also difficult to justify expenditures on a force that might not be
necessary.

In the postwar world, the geostrategic situation of Britain and the
United States is much as it was before 1939, even if the power relationship between the two has changed. In the Cold War, a Western
maritime coalition has faced a continentally based Eastern one. The
new factor has been the role of nuclear weapons and the question as
to what degree they alter the strategic situation for maritime power.
Some argued that the new weapons transformed the situation entirely, while others declared that they would be absorbed by the
armed forces in the usual way. Certainly the habits of Anglo-American cooperation learned during the Second World War remained in
place, despite the stress of crises (of which the worst was Suez).

Sea power as an element of national power has not disappeared in
the nuclear age, as some predicted. To the contrary, it has remained

an important factor, and a new power at sea has emerged from the Soviet Union. Maritime forces have been key elements in the global balance of power. The United States has found the need to keep its naval forces in distant seas to maintain its alliances and to be ready to deal with crises, while also preparing for a possible global war in which commerce requires protection. Maritime strategic planning has come to stress the relationship of sea power to the other elements of national power, thereby reflecting one of the great themes of the Anglo-American tradition.

In the twentieth century, both Britain and America have used maritime strategy as a subset of grand strategy in order to deal with balance of power issues. In regard to Europe, Britain was the traditional balancer who allied herself with the weaker powers threatened by continental land powers. Maritime power was always a key element of British policy, but it was rarely if ever used successfully without reference to the diplomatic, financial, commercial, and military factors of power. Thus, current practitioners in the Anglo-American tradition of maritime strategy have come to understand that the sea power does not stand alone among the factors which may be employed to achieve a balance of power, yet it is significant enough to deserve separate in-depth analysis.

The influence of British thinking on twentieth-century coalition warfare, on the development of the machinery of government, and on concepts of maritime power has been profound. British experience has illustrated, too, the fundamental debate about the appropriateness of balance of power politics. In nineteenth-century Britain, balance of power proponents contended that national security depended on European equilibrium. They insisted that Britain should intervene in various situations in order to prevent a rival from gaining dangerous power. Their political opponents were convinced that Britain's welfare had nothing to do with the balance of power. They believed that intervention was appropriate only when national interests were threatened directly. The balance of power proponents rested their case on traditional European power politics; their opponents rested theirs on Christian morality. The resulting political battle was between those who wanted to control the existing international political system and those who wanted to create a new order among nations. These same conflicting views have been a characteristic part of the American political tradition.

In the Anglo-American democratic tradition, there is an inbred suspicion of standing military forces. During peacetime, domestic public opinion may not be willing to accept the cost of wide-ranging, flexible preparations for war. Naval leaders have thus been caught in a dilemma: they must meet the immediate needs of peacetime naval operations, including crises; they must prudently predict what a future war may look like, in order to prevent it from breaking out; and they must provide an assessment of the most probable future war to persuade legislators to finance the basic long-range needs for equipment, training, and men. These are diverse efforts which do not always yield the same naval requirements. The Anglo-American experience shows that, in peacetime, the stress among such conflicting views can result in either an inappropriate compromise among them or an overemphasis on one aspect at the expense of another.

In the twentieth century, Anglo-American maritime strategy has evolved with change and experience, but it is still linked with the dominant naval power and with balance of power politics. It continues to embody a broad concept that ties together the control of shipping at sea and the use of that control to affect events on land. At the same time, as naval leaders prepare for future contingencies with the most modern equipment, one can discern traditional critics and traditional dilemmas.

Although these stresses will always be present, they need not be as difficult for American naval leaders as current trends may suggest. The public discussion of the U.S. Navy's Maritime Strategy in the mid-1980s left the mistaken impression in the popular imagination that American maritime power is formed around a strategy of aggressive power politics. While that impression may have been useful for rationalizing the Navy's force structure at that particular phase in America's international relations, it could well be counterproductive for the future. As American naval leaders contemplate this future and to look at possible arms control agreements, they need to keep in mind the fundamental concept of maritime strategy which links commercial and naval affairs in the context of international relations. The ultimate objective for a modern superpower navy is to contribute to world stability. It is this foundation upon which American naval strategy should be based, not the mistaken notion of aggressive attack.

NOTES

This essay was first published in the *Naval War College Review,* XLIII (Winter 1990), pp. 90–99. Originally, this was a contribution to the 1989 Williams College-Mystic Seaport Symposium on "the Atlantic Maritime

World." It is my selection of some of the themes from a book of essays I co-edited with Robert S. Jordan, *Maritime Strategy and the Balance of Power: Britain and America in the Twentieth Century.* (London: Macmillan Press in association with St Antony's College. Oxford: New York: St. Martin's Press, 1989). The contributors to that book were Norman H. Gibbs, Eric Grove, John Gooch, Hattendorf, Barry D. Hunt, Paul M. Kennedy, Robert S. Jordan, J. Kenneth McDonald, Marc Milner, Malcolm H. Murfett, Joel Sokolsky, Geoffrey Till, and Robert S. Wood. Although their detailed essays were the sources for this essay, they may or may not agree with the general interpretations presented.

1. N. H. Gibbs, "The Origins of Imperial Defence," in *Maritime Strategy and the Balance of Power,* p. 36.

2. Sir William Blackstone, *Commentaries of the Laws of England* (Oxford, 1765), volume 1, p. 151.

3. A. T. Mahan, *The Influence of Sea Power Upon The French Revolution and Empire.* (Boston, 1892), volume 2, p. 118.

4. A. T. Mahan, *The Influence of Sea Power Upon History 1660–1783,* 12th edition. (Boston, 1949), p. 209.

5. A. T. Mahan, *Naval Strategy Compared and Contrasted with the Principles and Practice of Military Operations on Land.* (Boston, 1918), p. 297.

6. Paul M. Kennedy, "The Relevance of the Pre-War British and American Maritime Strategies to the First World War and its Aftermath, 1898–1920," in *Maritime Strategy and the Balance of Power,* p. 183.

7. Malcolm H. Murfett, "Are We Ready? The Development of American and British Naval Strategy, 1922–39," in *Maritime Strategy and the Balance of Power,* p. 238.

8

American Strategies in the Pacific War, 1941–1945

Strategy is an essential aspect in the conduct of war, but it is something that is difficult to understand. The practitioners of strategy are those at the highest levels, who, in the crises of the moment, often do not explicitly record why they take the actions they do. Like all practical men, they usually think in concrete, not abstract, terms. On the other hand, students of strategy are commonly writers and historians, who often find patterns of action that the practitioners of strategy rarely realize are present. Writers are people of ideas and, perhaps too often in this area, ideas attract them and they see them as the driving forces of strategy. In order to try to understand strategy, people should to try to balance these divergent outlooks: the differing views of decisive leaders and of reflective minds. It is undeniably a difficult task, but it is not without hope. The armed forces of most nations have come to realize the importance and value in this task; it is the fundamental purpose for the existence of staff colleges, war colleges, and the large staffs that now support many commanders.

In the common understanding of the process for developing strategy, there is a rational hierarchy with descending levels of guidance, national interests creating the basis for policy, policy providing the guide for strategy, and strategy, in turn, informing tactics. More fundamentally, however, strategists think in the context of the prevailing cultural and national attitudes that surround them. Thus, there are fundamental differences in national outlook and there are national strategies that stretch beyond rational calculation. Emotion, comfortable delusion, and personal pride in both leaders and their people are matters to consider. No less important, the decision-making process, the structure and methods of command and administration, along with domestic politics, financial, and industrial resources with the capacity to transport men and equipment, are all equally important factors in understanding the strategy of a war.

Strategy reaches for an overarching idea, reflecting an understanding of an entire war. While strategy involves this conceptual dimension, it is, at the same time, the comprehensive and actual direction of national power, including armed force, to achieve some measure of control over an opponent, and, by that control, to achieve specific practical and political ends.[1]

There are hundreds, even thousands, of books written on the war in the Pacific. By and large, we know the general pattern of what happened. We have masses of data; nevertheless, there is even more to recover in the archives. There is much work yet to be done in bringing this data forward, with new interpretations and new insights. In this process, one can approach the war in the Pacific from a variety of levels and perspectives, ranging from the experience of individuals or the role of particular organizations, the outlook and reaction of individual nations, or even the broad range of world history.[2]

There are several aspects to consider in understanding the way the United States developed its strategy. One of these is the mindset, the intellectual baggage, which Americans had developed before 1941 and carried with them into the war years.

INTELLECTUAL BAGGAGE

The most often mentioned aspects are the ideas contained in "War Plan Orange," the contingency plan that the U.S. Navy began to develop as early as 1907, after anti-Asian riots in San Francisco first raised widespread fear of war with Japan.[3] In the decades that followed, naval officers working in the Navy Department offices in Washington, along with the faculty and staff at the Naval War College in Newport, began to formulate an idea of how to fight a war with Japan, should one arise. Like any such exercise, it was speculative. To tie the speculation to the realities of current equipment and capabilities, the Naval War College used its capability for war gaming. Discussions with Army staff officers brought understanding of military plans, problems, and capabilities. Through this continuing process, Army and Navy planners developed several versions of the Plan Orange in the 1920s and 30s and there are various mutations on specific points. It was neither a stagnant nor a set idea. Looking back on it, historians have found many similarities in the way Americans actually fought the war.

In essence, most of the early versions of the plan anticipated a long, expensive maritime war, aimed at the complete subjugation of

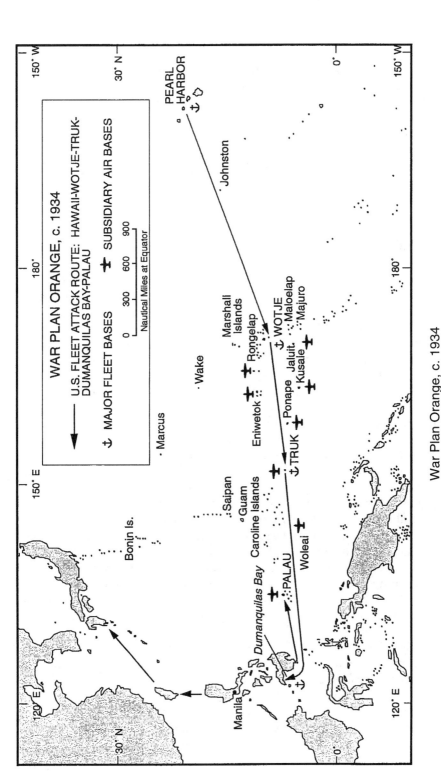

War Plan Orange, c. 1934

(Naval War College, based on Edward S. Miller, War Plan Orange [Annapolis, MD: Naval Institute Press, 1991] and Geoffrey Barraclough, eds., The Times Concise Atlas of World History. [Maplewood, NJ: Hammond, 1982])

Japan. Planners suggested that the war would have three phases. During the first phase, U.S. forces would be unable to prevent the Japanese from seizing American outposts in the Pacific.

In the second phase, American naval and air forces would move gradually westward across the Pacific, seizing isolated Japanese islands in the Central Pacific in a series of small battles that led to American forces recapturing the Philippines. Progressively developing a blockade on Japan's seaborne economic resources, the Japanese battleship fleet would eventually attack the U.S. fleet in a major fleet battle. In this, the American planners anticipated that the superiority of American battleship gunnery would prove to be the decisive factor, allowing the United States to defeat the Japan.

During the third phase, following the major battle-fleet action, American forces would move northward. During this phase, they would destroy Japan's economic capacity by blockading Japanese imports and using air bombardment to destroy her industry. Thus, the United States could force Japan to surrender, through American air and naval forces without directly assaulting the main units of the Japanese army on the Asian mainland and in the Japanese Home Islands.[4] Up to this stage, the planners anticipated a naval war, concentrated in the Central Pacific, executed completely by American forces, and barely touching the Southern Pacific area.

As the danger of war in the Pacific grew closer after 1938, American plans and expectations changed considerably. Considerations of the war in Europe, the influence of Allied needs, the possible needs of home defense, the limitations of American industrial capacity, and army reticence about the plans began to play a larger role in contingency planning for the Pacific. The strategic planners who developed Rainbow Five sought to restrain the offensive phase contained in the earlier versions of Plan Orange, and limited American Pacific forces to defensive operations off the American mainland and to minor counteroffensives in the Pacific, until the Allied powers defeated Germany. By dividing the fleet, the planners sought to conserve American naval forces for the battle of the Atlantic and for an offensive in Europe while, at the same time, providing a deterrent in the Pacific.[5]

By mid-1941, American military and naval planners had restricted their planned major fleet operations to go only as far as the eastern Caroline Islands, allowing, from that point, air and submarine raids on Japanese positions in the Marshalls, Wake, and the Gilberts. This change in American planning, along with the actual events of the war in Europe, silently altered an earlier and fundamental point that the British and American planners had counted on for the defense of Singapore, and with it, Australia and New Zealand. With reinforcements, they expected British forces in Singapore and Malaya to hold out for at least three months. Simultaneously, they expected American operations in the Central Pacific to cut off Japanese oil supplies from Southeast Asia.[6] At that point in the European war, however, British losses in the Mediterranean and in the Atlantic made it impossible to send a large reinforcement. Simultaneously, the United States Navy began to make plans to withdraw its forces to positions where they could no longer effectively cut off Japanese oil supplies. It is not clear whether British and American planners were deluding themselves on the situation or misunderstood each other. In any event, the respective national plans contained a logical defect.[7]

But all this was planning before the fact. As the naval theorist J. C. Wylie so clearly warned future military and naval planners, one "cannot predict with certainty the pattern of the war for which we prepare ourselves. We cannot, with reasonable certainty, forecast the time, the place, the scope, the intensity, the course, and the general tenor of a war."[8] No one ever has. Looking back over the plans, historians can piece together from the different variations some main features in the strategy that Americans actually used, but they find these concepts neither in any one of those plans nor expressed in any fully connected way. The best that the planners did, over the years, was to consider a range of likely situations. That was certainly a significant achievement, but it should not be mistaken for what actually took place.

There were several very important differences between America's prewar contingency planning for the Pacific and the United States conduct of the war in 1941–45. First, American planners had not seriously considered offensive operations against Japan from positions South of the equator. Prewar planners had looked briefly at a landing on Mindinao via a southern route in 1932, and the Rainbow Two and Three plans of 1939–40 had laid out plans for the fleet to reach Singapore via New Zealand and Australia, and in 1941 they briefly thought about the possibility of a fleet base at Rabaul. None of these, however, presaged either the South Pacific offensive in 1944 or the actual events in the recapture of Luzon. Additionally, the great effort that wartime strategists put into plans to open a theater of military operations in mainland Asia, Burma and China in 1943–44, and, again in 1945, in Korea and northern China, was the opposite of what the prewar planners considered.

To summarize, the events that occurred during the war led to six major departures from the prewar American planning;

1. the South Pacific amphibious offensive from Papua to Leyte;
2. American plans for an important land campaign in China;
3. the American decision to take Formosa and the reversal of that decision in 1944 in order to
4. recapture Luzon;
5. American plans for the final stage, bombing campaign based in Northern China and Korea; and
6. the reversal of plans for invading the Japanese Home Islands, and the use of the atomic bomb.[9]

In addition, no one had predicted the reaction of the American public to an attack like that at Pearl Harbor. No one foresaw that what most Americans in the 1920s and 1930s regarded as an abstruse issue in international affairs, involving relatively minor American trade in China and access to raw materials in Southeast Asia, would suddenly become, for many Americans, a crusade against an evil empire and a campaign that quickly mingled with racial hatred and the unavoidable emotion of war. The carefully analyzed issues of international relations in the prewar years were submerged by an overpowering emotional, public reaction, personalized by Roosevelt's graphic depiction in his long-remembered announcement: "Yesterday, December 7th, 1941, a date which will live in infamy, the United States of America was suddenly and deliberately attacked by naval and air forces of the Empire of Japan."

Despite these important differences, there were still considerable similarities with the mainstream in prewar American thinking.

- The Pacific War did take priority after the war in Europe.
- It was a strategy for the total defeat of Japan.
- It was fought in three phases: a defensive period of regrouping, followed by an offensive, and then a direct siege of Japan.
- American forces did cross the Pacific in a series of island-hopping moves, bypassing strongly defended Japanese positions and using mobile bases to arrive in the Philippines in great strength.
- It was a campaign that was air minded and amphibious minded, even while carrying with it some of the prewar dedication to battle fleet actions.
- It was a war designed to defeat Japan by attacking her economic resources.

- It was the long, difficult, expensive struggle that the planners had predicted.
- And in the end, the wartime strategists reverted to the prewar idea that direct amphibious assault on Japan was far too expensive and wasteful.
- The prewar planners were not always right, but their work gives some credence to the view that "an admiral may rely, for guidance in battle, upon the inspiration of the moment, only when that inspiration is due to long and conscientious self-culture in the line of his profession. . . . He who waits for war to learn his profession often acquired his knowledge at a frightful cost of human life."[10] Thus, War Plan Orange embodied many American predilections and much of the intellectual baggage that Americans carried with them into the war as they exercised strategy, reacting to the unexpected, dealing with the problems of the moment.

WARTIME STRATEGY

War Plan Orange and the Rainbow plans are parts of the prologue to the story, not the story itself. There are many ways to think about wartime strategy, but let me try to suggest some broad patterns involved.

First, the Japanese attack on Pearl Harbor made the most recent contingency plan, Rainbow-5, unworkable; the situation called for an entirely new approach. Japan controlled vast areas of the Central and Northern Pacific, and was rapidly widening her grasp, taking in American outposts in the Philippines, Wake and Guam as well as the Dutch East Indies, Hong Kong, Malaya, Singapore, and Rabaul in the Bismarck Archipelago. For the moment, Americans though that continental North America and the Panama Canal were also under an immediate threat.

Unlike some of the earliest planning scenarios, the war in the Pacific concerned more than just the United States. American leaders understood from the outset that it was to be a world war fought by allies. America's first concern in the war was in her relationship with Britain. Even before Congress declared war, Roosevelt showed to Churchill America's concern for Britain's survival in Hitler's war. Yet, many American leaders in 1941 remembered their own experiences in the first World War and were unwilling to allow the Pacific theater of the war to be entirely subservient to the war in Europe or for Britain to dominate completely American forces as she had in

1917–18. Given Britain's relative weakness in the Pacific, the series of defeats she had suffered, and the slim chances for Britain to make major contributions in the Pacific, Americans felt that they must retain strategic control of Allied operations in the Pacific.[11] For his part, Churchill had closely studied the experiences of his ancestor John Churchill, the first Duke of Marlborough, in the early eighteenth-century Grand Alliance during the War of the Spanish Succession.[12] Having seen, through Marlborough's experience in the years 1702–12, both the dangers of divided allied councils and the effects of a wartime election on the conduct of war, Churchill confirmed his own predilections more than two hundred years later in 1939–45 and he was not willing to allow either.

These two quite different influences on individual leaders were reflected in the hasty decisions that Roosevelt and Churchill jointly took to create the Anglo-American division of global responsibility and the creation of the Combined Chiefs of Staff, in which "it had unfortunately not been possible to consult all Governments concerned adequately beforehand."[13] It was something more than merely time and geography that did not allow for the type of direct participation that Australia, New Zealand, and the Netherlands wished to have. On the other hand, there was no sinister motive behind it.

As Japanese forces moved on to take advantage of their success at Pearl Harbor, Japanese leaders chose not to go on the defensive and preserve what they had already gained, but to expand their orbit. In the face of Japanese moves, the United States could only try to defend the threats against its position as Americans saw the Japanese moving in a triple threat, (1) toward Tulagi in the Solomons and to New Guinea trying to dominate the Coral Sea, (2) to capture Midway and to destroy the remainder of the U.S. fleet in Hawaii, and (3) to capture New Caledonia, the Fijis, and Samoa and to server American sea lines of communication with New Zealand and Australia.

Reacting to this situation, Allied war strategists developed what became the basis for two sequential strategies, one in the Central Pacific and one in the Southwest Pacific, each of which involved a series of discrete steps that could be planned ahead, the results of which led to the next series of steps.[14] The pattern of these two operations in their complementary moves under the separate commands of Admiral Nimitz and General MacArthur are so very well known that I will refrain from outlining them in detail here, except to mention the role of strategy in the division of those commands.

In one respect, the division of the American Pacific command into two parts and the geographical delineation of those commands rep-

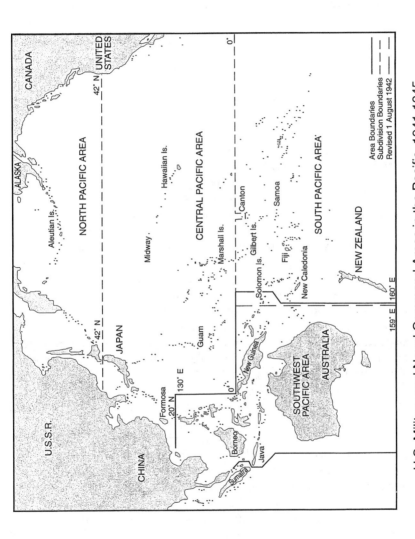

U.S. Military and Naval Command Areas in the Pacific, 1941-1945.

(Naval War College, based on Edward S. Miller, War Plan Orange [Annapolis, MD: Naval Institute Press 1991 and Geoffrey Barraclough, eds., *The Times Concise Atlas of World History.* [Maplewood, NJ: Hammond, 1982])

resent internal American disputes about strategy and interservice
rivalry between the Army and the Navy. Creating two commands
was the only solution to this issue. It was also a decision to remain
flexible in strategy. Observers today tend to personalize this issue
and think of the tensions between Nimitz and MacArthur as the
dominating issue. In fact, the personality issue followed and did not
precede the division. The two commands reflect an understanding of
American war strategy as it existed at the very outset of the war.
This is particularly true of the division of the South Pacific, allocat-
ing Australia to one command and New Zealand to the other. While
this division appeared illogical to those who saw the defense of the
two dominions as a single strategic objective, American leaders
looked at the issue in terms of strategic functions and the exigencies
of the moment when the commands were created. The issue was debated for a short period in Washington, but the consensus lay with
the view that the strategic interests of New Zealand were essentially
maritime and were integral part of the naval issues tied to the system of island bases stretching to Hawaii. In this, strategy involving
New Zealand was tied directly to the operations of the fleet. At the
outset of the war, strategists saw the defense of Australia as a very
different problem, primarily involving land-based air defense and
military operations. At the point in the war when these separate
commands were created, American Army strategists expected operations from Australia to be defensive and only planned to make limited, general preparations for mounting a defensive from that position. In contrast, while leaders in Washington directed Nimitz to be
on the defensive, they explicitly told him to begin to prepare for an
amphibious offensive across the Pacific, assuming that the main
thrust would come from New Zealand and the South Pacific.[15] These
initial thoughts on strategy changed over time, even if the command
structure remained.

   At its high point, Japan held an extremely strong position, controlling vast areas of the Pacific defended on its perimeter by a series of island bases that were strategic barriers to any Allied advance
against Japan. Once Japan's advance had halted at these points, the
strategic problem for the Allies was how to go on. Japan's advance,
up to this point, was a careful interplay between land, air and sea
forces. The Allies' response to it had to consider the same issues. To
do this, the Allies had to hold, contest and take advanced bases,
working out their defense, supply and future use. Thus, not surpris-
ingly, logistical matters in the establishment and supply of bases
came to dominate strategy in the Pacific. In contrast to the war in

the Atlantic, strategists in the Pacific, first, had to create the structure to support the operating forces, before the forces could undertake the operations. This was very clearly an essential feature of the sequential strategies in the Pacific, paralleling it in all strategic phases.[16]

In considering a strategy for the offensive stage of the war, Allied war strategists saw four major alternative options to attack Japan:

1. an approach through the Indian Ocean and Southeast Asia;
2. an approach across the Northern Pacific through Alaska and the Aleutians;
3. an approach from New Guinea and Mindinao, liberating the Philippines before attacking Japan directly and
4. a Central Pacific approach, taking key bases in the Gilbert, Marshall, and Caroline islands, before moving on to the Marinas and Formosa to create stepping stones for a base in China from which to assault Japan directly.

The fifth possibility of an assault from Northeast Asia and the Soviet Union did not arise until the final days of the war. Among the others, however, there were ardent proponents and considerable effort expended toward each strategic goal. From an analytical viewpoint, there were several combinations that were possible, but the linear extensions of sequential strategy require practical success on each step in order to move to the next. Thus, Allied operations in the China-Burma-India theater did not result in positions that could lead to a direct assault on Japan. So too, the Aleutians and Northern Pacific campaign found an even more formidable enemy than the Japanese in weather and climate, although it remained an important route for American sending supplies to the Soviet Union for the war against Germany.[17] It was not until late 1943 that it began to be clear that the Allies would not be able to assault Japan through China and Southeast Asia. At the Cairo Conference in December 1943, the Combined Chiefs of Staff developed a compromise between the Southwest Pacific strategy and the Central Pacific strategy. MacArthur's further successes in the Admiralty Islands and in New Guinea in 1944, paralleled Nimitz's successful operations in the Marianas, and pointed to the wisdom of a dual strategic concept, rather than a choice between the alternatives. Such a choice, however, was made possible by the luxury of additional resources becoming available to the allies. In this, the rapid development and employment of fast-carrier task forces, with their mobility and flexibility, were essential features in leapfrogging and neutralizing enemy bases in the Central Pacific.[18]

However, if the allied powers had not been so strong, economically, industrially, and militarily, these multipronged strategic approach could have been a disastrous choice that would have forced them to stretch their capacities too thinly, forcing defeat, not victory.

Simultaneously, the sequential nature of the complementary, Allied strategies allowed for several new steps to be taken. First, the capture of Saipan in the Marianas, in particular, allowed the Army-Air Force to use its newly developed B-29 bomber in 1944 and begin to make more effective air attacks on Japan itself. Second, Saipan was an ideal base for submarine operations, using newly redesigned torpedoes, against Japanese merchant ships. Both the submarine and the air attacks on Japanese resources represented an additional and complementary concept of strategy in the Pacific War. It was certainly the result of the sequential operations, allowing these weapons to be placed within effective range of meaningful targets, but their strategic function in the war was not sequential, but cumulative.

In cumulative strategy, one action does not depend on its predecessor; one action does not lead to another. Rather, each is a part of a larger pattern made up of a collection of small actions. "Each individual one is no more than a single statistic, an isolated plus or minus, in arriving at the final result."[19] Thus, the air raids on Japanese industry and the submarine attacks on Japan's unprotected merchant fleets produced a cumulative effect on her industrial and economic capacity to continue to fight the war. Like all such cumulative operations, the effects are slow to appear. Submarine operations had been under way since the beginning of the war and submarines had sunk more than 2.2 million tons of Japanese shipping in the period 1941–43. In 1944, however, this figure skyrocketed. In that year alone, submarines accounted for sinking more than 600 ships, 2.7 million tons. By then, Japan had lost two-thirds of her tanker fleet, while submarine attacks nearly cut off completely the flow of oil from the East Indies and reduced other imports by nearly 40 percent.[20] At the same time, the U.S. Navy's submarine force also did significant damage to the Japanese navy, accounting for the sinking of a battleship, eight aircraft carriers and eleven cruisers.

The air raids against Japan slowly became more effective. Until early 1945, however, daylight precision bombing was not as effective as had been hoped. By March, however, strategic bombing began to have devastating effects on Japanese cities, destroying industry and

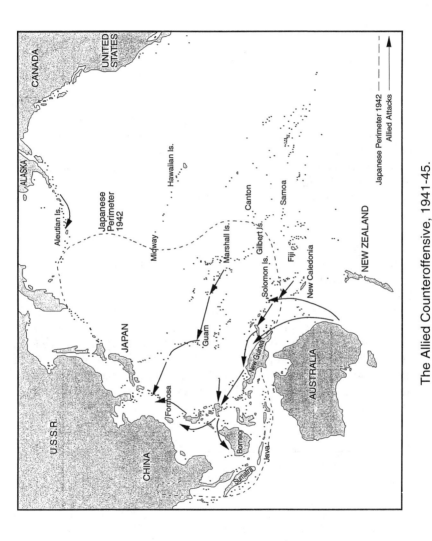

The Allied Counteroffensive, 1941-45.

(Naval War College, based on Edward S. Miller, War Plan Orange [Annapolis, MD: Naval Institute Press, 1991] and Geoffrey Barraclough, eds., *The Times Concise Atlas of World History*. [Maplewood, NJ: Hammond, 1982])

rendering thousands of civilians homeless. Together, the various air and submarine attacks slowly had a cumulative effect on Japanese capacity and morale. This cumulative strategy was not an alternative, but a complement to the sequential strategies in use, interacting to increase effectiveness.

The final attacks on Japanese cities with the atomic bomb also represented another change in strategy. It was a shift from the sequential strategy that led toward a direct amphibious assault on Japan, and it marked a shift from the cumulative effect of relatively small attacks. Although there were some similarities to the strategy of the bombing campaign, the devastating blows wrought by the atomic bomb were of an entirely different proportion and represented a significant change in American objectives through the employment of force. While many purists later objected quite rightly to labeling nuclear weapons as strategic weapons, the first and only use of them did represent a change in strategy.

In conclusion, then, the United States employed several strategies in the Pacific War. In doing so, Americans were not inflexibly tied to their prewar thinking, even if that prewar thinking showed clearly some of their predilections and, at one time or another, presaged the course of some events that occurred. The war created new situations and new opportunities while they also blocked what often seemed the most attractive objectives and fruitful paths during the war. Americans had not predicted with any certainty the pattern of the war for which they had prepared themselves. Neither had they been inflexible in their strategy. They had not forecast with any great accuracy the time, the scope, the intensity, or the course of the war. Finally, America with her Allies had pragmatically attempted several alternatives and used several complementary strategies to achieve their ends.

NOTES

This essay was presented as a paper on the strategic background in the Pacific at "Kia Kaha—Forever Strong: A Conference to Examine New Zealand's Role in the Second World War," held at the National Library of New Zealand, Wellington, 4–7 May 1995.

1. J. C. Wylie, *Military Strategy: A General Theory of Power Control. Classics of Sea Power* (Annapolis: Naval Institute Press, 1989), pp. 66–67; Henry E. Eccles, *Military Concepts and Philosophy* (New Brunswick, NJ: Rutgers University Press, 1965), p. 18.
2. See Paul M. Kennedy, "Levels of Approach and Contexts in Naval His-

tory," in John B. Hattendorf, ed., *Doing Naval History: Essays Toward Improvement* (Newport: Naval War College Press, 1995), pp. 143–149.

3. Edward S. Miller, *War Plan Orange: The U.S. Strategy to Defeat Japan, 1897–1945* (Annapolis, MD: Naval Institute Press, 1991), p. 21. The illustrations in this chapter are derived from the information in this book.

4. Ibid. p. 4.

5. Ibid. p. 276.

6. On the Singapore Strategy, see I. C. McGibbon, *Blue Water Rationale: The Naval Defence of New Zealand, 1914–1942* (Wellington: Government Printer, 1981), chapter V; Paul Haggie, *Britannia at Bay: The Defence of the British Empire Against Japan, 1931–1941* (Oxford: Oxford University Press, 1981), chapter VIII; James Neidpath, *The Singapore Naval Base and the Defence of Britain's Eastern Empire, 1919–1941* (Oxford: Oxford University Press, 1981), chapter VIII. For Anglo-American agreements, see James R. Leutze, *Bargaining for Supremacy: Anglo-American Naval Collaboration, 1937–1941* (Chapel Hill: University of North Carolina Press, 1977) and especially, Malcolm H. Murfett, *Fool-Proof relations: The Search for Anglo-American Naval Cooperation during the Chamberlain Years, 1937–1930* (Singapore: Singapore University Press, 1984)).

7. Edward S. Miller, *War Plan Orange: The U.S. Strategy to Defeat Japan, 1897-1945* (Annapolis, MD: Naval Institute Press, 1991) p. 284.

8. Ibid. p. 70.

9. Ibid. chapter 30.

10. Rear Admiral Stephen B. Luce, "An Address delivered at the United States Naval War College . . . 1903," reprinted in John D. Hayes and John B. Hattendorf, eds., *The Writings of Stephen B. Luce.* (Newport, RI: Naval War College, 1975), pp. 39, 40.

11. Christopher Thorne, *Allies of a Kind: The United States, Britain, and the War Against Japan, 1941–45.* (Oxford: Oxford University Press, 1978), chapter 5.

12. Winston S. Churchill, *Marlborough: His Life and Times.* 4 volumes. (London: Harrap, 1933–38).

13. Richard Cases reporting his conversation with Roosevelt to the Australian Minister for External Affairs, Herbert Evatt, 13 January 1942, in John Robertson and John McCarthy, eds., *Australian War Strategy, 1939–1945: A Documentary History* (St Lucia: Heinemann, 1985), Document 144, p. 181.

14. J. C. Wylie, *Military Strategy*, p. 23.

15. Louis Morton, *Strategy and Command: The First Two Years.The United States Army in World War II. War in the Pacific.* (Washington: GPO, 1962), pp. 245–246, 251–252.

16. Duncan S. Ballantine, *U.S. Naval Logistics in the Second World War* (Princeton, NJ: Princeton University Press, 1949), p. 45.

17. Dean C. Allard, "The North Pacific Campaign in Perspective," *The Northern Mariner,* V, no. 3 (July 1995), pp. 1–14.

18. Clark G. Reynolds, *The Fast Carriers: The Forging of an Air Navy* (New York: McGraw-Hill, 1968), pp. 380–384.

19. J. C. Wylie, *Military Strategy*, p. 118.

20. Clay Blair, Jr., *Silent Victory: The U.S. Submarine War Against Japan* (Philadelphia: Lippincott, 1975), p. 792.

9

Rear Admiral J. C. Wylie:
Naval Thinker

Rear Admiral J. C. Wylie was a rarity among American naval officers. He was the first serving officer since Luce and Mahan, half a century before him, to become known for writing about military and naval theory. First and foremost Wylie was a sailor, a sea officer, and an accomplished ship-handler, but at the same time he became a careful thinker about strategy.

Wylie came to be interested in abstract theory gradually, through experience and observation during his naval career.[1] Wylie's book, *Military Strategy: A General Theory of Power Control,* was clearly a product of his experience and his professional development as a naval officer. Looking back over his career, one can find in it the ideas and thought processes that led him to write the book. The key influences on his thought came first through an appreciation of cultural differences, which he obtained in his early years with the Asiatic Fleet. This was followed by his combat experience in the Second World War, his role in the development of the Combat Information Center and his postwar experience with ergonomics. The stimulation and the time for reflection that he had at the Naval War College during the period when the U.S. Navy was struggling through the bureaucratic battles of service unification were also important elements of his development. All of the separate influences combined to bear fruit through his work with the strategy and sea power study group at the Naval War College in the 1950s. These were Wylie's intellectual steps that led to *Military Strategy.*

Wylie's father, Joseph Caldwell Wylie, Sr., had been graduated from Clemson College in his home state of South Carolina. He went to the New York City area to engage in business, rising to become vice president, secretary, and a director of the Lovell-Dressel Company, manufacturers of marine lighting and signaling equipment.[2] He and his wife had three children, first a son and then two daugh-

Rear Admiral J. C. Wylie

Photograph taken as a Captain, U.S. Navy, in command of the heavy cruiser, USS *Macon* (CA-132), on 30 June 1959, as his ship led the U.S. Navy's contingent at the opening of the St. Lawrence Seaway in Canada. (*Photo by Bill Ray*)

ters. The boy, named for his father, but known as "Bill," was born in Newark, New Jersey, on 20 March 1911 and grew up in Newark and the neighboring town of Glen Ridge.

Reminiscing about his childhood, Wylie was fond of saying "I am a high school dropout who never went to college," because he never graduated from high school and, in his day, the U.S. Naval Academy did not award an academic degree. In January 1928, he left Barringer High School in Newark, New Jersey, for several weeks to attend Werntz's preparatory course in Annapolis. Upon its completion, Wylie returned home and took a competitive examination offered by his congressman. This examination was also the academy's entrance exam, and through scoring the highest, he earned his appointment. After receiving news of his appointment to the academy in April, Wylie left high school before his graduation and spent the remainder of that spring sailing on Barnegat Bay, where his parents had a summer home and where had he learned to love sailing and the sea from an early age.

Having just turned seventeen,Wylie was younger than most of the other midshipmen who entered the academy during the summer of 1928. In the years that followed, he did well at Annapolis. As the Academy year-book, *The Lucky Bag,* commented in his final year, "Academics have never bothered him. At any rate he always stays well above the 3.0 mark with plenty of time to read all the good magazines and books. . . . " His main extracurricular activity was rowing. "When he found out he was too light for the Varsity and too heavy for the Lightweights, he set his eye on crew managership and attained that difficult position after months of hard work."[3]

Upon receiving his commission in June 1932, Wylie got his orders to the heavy cruiser USS *Augusta* (CA-31). The ship had entered service only eighteen months earlier, and Wylie joined her shortly before she sailed to become flagship of the U.S. Asiatic Fleet. In his first four years on board the *Augusta,* Wylie saw his initial service as an officer in circumstances different from those in other parts of the Navy. A small force, the Asiatic Fleet operated as a separate entity, reporting directly to the Navy Department and not through the commander in chief of the U.S. Fleet, as did other major commands. Its primary purpose was diplomatic. Should war break out, the small Asiatic Fleet was to be augmented by the much larger U.S. Pacific Fleet. Thus, the time that the flagship spent on competitive fleet exercises was limited. In Wylie's time, exercises usually took place in January and February each year, leaving the ship free to cruise in a fairly well-established pattern: a few weeks in Hong Kong, visits to

ports such as Amoy and Foochow along the China coast up to the
mouth of the Yangtze, occasionally up the river as far as Nanking,
then north to Tsingtao as a base for three summer months. In the autumn, the flagship cruised south to spend the winter in the Philippines. During the winter, there were cruises to Singapore, the
Netherlands East Indies, and, in 1934, a visit to Australia.

The most dramatic even that influenced Wylie's appreciation of differing cultural perceptions occurred in the summer of 1934. Admiral
Frank B. Upham, the commander in chief of the Asiatic Fleet, broke
the usual pattern of routine visits and sailed in the *Augusta* from Tsingtao to Yokohama in order to represent the United States at the funeral of Admiral of the Fleet Heihachiro Togo, the Japanese admiral
who had defeated the Russian Fleet at Tsushima in 1905. Protocol
required that the ship send a platoon of forty bluejackets and two officers to march in the parade. Captain Chester Nimitz decided not to
use the regular landing force, and he mustered a special detail of
men, all of whom were over six feet tall. Wylie was the ensign, march-
ing along behind the American contingent. Ahead of them were the
Japanese and the British. Along the long line of march with the cas-
ket and the detachments from many countries, Wylie could hear
whispered comments from the spectators, noting that the Americans
were a head and a half taller than anyone else in the parade.

When Wylie was ashore in those years, he had an experience of exotic cultures, but one in which two cultures operated in different
spheres, each by its own standards. On board ship, Wylie found that
the Asiatic Fleet's mission gave service with it a different tone than
one found elsewhere in the U.S. Navy. The frequent and conscious
connection of fleet operations with diplomacy and international relations made its impact, although the emphasis was on professional
naval duties. In this, his first practical experience was guided by a
series of very successful officers. His first three commanding officers
in the *Augusta* were Captains James O. Richardson, Royal E. Inger-
soll, and Chester W. Nimitz, each to rise to admiral within a decade.

In May 1936, at the end of his tour of duty in the *Augusta,* the Bureau of Navigation ordered Wylie to the destroyer *Reid* (DD-369),
then under construction at the Federal Shipbuilding and Dry Dock
Company in Kearney, New Jersey. The *Reid's* commanding officer
was Robert B. Carney, another future chief of naval operations.
Thinking back over those years, Wylie exclaimed, "You wonder I
thought it was a good navy?"

While he was serving in the *Reid,* he became engaged to Harriett
Bahney, daughter of Mr. and Mrs. Luther W. Bahney of Elizabeth,

New Jersey. She was a graduate of St. Margaret's School in Water-
bury, Connecticut, and the Connecticut College for Women. The couple married on 27 November 1937; they had two children, Elizabeth
and Peter, both of whom eventually became naval officers.[4]

After six years at sea, Wylie was transferred to the destroyer tender USS *Altair* (AD-11), based at San Diego. Serving as the ship's
communications officer, he remained in her from July 1938 until
June 1939, after which he returned to Annapolis for shore duty in the
Executive Department at the Naval Academy. In July 1941 Wylie reported to the USS *Bristol* (DD-453), lead ship in a new group of
1,700-ton destroyers built under the "Two-Ocean Navy" Act of 1940.
When Wylie reported onboard, she was then fitting out for her commissioning at Kearney. During her first year at sea, Wylie participated in patrol and convoy operations in the North Atlantic between
Canada and Ireland. The *Bristol's* commanding officer occasionally
served as senior escort commander with Canadian, Free French, and
Polish corvettes in company.

In May 1942 Wylie was ordered back to the shipyard at Kearney,
this time to be executive officer of the USS *Fletcher* (DD-445), the
lead ship in a new class of 2,100-ton destroyers, under the command
of William M. Cole. Commissioned in June 1942, the *Fletcher* sailed
from the East Coast, arriving at Noumea, New Caledonia, in October, and immediately began patrol and escort duties for the Guadalcanal operation. She bombarded Lunga Point on 30 October, covered
reinforcements landing on Guadalcanal on 9 November, and helped
to drive off heavy enemy air attacks on the transport ships on 12 November in the first phase of the battle of Guadalcanal.

The *Fletcher* played an important role in the night action off
Guadalcanal on Friday, 13 November, firing her guns and torpedoes
in the general action that sank two Japanese destroyers and damaged the battleship *Hiei*. Amazingly, the *Fletcher* received only slight
damage in the intense battle which, a Naval Academy history textbook notes, "for confusion and fury is scarcely parallelled in naval
history."[5] Despite the superior number of Japanese ships and the loss
of eight U.S. ships, the Americans drove the Japanese battle force
and transports back to their base. After the action, the *Fletcher*
sailed eastward for Espiritu Santo in the New Hebrides Islands to
refuel and rearm.

On 30 November, she put to sea with Task Force 67, a group of
cruisers and destroyers, to intercept Japanese ships in another attempt to bring troops to reinforce their positions on Guadalcanal.
The *Fletcher* led the American formation westward through the

Lengo Channel into Iron Bottom Sound and approached the westerly end of Guadalcanal's north coast. Taking advantage of the latest surface search radar with a Plan Position Indicator display, the *Fletcher* was the first to make radar contact with the Japanese off Tassafaronga Point, just before midnight, and to pass on recommendations to Rear Admiral Carleton Wright, the officer in tactical command. Wright, hesitating to use the new technical capability that the *Fletcher's* radar offered, lost his opportunity as the Japanese seized the initiative. Hampered by faulty exploders and depth-control mechanisms, not one of the American torpedoes found its mark, although one destroyer was sunk by gunfire. The Japanese sank one of the American ships and severely damaged three others.

Wylie was awarded the Silver Star Medal for "gallantry and intrepidity in action" as the Fletcher's executive officer during the two actions off Guadalcanal. "Using discriminating judgement and quick resourcefulness," the citation reads, "Lieutenant Commander Wylie directed the ship, gun and torpedo control of his vessel with outstanding success, inflicting heavy damage on two enemy cruisers and sinking a third. . . . "

During these actions, Wylie's battle station was in the ship's chart house, just abaft the bridge, where he operated the surface search radar. Knowing better than the newly trained radar operators what sort of information the captain needed to correlate the radar information for the best offensive use of the guns and torpedoes, Wylie could talk to the captain through a louvered light screen in the porthole between the bridge and the chart room. While watching the radar scope, he wore split sound-powered telephones, one to the gunnery officer and the other to the torpedo officer. Close at hand, he had a microphone to use the TBS voice radio. It was a jury-rigged arrangement, radical in the light of current doctrine, yet as one historian has commented, "Thus, Wylie was himself the Navy's first Combat Information Center, or CIC, a concept and term that had yet to be invented."[6]

In January 1943 Wylie took command of his first ship, the USS *Trever* (DMS-16), a First World War flush-deck destroyer converted into a fast minesweeper. The *Trever* received the Navy Unit Commendation for her action in the Solomon Islands campaign, which at that point involved little minesweeping and was devoted to carrying troops from Guadalcanal up the Slot for clandestine rubber-boat landings at night.

After only six months in command, Wylie was unexpectedly ordered to Pearl Harbor for duty on the staff of Rear Admiral M. S. Tis-

dale, commander, destroyers, Pacific Fleet. Wylie was angry that he
had been ordered ashore after so short a time in his first command.
Tisdale promised him a new command, but explained that the fleet
had a higher priority. Tisdale saw the urgent need for commanding
officers to use and to correlate the rapidly increasing quantity of information that was becoming available to ships. Impressed by the
Fletcher's action report on the Guadalcanal operation, the staff in
Pearl Harbor believed that Wylie might be the right man to help in
quickly reaching to the heart of the issue. At Pearl Harbor, the question was not merely one of radar and sonar information, but also of
air and surface scouting reports, electronic and code-breaking intelligence, and basic navigational and piloting data.

Joining others on the staff who were dealing with this same problem, including Commander Caleb B. Laning and Lieutenant Commanders Edward Day, George Phillips and Lieutenant (j.g.) Robert
E. Bookman, Wylie got the job of preparing a short handbook. Within
two months, he produced the text for the *CIC Handbook for Destroyers*. The destroyer tender at Pearl Harbor printed the first run
of about five hundred copies for all Pacific Fleet destroyers and their
staffs. It was an immediate success and within a short time was
widely reprinted and distributed throughout the Navy.

The basic concept that Wylie and his colleagues developed was
more than just the thought of having a space and the equipment
aboard ship to deal with the vast expansion of available information.
Their original concept included an arrangement of positions and
equipment to correlate the data most profitably. They devised a general plan that could be adapted to whatever ship would use it, bas-
ing it on a hypothetical square compartment. Dividing the square
compartment in half with a fore and aft line, they assigned the starboard side to air action, or in the case of destroyers at that time, air
defense. The port side was devoted to surface and subsurface action.
Having established this division, they divided the square compartment the other way, from side to side. The forward half was allocated
to "history," anything that preceded the current situation, while "current events" was assigned to the after half.

Using this basic concept, the Destroyer Force staff placed the surface search radar in the after port side for surface current events and
recommended that the sonar control console be placed there also. In
the forward port side they located the Dead Reckoning Tracer, which
showed where the ships and its targets had been. On the starboard
side they placed the air search radar in the after portion for "current
events," and the air plotting boards forward with "history." They

called the officer who controlled all this the "evaluator." His station was between the two radar screens and both surface and air plots. After outlining the basic idea of this arrangement, Wylie and his colleagues went on to work out the duties and responsibilities of the team who would operate the equipment, keep the plots, and man the radios and sound-powered telephone circuits. The Pacific Fleet Destroyer Force staff wanted to call this new coordinating center the Combat Operations Center. This suggested name did not sit well with the destroyer captains of the day, who could not imagine a captain anywhere but on the bridge. Thus the name Combat Information Center came into use in the U.S. Navy.

Upon the *CIC Handbook's* completion, Admiral Tisdale sent Wylie to muster support for the *Handbook* at the Bureau of Ships in Washington and the staff of Rear Admiral M. L. Deyo, commander, Destroyer Force, Atlantic Fleet. Despite some opposition from the staff of the commander in chief, U.S. Fleet, Deyo accepted the *Handbook* and the two force commanders agreed to unified requirements. The Bureau of ships approved the remodeling of the commodore's cabin into a CIC, while the ships' captains were given a Pullman-type roomette arrangement in their sea cabins.

Returning to the Pacific, Wylie went to Espiritu Santo in the late summer of 1943 to start a combat indoctrination school for newly arriving destroyers. Nicknamed "Cocoanut College" because it was located in the cocoanut grove on Aore Island, it was not a formal school in the strict sense. Instead, it was composed of a team of five or six officers who had been in recent combat and could teach officers and leading petty officers the latest ideas based on experience with using the PPI radar scope and coordinating information during combat. The most difficult task they faced was to change ingrained patterns of thought and teach people to solve relative motion problems with their own ship at the center of the plot, rather than the guide of the formation-a key task if the U.S. Navy was to use the new PPI radar scopes effectively.

In December 1943, Wylie left the Pacific and returned to Kearney, New Jersey, to take command of a destroyer under construction, the USS *Ault* (DD-698). Through his long experience with that shipyard, Wylie had developed a close relationship with yard workers. Some of the men that he had worked with during his three earlier assignments at Federal Shipbuilding in Kearney, New Jersey, outfitting the destroyers *Reid, Bristol,* and *Fletcher,* had now become shipyard foremen. This personal connection made for good relations with the yard and high quality in outfitting his new ship.

The *Ault* was commissioned on 31 May 1944, and after a shake-down period, Wylie returned with her to the Pacific. As flagship for Destroyer Squadron 62, she sailed from Pearl Harbor to join Task Force 38 at the end of 1944. Beginning in January 1945, the *Ault* entered combat operations. Providing screening, plane guard, and shore bombardment duties, she participated in the Formosa Raids on 3–4, 9, 15 and 21 January; the China Coast Raids on 12 and 16 January; the Nansei Shoto raid on 22 January; the Iwo Jima operation from 15 February to 5 March; the Fifth Fleet raid on Honshu and Nansei Shoto from 15 to 16 February and 25 February to 1 March; and the Okinawa operation from 17 March to 30 May. In connection with the first carrier raids on Tokyo in mid-February and early March, the *Ault* participated as a radar picket for the "delousing" destroyers, providing antiaircraft fire against Japanese planes that followed the raiders back to the fleet.

Detached from command of the *Ault* in July, Wylie was assigned to duty in Washington, where he reported to Commodore Arleigh Burke in the Special Defense Section on the staff of the commander in chief, U.S. Fleet. This group under Burke's direction had the duty to develop countermeasures to the Japanese kamikazes in preparation for the planned invasions of Kyushu and Honshu. The war ended in August before the group had developed a plan, and it was disbanded.

During the general demobilization of U.S. forces, Wylie served with the Office of Naval research as a special project officer. Based at Beavertail in Jamestown, Rhode Island, Wylie was project officer for a group of experimental psychologists from Johns Hopkins University, and a number of other academics who had subcontracted with Johns Hopkins, in studies to develop the most efficient control mechanisms for a naval officer to use in controlling complex machinery. Eventually they produced a handbook that could be used by design engineers in developing airplane cockpits and other key control positions. This publication on "human engineering" was an early contribution to what is now referred to as ergonomics, that aspect of technology concerned with the study of problems relating to the mutual adjustment of men and machines.

In June 1948, Wylie reported to the Naval War College as a student in the Strategy and Tactics Course. Toward the end of his year there, he and five or six of his colleagues had a discussion about the navy's situation in the unification of the armed forces. All agreed that what the navy needed most, in order to avoid being sunk in unification, was a clear and succinct understanding of the reason for its existence. They could see that the navy's leaders were not stating any rationale for the navy's role. As the discussion broke up, the students agreed that the first of them to return to Newport on the staff of the Naval War College would try to make some kind of study that could create an intellectually sound rationale for a modern navy.

After Wylie left Newport in 1949 to serve as staff operations officer for Rear Admiral John Higgins, commander, Destroyer Flotilla One, based at San Diego, Admiral Richard L. Conolly received orders to be president of the Naval War College. He had been a student and a staff member in Newport from 1929 to 1931, had extensive experience afloat as a destroyer squadron and amphibious commander during World War II, and in the postwar years had been Deputy Chief of Naval Operations for operations. Since 1946 he had been based in London while serving as commander in chief, U.S. Naval Forces, Eastern Atlantic and Mediterranean. Conolly had his own strong ideas about naval strategy and saw clearly the need for new work in this area.[7]

By chance, Wylie received orders to return to the Naval War College as the staff member for the Advanced Course in Strategy and Sea Power in the summer of 1950, just as war began in Korea. Some weeks after Conolly's arrival in Newport in December 1950, Wylie had the opportunity to speak at length with him and discuss his idea for a study of the navy's reason for existence. The idea was very much in tune with Conolly's views, and he instantly seized on a name: the School of Advanced Study in Strategy and Sea Power. This became one of the major efforts in Conolly's initial recommendations for change in the Naval War College curriculum.

By 1 May 1951 Conolly had completed his letter recommending changes to Admiral Forrest Sherman, the chief of naval operations. Incorporating many of Wylie's thoughts, Conolly proposed to extend the usefulness of the Naval War College. Conolly wrote, "while the primary function of the Naval War College must remain the education of naval leaders in command, strategy, tactics, logistics and staff work, its mission is incomplete and unfilled if it does not generate progressive ideas, foster creative thinking in its own field of education and produce an accumulation of knowledge and understanding of the basic elements of the 'Art and Science of Naval Warfare.'" To achieve this, Conolly proposed to establish a Research and Analysis Department as well as the School for Advanced Study. Noting that nowhere in the navy's curriculum was there an opportunity "for a mature, adult appreciation of the orderly intellectual process evolved for the study and solution of problems in the social and physical sciences," he went on to declare that the lack of understanding of the naval profession and general lack of intellectual discipline had been convincingly demonstrated in recent years. Summarizing his view of the situation, he wrote:

> . . . we are, as naval officers today, a breed of fine seamen, of able airmen, efficient administrators, and of superb tacticians and technicians. But very few of us, until the forces of naked power stared the nation in the face, were able to reason with the Congress or present our case convincingly to the people so that our own service should be saved from comparative oblivion. Our understanding and our exposition of the indispensable character of our profession and the undiminished and vital nature of Sea Power have been dangerously superficial and elementary.[8]

In this proposal, Conolly and Wylie saw the importance of history. Wylie, in particular, seized upon his suggestion that Admiral Raymond Spruance had made some years earlier to establish a civilian chair of history at the Naval War College. This position had been approved by the Secretary of the Navy in 1948, but for lack of funds it had never been filled. Wylie saw the importance of history for broad understanding of strategy. Conolly incorporated Wylie's ideas on this subject in his letter to the Chief of Naval Operations:

> All of us have, at one time or another, uttered or acquiesced in the cliché that we learn from history. But few, if any, of us know any history; and none of us now has the time or inducement to study any history on other than a desultory catch-as-catch-can basis. Very few of us have even come to realize that there are three types of knowledge to be had from military history. One is simple knowledge of events that took place; the second is a knowledge of how to fight better; and the third (and generally neglected) is a knowledge of how to think more clearly in order to properly analyze the situations and assess and evaluate the various factors that produce success or failure, victory or defeat.

Emphasizing his point, Conolly wrote, "In this connection, it should be noted that the history we need is a rather unknown, little understood, facet of the broad chronology. It is interpretative history and there have not been very many interpretive historians who have chosen our profession as their field of study."[9]

The study of history played an important role in the proposed new course, alongside other complementary approaches to understanding modern warfare at sea. Although Wylie was unhappy with Conolly's choice for the name of the course, since it seemed to imply a course that was superior to the other resident courses rather than one that was merely different, he acquiesced. The Chief of Naval Operations, Admiral Forest Sherman, approved Conolly's suggestions in early July 1951 and Wylie was given responsibility for its administration.[10] At Wylie's request, he obtained as his assistant Lieutenant Commander Eugene Burdick, later to become famous as the coauthor of the novel *The Ugly American.* Together, they laid the groundwork for the new course.[11] In the process, they consulted a number of university professors, including Harold Sprout of Princeton, Edward M. Earle of the Institute for Advanced Study, William Reitzel of the Brookings Institution, Robert G. Albion of Harvard, and James Phinney Baxter of Williams College. All made useful contributions, but on reflection Wylie found that the advice they had received from John von Neumann of the Institute for Advanced Study and Harold Lasswell at Yale proved to be most influential. Wylie designed the work to be that of a study group, rather than a course. The early structured part was a means of preparing group members for the primary purpose of their work, which was to be research, study, and the increase of basic knowledge. In the fall of 1951, after the first group of eight officers had arrived, Burdick began the course with a study of intellectual methods. In actuality this was an appreciation of some of the basic concepts of philosophy and logic.

This approach paralleled a course in maritime history for the period 1500–1900, which was taught on a part-time basis by Professor Thomas C. Mendenhall of Yale University. The purpose of his course was not to examine the usual chronological pattern, but the relationship of maritime matters to events in other fields of human activity-the political, social, economic, and cultural. Mendenhall concluded his course with a two-day session in which the group attempted to define the role of contemporary sea power in the light of their historical studies. In this, Mendenhall was the first to serve as the college's professor of maritime history. In the following year, he was succeeded by Professor John H. Kemble of Pomona College, who held the position in 1953 as its first full-time occupant when it was named the Ernest J. King Chair of Maritime History. At the same time, the Naval War College established the Chester W. Nimitz Chair of Social and Political Philosophy. These were the Naval War college's first civilian academic chairs.

To sharpen themselves, each member of Wylie's group wrote a weekly paper and then defended it in a seminar meeting in which invited guests could participate. The guests ranged from members of the War College staff, such as Vice Admiral Conolly and retired Rear Admiral Henry E. Eccles, to outside experts, such as Captain Basil Liddell Hart, Dr. Herbert Rosinski, Professor John Masland of Dart-

mouth College, and Vice Admiral Friedrich Ruge, who in 1956 as In-
spekteur der Marine became the first head of the Federal German
Navy.

During this first year, Wylie published some of his own work in
connection with the study course. He delivered "Reflections on the
War in the Pacific," first as a lecture at the Naval War College in November 1951 while he and his colleagues were examining the historical context of maritime strategy. It was much more than a personal reflection on a segment of the war in which he had a great
interest; Wylie took seven events in the war and looked at them as
matters that could be usefully studied for reference in improving the
strategic conduct of a future war. Considering the use of strategy in
the light of his Naval War College discussions of theory and logic,
Wylie laid part of the groundwork for his later book, *Military Strategy*.

Most significantly, he developed an idea that had been suggested
by Dr. Herbert Rosinski in conversations during the spring of 1951.
At that time, Rosinski had tried to identify two different types of
strategy: "directive" and "cumulative." Wylie went on to develop
Rosinski's ideas further and classified them as "sequential" and "cumulative" strategies. This point was an important one for his later
work.[12] Wylie submitted his article to the U.S. Naval Institute,
where it earned an honorable mention in that year's prize essay contest and was published in *Proceedings* the following spring.

Following this work, Wylie began during the latter part of the first
year to develop his first general statement of maritime strategy. He
organized it into an essay that was discussed in the seminar group
and then given as a lecture to the Naval War College students on
11–12 September 1952. This, too, he submitted to the Naval Institute, where he again won an honorable mention and publication in
Proceedings under the title "On Maritime Strategy." Clearly demonstrating the results of his first year's work, Wylie explored the subject in terms of theory, past experience, complicating current factors,
and finally, the contemporary use of military and naval power. His
ideas on maritime strategy are very briefly summarized in *Military
Strategy* and show their basis in this work.[13] Most important, Wylie
focused on the idea of control as the aim of warfare. He argued that
the division of strategy by service, into maritime, continental, and
air strategies was artificial and should be made only for the purpose
of study and analysis. "In practice there is, and must be, a good deal
of overlap and merging," he wrote. The most important part of this
article was Wylie's development of the idea that the purpose of sea

power is to project control over the land. In this, he noted, there are
two methods:

> a victory by a sea power exploiting her power at sea to project a frequently
> smaller but strategically decisive ground force for the actual establish-
> ment of control on land; and a victory by a sea power exploiting her power
> at sea to project an economic force toward the eventual establishment of
> governing control over the enemy in his own land.

Wylie went on to say,

> It should be noted that, in practice that the exploitation of sea power is
> usually a combination of general slow stiflings with a few critical thrusts.
> These latter are frequently spectacular and draw our attention to the ex-
> clusion of the former, while in point of fact the critical thrusts would not
> be critical were it not for the tedious and constant tightening of the screws
> that makes them possible.[14]

In the second year, each member of the group selected a subject for
research and defended it in rigorous seminars. As the year wore on,
the students decided what they wanted to do with the results of their
work. They knew that while few in the Navy took the time to ponder
the abstract statements in professional and academic journals, naval
officers did listen to what their senior officers were saying and read
their operational orders carefully. Therefore, the group decided that
the most influential way in which to get their ideas across was to
write speeches for senior officers in Washington and to contribute
phrases and paragraphs to fleet operation plans and basic orders. In
this way, many of the basic ideas that Wylie and his study group developed received widespread currency in the 1950s and 1960s, penetrating all levels of the service and being borrowed by writers of
speeches and operation plans.

While this work was in progress, Wylie published a small piece
that revealed the value he placed on the use of careful terminology
in discussing strategy. In the spring of 1953, as the study group completed its second year, the Navy was doing very badly in the budget
hearings in Congress. One of the Army's most effective and persuasive advocates repeatedly replied to difficult questions by saying,
"Mr. Congressman, that is a calculated risk." Since no one knew
what the phrase meant and no one in Congress wanted to gamble on
a risk that was not carefully calculated, Wylie teasingly devised a
mathematical expression of the phrase in a one-page article for *Proceedings*. Wylie wrote about this formula:

For the victor it will add a rare quality of intellectual brilliance to his assured rank of major or minor genius. To the unfortunate victim-of-cir-
cumstances-beyond-his-control it offers dignified justification. The critics
will be so involved in recalculation that their audiences will soon give up
in sheer boredom. The ones who were already in accord with the victim's
decision will have long since understood it anyway.[15]

A commentator, Walter Millis, picked up on Wylie's piece and wrote
a column on it in the *New York Herald Tribune* that summer. As
Wylie later commented, "The result was that no one ever mentioned
the calculation of risk before Congress again for at least five years.
So it did serve its purpose."

Before Wylie left the Naval War College in the summer of 1953, he
reflected on the course and his suggestions for its future. Among
them was a point that guided his own thinking:

Rather than rediscovery of the areas of continental, maritime and air
strategies, use these as a point of departure in appreciation of the problem of the study of strategy. Introduce at this time in the spring term other
known or suggested methods of studying or analyzing strategy such as by
means of the so called principles, by situational analyses, by other theoretical divisions such as sequential and cumulative classifications, by the
doctrinal approach, and by that odd but prevalent joining of faith and os-
mosis down a path toward a hoped-for understanding.[16]

Concluding his recommendations, Wylie wrote:

I can not too strongly state my belief that study of this nature is the primary hope for a continued and expanded contribution of the navy to the
nation. We can count with reasonable surety on the technical and industrial strength of the nation and its reflection in the technical improvement
of the navy. For a better understanding of when, where, and how to apply
these technical advances we can turn to no one outside the service. For
that deeper understanding of the nature of our profession only we can
help ourselves.[17]

In July 1953, Wylie took command of the attack transport USS
Arneb (AKA-56). It was while in command of the *Arneb* during long
passages at sea that Wylie wrote the basis for what, fourteen years
later, was to become his book *Military Strategy*. In 1954 he joined the
staff of Rear Admiral H. Page Smith, commander, Amphibious Group
Two, as operations officer and later as chief of staff. The next year he
was ordered to duty in the Office of the Chief of Naval Operations.
During this tour of duty in Washington he had the opportunity to see

the Navy budget process at work and to observe naval officers as they defended the Navy's role. As he watched officers from the other services and listened to their logic, he saw that the naval officers reflected a different manner of thinking than the others. He took this topic as the subject for another article in *Proceedings* entitled "Why a Sailor Thinks Like a Sailor."[18] In October 1958, he took command of the heavy cruiser USS *Macon* (CA-132). Command of this ship marked a high point in Wylie's career. During his period of command, he took the *Macon* through the St. Lawrence Seaway for the opening ceremonies and continued on through the Great Lakes to Chicago, the first (and still the only) cruiser to make such a trip. "Taking a ship the size of *Macon* halfway across a continent was probably the most exhilarating experience that a cruiser captain could ever hope for," Wylie wrote.[19]

From November 1959 to December 1960, Wylie served on the staff of Admiral Robert L. Dennison, the Supreme Allied Commander, Atlantic. Selected for promotion to rear admiral during this period, Wylie pinned on his new insignia on 1 December when he took command of Cruiser Division Three (later renamed Cruiser Destroyer Flotilla Nine). Wylie was appointed Deputy Inspector General of the Navy in November 1961 and remained in that position until August 1962, when he was assigned to the joint Strategic-Survey Council of the Joint Chiefs of Staff. For his service in that position, between 1962 and 1964, he was awarded the Joint Service Commendation Medal.

In July 1964, Wylie reported as deputy chief of staff and deputy chief of staff for plans and operations to Admiral H. P. Smith, the Commander in Chief, U.S. Atlantic Fleet. He was awarded the Legion of Merit "for . . . outstanding service . . . during Operation Power Pack in the Dominican Republic crisis in April and May 1965. . . . [He] provided invaluable assistance to the Commander in Chief United States Atlantic Fleet during a period when rapid, decisive planning and execution of joint military operations in the Dominican Republic were of the utmost importance to our national interests."

In March 1966, he became deputy commander in chief, U.S. Naval Forces, Europe, and chief of staff to Admiral James S. Thach, the Commander in Chief, U.S. Naval Forces Europe. Wylie was serving in this position when his book, *Military Strategy,* was first published by Rutgers University Press. Completing his assignment in London, Wylie became chief of staff to Vice Admiral John T. Hayward, the President of the Naval War College, and he remained in that position for a year, until he became commander of the Naval Base, Newport, Rhode Island. After only three months, he took up the additional responsibilities of the commandant of the First Naval District, with headquarters in Boston, Massachusetts, and with further duty as commander of the naval base, Boston.

Rear Admiral J. C. Wylie retired from active duty on 1 July 1972, after more than forty-four years in uniform. Upon his retirement, he received a Gold Star in lieu of a second Legion of Merit for meritorious conduct as commandant of the First Naval District.

In 1974, following the translation of a series of articles that had appeared during 1972 in *Morskoi Sbornik* by Admiral of the Fleet of the Soviet Union Sergei Gorshkov, Wylie was one of eleven prominent U.S. flag officers invited by the Naval Institute to comment upon Gorshkov's work as it appeared in monthly installments of *Proceedings.* Wylie took Gorshkov's piece on *Analysis of Navies in the Second World War"* for comment, and noted that through this series, "We have gotten a glimpse of a very important mind at work. We should profit by it."[20]

Upon his retirement, Wylie and his wife moved to Portsmouth, Rhode Island. Admiral Wylie remained active, starting work on an analysis of strategy in terms of its historical development. In addition, he served as the first chairman of the USS *Constitution* Museum Foundation, an organization established to provide support for a museum that opened in 1976 in a restored machinery building for the 1832 drydock in the Boston Navy Yard.

At the same time, in the autumn of 1972, he became the first chairman of the American Sail Training Association, which in June 1976 brought 102 sail-training ships to a race from Bermuda to Newport, Rhode Island, in connection with the celebration of the bicentennial of American independence. He retired from these activities in he late 1970s, but has remained an active member of the New York Yacht Club, the Ida Lewis Yacht Club, the Navy Sailing Association, the Coaster's Harbor Navy Yacht Club, the Newport Reading Room, and Quindecim and participated in a variety of community service activities.

Wylie wrote *Military Strategy* while he was in command of the USS *Arneb* in 1953, but he did not submit it for publication until 1966. After expanding and revising the book during the intervening years, Wylie eventually submitted it under the title *The Military Mind* to Rutgers University Press, which had recently published a number of books on military subjects. They agreed to publish it as *Military Strategy.* The editor suggested the new title so that libraries could more easily index it by its subject.

On 17 April 1967, Rutgers University Press published 2,500 copies of the 111-page *Military Strategy* at four dollars a copy. In recommending the book, *The Library Journal's* reviewer commented, "Although the price is slightly high for such a small book, the relevance of the topic to today's unstable world and Admiral Wylie's thoughtful discussion of it makes the book essential reading for public and academic libraries."[21]

Reviewing the book for the *New York Times Book Review,* defense correspondent Hanson Baldwin noted:

> No military service can long remain effective without searching self-criticism and continuous re-examination of its own ideas. . . . Wylie, well known in the Navy, is a refreshingly outspoken and thoughtful individual, thoroughly at home on the bridge of a ship, but equally at home in the semantics of dialectical discussion. He has produced a simple but relevant little work in an attempt to promote order in the discussion of strategy.[22]

Shortly after the book appeared, Rear Admiral Henry E. Eccles prepared a review in which he summarized Wylie's main arguments. "On the staff of the Naval War College and in his other assignments, he demonstrated his imagination and his independence of mind in a continuing challenge of conventional assumptions and routine formulations," Eccles noted. "It is a tribute to his dedication that while serving in demanding high-level positions, he was able to produce even a short reflective and imaginative work."[23] Eccles pointed out the debt that Wylie owed to Dr. Herbert Rosinski in developing the analytical classification of sequential and cumulative strategies. Interestingly, he also pointed out a similarity with that of André Beaufre, Eccles found a harmony of thought that "is the natural, if not frequently expressed, result of the combination of hard practical experience in combat command, responsible high-level planning, innate scholarly bent, a receptive speculative mind an a dissatisfaction with mediocrity."[24]

In 1968, Wylie's move to the Naval War College as Chief of Staff to Vice Admiral John T. Hayward prompted other reviews. Most prominent among them was by Neil Ulman in the *Wall Street Journal.*[25] "No attempt to proclaim the last word on warfare," Ulman wrote, "it is a fine introduction to strategic thought and chiefly fascinating as the forging of a thinker's tool." Underscoring Wylie's point that the service-oriented theories of strategies create barriers between their proponents and make it more difficult for them to understand one another, Ulman found Wylie's general theory of strategy "a very broad statement of strategy, but worth a book to develop if the power

of Admiral Wylie's arguments can wean planners from hitherto
parochial outlooks to a broader, more flexible approach." In concluding his review, Ulman wrote that Wylie "clears much of the irrelevant debris from the foundations of strategic thought and offers
planners a logical point of departure.

Among readers of strategic theory, Wylie's book became well
known. By 1970, Rutgers University Press had exhausted the initial
printing. The press reprinted the book in 1970, 1972, and 1977, each
time printing 1,500 additional copies. In 1978 the Escuela de Guerra
Naval in Buenos Aires, Argentina, translated the book into Spanish.
Rutgers sold rights to Greenwood Press in 1980 for a clothbound edition, and in 1987 to the Australian Naval Institute in Sydney for a
paperback edition.

Commenting on the Australian edition, Professor Peter Nailor of
the Royal Naval College, Greenwich, wrote:

> The book itself was first published in 1967, and it is fair to say that it
> never received the attention it might have done. The American strategic
> community was then preoccupied with more specific issues than general
> theories of strategy; and the reflective cast of the argument-and its
> brevity, perhaps-somehow eluded the general notice. Nevertheless, the
> book has many virtues, which are not out of place today, and it is good to
> be reminded of Wylie's professionalism and clarity.[26]

Although the book did not receive widespread attention in the larger
defense community, it did have a major role within the Navy. As Nailor
commented, "Wylie has many claims to be thought of as an intellectual influence upon military, specifically naval, staff thinking."[27]

In the 1980s, as leaders and staff officers within the Navy were developing the U.S. Navy's maritime strategy, Wylie's book had an impact on their approach. Some of the staff officers dealing with the detailed development of the maritime strategy were deeply influenced
by his ideas and tried to apply his concepts of control, cumulative,
and sequential strategy in their work. One of the active participants,
Captain Peter M. Swartz, USN, wrote about one of Wylie's essays
that it was "by the Navy's leading public strategist of the 1950s and
60s. Remarkable similar to the views expressed in the Maritime
Strategy a generation later."[28] Reflecting the increasing interest and
importance of the book, the U.S. Naval Institute republished it in
1989, in its Classics of Sea Power series.

In his last years, Wylie retained his intellectual curiosity in a wide
range of areas, occasionally traveling to places such as off-beat
places as the Massif Central in France and becoming involved in

such age-old questions as "Who wrote Shakespeare's plays?" He remained heavily involved in volunteer activities throughout the community, but when his wife became ill in the late 1970s, he searched for a project that he could do at home. Returning to his interest in strategic thought, he devoted considerable time to preparing a long manuscript that described the evolution of maritime strategy from the middle ages and the renaissance to the present, "an effort to set forth the sailor's ideas within the matrix of other concepts"[29] expressed in what he always called "tight, but readable prose." Intended as a study for "plain sailors," the work brought him both personal pleasure and a deeper appreciation of events in military history. Nevertheless, he was disappointed by his inability to find a publisher for the book and frustrated by the criticism of readers that it did not stand up to the standards of professional historians nor reflected the latest literature. At first, he felt that his wife's increasing illness had preoccupied him, but later he saw that the basic defect was that he had treated technology and social conditions as separate subjects. "I doubt that I'll try again," he wrote, " but, if I do, I'll treat the entire socio-techno fabric as an encompassing entity in which strategy is embedded and by which the shape of strategy is set."[30]

In 1990, he played an important role in a conference held at the Naval War College to mark the centenary of the publication of Mahan's *The Influence of Sea Power Upon History, 1660–1783*. In an address, "Mahan: Then and Now," Wylie noted, "Sea Power, this essentially benign, ubiquitous, worldwide maritime presence, is the indispensable *basis* for many of the different aspects of our American foreign policies all around the world."[31] This thought came to occupy much of his attention in his final years, while his participation in the Mahan Centenary conference had stimulated him to return to his unpublished manuscript on "The Evolution of Maritime Strategy" In July 1992, just six months before his death, he felt that this concept was the most important practical notion that one could get from his manuscript. "The postulate that the maritime strength of the United States is an important under-pinning of United States policies has at least three direct effects," Wylie wrote:

It means closer coordination of maritime activities overseas with non-military foreign policies of the United States.
It provides one basis for maritime force planning that, for fifty years, has been buried in the more urgent needs of the super-power confrontation.
And it provides one basis for budget planning that is not only valid for maritime forces, but, by extrapolation, might possibly be a new point of

departure for reassessment of other national policies in this novel and literally singular role of world leadership.[32]

Above all, he believed, that both the Navy and key civilian agencies—particularly those dealing with foreign policy, international finance, and commerce—must develop far greater practical cooperation than any of them had previously considered.[33]

On 29 January 1993, Rear Admiral Wylie died of lung cancer at his home in Portsmouth, Rhode Island. At his funeral in Emmanuel Episcopal Church in Newport, some of the music from the film series "Victory at Sea," poignantly echoed a high point in his World War II combat career: Rogers and Hammerstein's "Under The Southern Cross." He was buried in Trinity Cemetery in Portsmouth.

As the United States Navy moved toward the last decade of the twentieth century, it came to focus more explicitly on the question of national strategy and the role of the Navy within it. Along with this, came and renewed emphasis on joint operations and cooperation among the services. In dealing with these matters, Wylie's basic analysis, his statement of a general theory of strategy, and his thoughts for practical future directions stand as clear and eloquent statements from which innovative thought may proceed.

NOTES

This is a revised version of the "Introduction" to J. C. Wylie, *Military Strategy: A General Theory of Power Control*. Classics of Sea Power Series. (Annapolis, MD: Naval Institute Press, 1989), pp. ix-xxxv.

1. Except where noted, this outline of Wylie's intellectual development is based on the U.S. Navy's Office of Information biographical sketch of Rear Admiral J. C. Wylie, Jr., dated 22 August 1972, supplemented by the U.S. Naval Institute Oral History, conducted by Paul Stillwell, 21–22 May 1985; Naval War College Oral History No. 7, conducted by Dr. Evelyn Cherpak, 21 November 1985–5 February 1986; and information supplied to the author by Admiral Wylie.
2. Obituary: J. Caldwell Wylie, *The New York Times*, 16 January 1958, p. 29:4.
3. *The Lucky Bag of the Service: The Annual of the Regiment of Midshipmen* (U.S. Naval Academy: Annapolis, MD, 1932), p. 248.
4. "Harriette Bahney to Wed," *The New York Times*, 10 October 1937, sec. vi, p. 4:7; "Harriette Bahney Wed to Navy Man," *The New York Times*, 28 November 1937, sec. vi, p. 5:1.
5. E. B. Potter and C. W. Nimitz, eds., *Sea Power: A Naval History*. (Englewood Cliffs, NJ: Prentice Hall, 1960), p. 704.
6. Eric Hammel, *Guadalcanal: Decision at Sea*. (New York: Crown, 1988), p. 253.

7. For a summary of his ideas, see Donald G. White, "Admiral Richard L. Conolly: A Perspective on His Notions of Strategy," *Naval War College Review,* November 1971, pp. 73–79, and Oral History: Columbia University Oral History Program.

8. Naval War College Archives, Records of the Course of Advanced Study: President, Naval War College, letter to Chief of Naval Operations, A3–1 serial 2354–51, 1 May 1951.

9. *Loc. cit.* J. C. Wylie, Memorandum [for the President, Naval War College], Subj: Chair of Military History, 2 April 1951.

10. *Loc. cit:* CNO to President, Naval War College, OP-03 serial 130P03, 3 July 1951; J. C. Wylie, Memorandum for Admiral Conolly, 1245, 5 July 1951.

11. On this, see Wylie's postscript " Twenty Years Later" to *Military Strategy: A General Theory of Power Control.* Classics of Sea Power Series. (Annapolis, MD: Naval Institute Press, 1989), pp. 95–115.

12. The key excerpt from this essay appears as Appendix A to Ibid., pp. 117–121. It originally appeared in the U.S. Naval Institute *Proceedings,* 78 (1952), pp. 351–361.

13. Reprinted as Appendix B in Ibid., pp. 123–147. It originally appeared in the U.S. Naval Institute *Proceedings,* 79 (1953), pp. 467–477.

14. Ibid.

15. J. C. Wylie, "The Calculation of Risk," Naval Institute *Proceedings,* 79 (1953), p. 725.

16. Naval War College Archives, Staff File: J. C. Wylie, Memorandum to the President [Naval War College], Subj: Conduct of the Course in Advanced Strategy and Sea Power, 9 June 1953.

17. *Ibid.*

18. Reprinted as Appendix C in *Military Strategy: A General Theory of Power Control.* Classics of Sea Power Series. (Annapolis, MD: Naval Institute Press, 1989), pp. 149–162. It originally appeared in the U.S. Naval Institute *Proceedings,* 83 (1957), pp. 811–817.

19. J. C. Wylie, "The Freshwater Cruise of the USS *Macon,*" U.S. Naval Institute *Proceedings,* 86 (April 1960), p. 61.

20. The series was later collected in book form: Sergei Gorshkov, *Red Star Rising at Sea.* (Annapolis: Naval Institute Press, 1978). Wylie's contribution may be found following Part 9 on pages 110–111.

21. K. G. Madison in *The Library Journal,* vol. 92 (May 15, 1967), p. 1930, quoted in *Book Review Digest 1967,* p. 1430.

22. *New York Times Book Review,* November 5, 1967, p. 62.

23. Naval Historical Collection, Naval War College; Manuscript Collection 52, box 7, folder 15: Papers of H. E. Eccles, Enclosure to Henry E. Eccles letter to Wylie, 27 March 1967.

24. Ibid.

25. "The Bookshelf: Flexible Strategy," *The Wall Street Journal,* 10 July 1968, p. 16.

26. *The Naval Review,* 76 (January 1988), pp. 88–89.

27. Ibid.

28. "Addendum to 'Contemporary U.S. Naval Strategy: A Bibliography,'" p. 53, published in April 1987 as an addendum to the "Maritime Strategy Supplement," U.S. Naval Institute *Proceedings,* January 1986. For a detailed discussion of Swartz's role, see Chapter 12, below.

29. Draft Introduction to "The Evolution of Maritime Strategy," 9 June 1990.
30. J. C. Wylie, letter to Hattendorf, 2 February 1989.
31. J. C. Wylie, "Mahan: Then and Now," in Hattendorf. ed., *The Influence of History on Mahan: The Proceedings of a Conference Marking the Centenary of Alfred Thayer Mahan's* The Influence of History Upon History, 1660–1783. (Newport, RI: Naval War College Press, 1991), pp. 37–45. Quote from p. 45.
32. J. C. Wylie, letter to Hattendorf, 21 July 1992. with enclosed revision to the conclusion of "The Evolution of Maritime Strategy," Chapter XII, pp. 14–17.
33. J. C. Wylie, letter to Hattendorf, 22 July 1992.

10

International Naval Cooperation and Admiral Richard G. Colbert: The Intertwining of a Career with an Idea

Most people who serve in navies or devote their days to writing and thinking about naval power take almost for granted the concept that navies are an expression of national power and therefore, in modern terminology, reinforce nationalism. We have become almost hypnotized with the idea that there is a continuum from national policy to naval strategy and tactics. Indeed, that is one powerful thought that lies at the foundation of Mahan's writings and Corbett's analysis. Yet it is not the only way to view the matter. Mahan and William S. Sims in the U.S. Navy of the early twentieth century had thought about possibilities for an Anglo-American maritime alliance. But, there is an even older thought: the idea that there is an essential commonality among those who go down to the sea in ships. Richard Colbert has been one of a very few senior admirals in the United States Navy to champion this other view. At the first International Sea Power Symposium in 1969, an occasion which brought together for the first time many heads of free world navies, Colbert outlined his own view:

> The experience of this conference has strongly confirmed what all of us already knew by instinct and experience: that the common aspects of so many of the problems we each face in operating at sea creates a strong fraternal bond. This unites all of us in blue suits who share similar professional concerns.
>
> We recognize that there are political problems and interests which sometimes limit our co-operation. But it is equally clear that the broad interests of the world community we serve are enhanced by bringing our common perspective to bear on common problems. Much can be done on a Navy-to-Navy basis.[1]

Admiral Richard G. Colbert
Photograph taken as a Vice Admiral in c. 1970–71, while serving as President
of the Naval War College. (*Naval War College Museum*)

An acquaintance of Colbert's in the Italian Navy defined the concept even more sharply when he wrote, "probably the underlying philosophy lies in the *Idea of Considering Navies of the World as a Social System* to a degree separated or divorced from the states they defend."[2] In other words, it is possible to discern a kind of global brotherhood of naval officers, indoctrinated with a concept of international naval cooperation and nurtured by close, personal relations.

In a sense it seems an idealistic concept founded on a belief in peace and friendship on a global scale that should be the basis for all human relations.[3] Yet at the same time, Colbert's notion can be viewed as a realistic, pragmatic strategy for the free world as the United States and its Allies faced Soviet naval power.[4] As some of his contemporaries noted, Colbert was not a theoretician given to working out new concepts in abstract form, but once someone else had formed a concept, he was superb at developing it further and bringing it to fruition.[5] It is in this sense that Colbert was accurately described in an honorary degree citation as "Sailor-Statesman of the Navy, creator, innovator, educator."[6]

In the thirty-six years of his naval career, Colbert slowly but increasingly became interested in concepts and ideas relating to international naval cooperation. By the time of his death in 1973, he had reached the rank of full admiral and had truly earned the title which Admiral Elmo Zumwalt gave him: "Mr. International Navy."[7]

EARLY CAREER

Colbert came from unusual family background. He was born in Brownsville, Pennsylvania, on 12 February 1915, the son of Charles F. Colbert, Jr., and Mary Louis Benford Colbert. His father, a prominent leader in the coke, coal, and alloy business, was president of the Pittsburgh Metallurgical Company. Colbert attended Shady Side Academy, an established college preparatory school in Pittsburgh. During his years there, he developed a passionate desire to become a naval officer, despite his father's fond hope that he would join the family business. Young Colbert decided to test out his desire and, with his father's help, obtained a berth on board the steamship *Robert Luckenbach* for the summer of 1931, on a voyage from New York to Seattle and back via the Panama Canal. It was an eventful trip which gave Colbert the experience of a hurricane and of hard work at sea. At the end of it, having firmly established his love for ships and the sea, the sixteen-year-old boy wrote his diary: "I can honestly say I have never enjoyed a summer as much as this one."[8]

After proving himself at sea, the next hurdle was to obtain an appointment to the Naval Academy following his graduation from school in June 1933. It was no easy task. Starting more than a year in advance, his father began writing letters to friends, business associates, local politicians, and his congressman asking their help. Disappointedly, they all replied that no appointments were available that had not already been promised to other equally good candidates.[9] Finally in desperation, a friend of the family and the Chancellor of Syracuse University, Charles W. Flint, wrote to President-elect Franklin D. Roosevelt asking his assistance. Roosevelt gave Flint the formula which eventually won the boy his commission: "The only chance for young Colbert," Roosevelt wrote, "is to find some other Congressman or Senator who has a vacancy and who would be willing to have him move into the district or state in which the vacancy exists for the purpose of establishing a residence there, even though it be a temporary one."[10] In the end, Colbert did not have to look too far afield. Congressman Harry A. Estrep of Pennsylvania's 35th District appointed Colbert to the U.S. Naval Academy in the class of 1937. This early incident is illuminating because it reveals the Colbert family's ease in approaching influential people, a skill which Richard Colbert often used later in life.

Colbert was a Naval Academy midshipman from 1933 to 1937; his class started with 440 and graduated 331. On graduation, he stood only 247 in the class. He was neither a great scholar nor an athlete, but he clearly stood out as a leader and as someone well trained in the social graces. He commanded the Third Battalion of Midshipmen in the first third of his senior year and again for the final third of the year, when the best and most successful leaders of the class were chosen. Throughout his academy years, he was busy in extracurricular activities, particularly social ones. On one occasion during the Midshipman's Practice Cruise in 1936, Colbert was selected from among the other midshipmen on board the flagship USS *Arkansas* to receive distinguished civilian guests. "I seem to be getting a name for being a Majordomo," he wrote to his father.[11] Indeed, he served on the hop committee and the Christmas card committee, was codirector of the musical clubs show, and finally, served as chairman of the most important social event of his four years at Annapolis, the Ring Dance.[12] Those experiences and social training helped Colbert develop his approach and style, so important later in his life.

While social events were prominent, one can find even in his midshipman days the first traces of his interest in foreign affairs.[13] He reflected this in a speech he prepared for the academy's public speaking group, the Quarterdeck Society, in January 1935. The prize-winning speech, entitled "The War Peril," reflected for the first time Colbert's appreciation of foreign opinion. In his speech, he declared that there was one great overwhelming fear in Europe, the fear of a war that, no matter where it started, would spread and destroy the Western world. "America cannot afford to be indifferent to this universal opinion of Europe," Colbert concluded.[14] It was a thought that echoed throughout his career.

Upon graduation from Annapolis in June 1937, Colbert went to his first sea assignment, the commissioning crew of the new aircraft carrier USS *Yorktown*. In 1939, he was reassigned, this time to the Asiatic Fleet, where he received orders to the flush-deck four-piper USS *Barker*. Colbert served in the *Barker* for five years, rising from junior ensign to Lieutenant Commander and commanding officer. The ship saw duty in Southeast Asian and Australian waters as well as escort duty in the Atlantic and as part of the carrier USS *Core's* successful hunter-killer group. His years in *Barker* brought him the first experience of cooperation with other navies. In early 1942, *Barker* was one of the ships in ABDA-Float (American, British, Dutch, Australian) the allied naval command under Admiral Thomas C. Hart, USN, and later under Vice-Admiral C. E. L. Helfrich, Royal Netherlands Navy. *Barker* served in the striking force along with British, Dutch, and Australian ships in the unsuccessful attempts to intercept the Japanese invasion fleet off Bali and Banka Island in February 1942. The experience of those actions impressed Colbert, who was then the ship's communications officer. Despite the current view of historians who see the Java Sea campaign as a mismanaged affair, Colbert often discussed with his colleagues how relatively smoothly he believed the ship-to-ship communications between ships of different navies had functioned in that critical situation.[15]

Despite the defeat of ABDA command, Colbert's memory of his experience stayed with him and convinced him not only of the practicality of multinational forces but also of the real advantage that multinational arrangements had for securing the seas. Looking back in 1966, he argued against those who wished to replace NATO with a series of bilateral treaties, saying that such treaties had not worked in "slow-motion" wars such as the Second World War. They could not be responsive to the complex, fast-moving events that could lead to nuclear war. Thinking of the events leading up to the Second World War naval engagements in the Dutch East Indies, Colbert commented that those were "desperate times, and I saw this lesson first hand. It was a bitter lesson."[16] Through that experience, Colbert came to believe that there was greater potential for success through the combined efforts of many nations than through following only the individual interests of single nations.

From *Barker,* Colbert went on to command the destroyer *Meade* in both the Atlantic and the Pacific, remaining in command of her until the end of the war. Promoted to commander, Colbert was assigned after the war to the Bureau of Naval Personnel, where he worked on plans for the postwar naval reserve. During that period, he also served as a social aide in the Truman White House. He kept up his interest in foreign affairs through membership in the United Nations Club, but in these years he had not settled down fully to concentrate on international issues.

MATURATION OF A CONCEPT

The real turning point in Colbert's career came in 1948, when he was selected as aide and flag secretary to Admiral Richard L. Conolly, USN, Commander-in-Chief US Naval Forces Eastern Atlantic and Mediterranean, based in London. Commenting on his new orders, Colbert told a friend, "Am not sure whether I like it or not. I guess I will find out."[17] He did, and Conolly's ideas and approach came to have a marked influence on Colbert.

Conolly was a superb negotiator, and Colbert accompanied him in meetings with naval leaders in most of the Western European and Mediterranean nations and learned much from the way Conolly handled problems and dealt with other leaders. One incident in particular seemed to summarize Conolly's approach and influenced Colbert's way of thinking. During a cruise in the Mediterranean on board his flagship in 1949, USS *Columbus,* Conolly arranged a table-top war game in which he posed the problem of an allied naval command in the Mediterranean; it was one of the first steps in the arduous process of creating what would become the NATO Mediterranean naval command. In order to examine carefully the issue of whether the command headquarters should be afloat or ashore, and what forces should participate, Conolly gathered senior officers from a number of countries. Each cooperated but clearly showed his national bias. Conolly finished the exercise without solutions but made all who participated feel that they were part of a team dealing with a common problem.[18] That was a theme basic to Richard Colbert's way of thinking.

By all accounts, Colbert's association with Conolly provided the basic insight upon which he built his later work. At the same time, there was a parallel and personal development which helped to shape his international outlook further. At a New Year's ball in 1949, Colbert met Prudence Ann Robertson, daughter of E. J. Robertson, the managing director of Lord Beaverbrook's newspapers *The London Daily Express, The Evening Standard,* and two Scottish newspapers. A Canadian who had gone to live in London after the First World War, E. J. Robertson nurtured Colbert's instinctive feeling for international cooperation as the most viable means of achieving world peace, and Colbert returned his interest with admiration and devotion. At the end of Colbert's tour of duty in London, he and Prudence Robertson were married at St Paul's Church, Knightsbridge. Throughout their married life, Colbert felt that England was his second home; at the same time, he learned from his wife how to be sensitive to differences in points of view between Europeans and North Americans.[19]

COLBERT IN WASHINGTON

Leaving England in December 1950, Colbert accompanied Admiral Conolly to his new position as President of the Naval War College, then Colbert moved on to his own new assignment in the political-military affairs division of the office of the Chief of Naval Operations.

Shortly after Colbert's arrival, the division received a new director, Rear Admiral Bernard L. Austin. Colbert obviously liked the work in his new assignment under Austin, much of which was dealing with foreign issues and with people of other nationalities.[20] During this period Admiral Austin became concerned with the problem of providing instruction for naval officers from nations who wanted training in the United States. There had already been a move to put service education on a more systematized basis through the establishment of the NATO Defense College in Paris, but this was not sufficient to meet all the demand. In the late 1940s and early 1950s, there were many requests made to the US Navy for use of its service schools, but no regularized arrangements had been made. In light of this, Austin directed Colbert to make a staff study of the best way in which a course could be developed for foreign naval officers.[21] This work was the seed from which much would grow later in Colbert's career.

While Colbert was at work on this and other projects, he came to the attention of Admiral Forrest Sherman, Chief of Naval Operations. Sherman selected Colbert to become his aide later in the year, undoubtedly on Admiral Conolly's recommendation. Before that could become a permanent assignment, however, Sherman needed an experienced and knowledgeable aide on temporary assignment with him for an overseas trips. One important assignment came in 1950–51, when Sherman was a member of an inter-allied committee negotiating how the new NATO military commands would be structured. After each negotiating session, Sherman would relax with his aides and unwind by discussing the events of the day. Through this method Sherman taught Colbert about national sensitivities and current issues as well as successful methods of international negotiation.[22]

In July 1951, another issue arose in which Admiral Sherman used Colbert's experience and expertise. Some years earlier, while with Admiral Conolly, Colbert had been closely involved in the staff work leading to the U.S. proposal for obtaining American naval base rights in Spain. As early as 1948, Franco had said that he would make bases available, but President Truman and the National Security Council had initially rejected the proposal.[23] Despite qualms about associating their country with fascist Spain, Sherman and Conolly, among others, believed that NATO's southern flank would be vulnerable without friendly bases in Spain. As the only member of the joint chiefs to take this view, Sherman went ahead, having finally persuaded Truman that it was an important strategic issue.[24] With Colbert at his side, Sherman traveled to Spain for talks with Franco, and afterwards he filled in the details and the rationale behind all his agreements in discussion with his aide. Continuing on from Spain to Naples for further talks with European leaders, Admiral Sherman suddenly died of a heart attack before he could prepare any written reports of his conversations. Colbert was the U.S. naval officer with the most thorough knowledge of what Sherman and Franco agreed upon[25] and thereby Colbert became a direct link in the chain that led to the U.S. Navy's use of Rota, Spain, as a naval base.

COLBERT AT THE NAVAL WAR COLLEGE

Upon completion of his tour of duty in Washington, Commander Colbert reported to the heavy cruiser USS *Albany* as executive officer. During his two years onboard, the *Albany* served as flagship for Commander, Battleship-Cruiser Force, Atlantic, and was deployed to the Mediterranean. Colbert distinguished himself as an exceptionally capable administrator, a good shipmate,[26] and, as one of his commanding officers recalled, "the best executive officer any ship had had (or the good fortune to have)."[27]

Upon completion of his sea duty, Colbert had to choose between assignment as either head of an academic section at the Naval Academy or a student at the Naval War College. Seeking advice, Colbert wrote to his old boss, Admiral Conolly, then retired. Conolly gave him the sound advice which was to prove remarkably true. "In regard to the possibilities for duty," Conolly wrote, "I would say by all means take the Naval War College if you have the opportunity . . . I have always considered it a turning point in a naval career."[28] In the autumn of 1955, Colbert reported to the Naval War College as a student in the naval warfare course. Recently promoted to captain, Colbert stayed on for two more years as a staff member.

The background for Colbert's new assignment stretched back to the early 1950s when he had done his staff study on training foreign naval officers under Admiral Austin in the political-military affairs branch. In 1955–56, the president of the Naval War College was Vice Admiral Lynde McCormick, who had taken up the college presidency after having been the first Supreme Allied Commander, Atlantic. In this role, McCormick had commanded several NATO exercises, including Mainbrace, the largest allied peacetime exercise up to that time. These experiences taught McCormick the fundamental need for developing better understanding among NATO navies. His experience paralleled that of Admiral Arleigh Burke.

During 1955, Burke's first year as Chief of Naval Operations, he began to lay the groundwork for closer coordination between the United States and other NATO navies. At the same time, he saw the need for similar coordination with friendly navies in Asia, Africa, and throughout the Americas. In addition, he wanted to create a way in which naval officers from nations that had fought against the United States during the Second World War could shed their unspoken sense of inferiority following defeat and become full-fledged Allies.

One of the options Burke saw was the chance to offer a year's study at the Naval War College, modeled upon the lines of the curriculum already in place for the first year of the naval warfare course. Burke made contact with the leaders of several allied navies, who were generally enthusiastic about this idea. By the spring of 1956, twenty-three navies had accepted Burke's invitation, with Admiral Mc-Cormick's full cooperation to implement the course at the Naval War College.

At the time these plans were coming to fruition, Colbert was just finishing his first year as a student in the naval warfare course. When Burke selected Colbert to head up the new course, there was some jealousy on the part of others at the college. But Burke had full confidence in Colbert, having known him while he was in the political-military affairs division where his office had been directly across the hall from Burke's.[29]

Colbert's first task was to choose a name for the course. He was firmly opposed to the idea of using the word "foreign" in the name, wanting instead to select a name which would reflect a positive and mutual goal. After about a month, he selected the name Naval Command Course for Free World Naval Officers.[30]

The purpose of the course was multifaceted. Basically it was to prepare officers for higher command responsibilities within their own navies, while at the same time familiarizing them with U.S. Navy doctrines, methods, and practices. But its purpose was much broader than that, as Professor August Miller reflected after his first year's experience under Colbert's direction:

> At the Naval War College in an atmosphere of complete freedom of thought and expression, the foreign officers both symbolize and interpret their own navies and their countries not only to Americans but to each other; and on the basis of this free inquiry it can be readily recognized that such an open exchange of ideas will help to allow friendly nations to cooperate with one another in maximum efficiency in time o world stress.[31]

Colbert himself was well satisfied with the course and privately wrote to a friend, "all goes well-almost too smoothly. The capability of the students is far beyond our expectations-they really look like the future CNO's [Chiefs of Naval Operations] of the Free World' as Admiral Burke describes them."[32]

Colbert took great pains with the course, designing an appropriate curriculum and nurturing close personal contacts among the students. The social side of the course was an essential element, and the Colberts spent a large sum of their own money to ensure that all went well, not only with cocktail parties but also with flowers for sick family members or small farewell gifts. For all of this, Burke consistently gave Colbert full credit for the course's success. As he wrote to Colbert privately a decade later, "the idea was good, but a lot of good ideas come a cropper, and this one did not because of you. You were the man who started it properly, who nursed it and nurtured it along the proper lines."[33]

Yet in this period, Colbert's ideas were very much in the process of development. The experience of being the director of the naval command course for its first two classes very clearly became the foundation upon which his later career was built. At this stage, however, he did not seem to have a clear vision of what could practicably be done with the cooperation he was then nurturing.

EXPERIENCE IN INTER-ALLIED AND INTER-AGENCY NAVAL ASSIGNMENTS

After three years at the Naval War College, Colbert left for Washington where he was assigned to the staff of the Joint Chiefs of Staff in the Long Range Plans and Basic War Plans Branch. In 1960, Colbert became commanding officer of the Sixth Fleet's general stores ship, USS *Altair,* based in Barcelona, Spain. This proved a formative and influential phase of his career, which reinforced some of his experience with the Naval Command Course. The ship spent much time at sea in support of the operations of the Sixth Fleet and developing an early approach to vertical replenishment at sea by helicopter; Colbert's experimentation with this new idea was a major contribution to its use and led to its becoming a standard operation for ships at sea. While engaged in these operations, Colbert was also intensely concerned with his ship's relationship to its home port and in developing cooperation with the Spanish navy. This, he thought, was a key element in the alliance system.

When word reached him that the very small U.S. naval facility at Barcelona might be abolished and the fleet supported by a more "cost-effective," larger base, Colbert objected strongly. His reasoning reflected his growing belief in the importance of personal relationships across national and cultural boundaries. He pointed out to his superiors that it was important for the U.S. Navy's sailors and their families to develop a close relationship with the people of the country in which their base was located, through an appreciation and recognition of their host's customs and way of life. *Altair's* home port in Barcelona gave such an opportunity. "It would appear," Colbert wrote, "that every opportunity should be grasped by the U.S. Navy to establish and maintain more small unobtrusive United States representation of this type in friendly countries, rather than closing them and concentration at installations which already are criticized as large and conspicuous overseas bases."[34]

Colbert was selected for his major command while still in command of *Altair.* He had asked for assignment to "a cruiser out of Boston," and the Bureau of Naval Personnel had obliged by giving him command of the guided missile heavy cruiser USS *Boston.* Under Colbert's command, *Boston* deployed to the Mediterranean and, for a brief period, served as the flagship for Commander Sixth Fleet. Admiral David L. McDonald later recalled that "Colbert and his crew in the *Boston* went out of their way to make their ship a most outstanding Flagship."[35]

It was while in command of *Boston* that Colbert decided he wanted to develop his experience further in political-military affairs. In 1962, Colbert became interested in the possibility of obtaining one of the two military billets on the State Department's Policy Planning Council, then headed by Walt W. Rostow. The council had been established in 1947 by Secretary of State General George C. Marshall to be a long-range planning and advisory staff whose task would be to analyze major foreign policy problems. Among its functional responsibilities the council was particularly charged with coordinating political-military policy and inter-agency planning.

Rostow wanted to fill his military billets with the best qualified officers. Because he did not want to accept just any officer that the Department of Defense might assign, Rostow wanted to have a competition that would produce "real Rhodes Scholarship type of thinking." During his search, Rostow recalled that Colbert wanted to have the experience which the Policy Planning Council assignment would give him, but Colbert was aware that the Navy's personnel bureau did not think it was good for his career. However, Colbert persisted in applying, believing that military and naval officers needed to have a deep knowledge of the problems of diplomacy. In his letter to Rostow, Colbert remarked that at the Naval War College he had been closely involved with officers from other countries and the experience had a marked effect on his attitude. Above all, he wanted to build upon the sense of fraternity that he had experienced.[36]

In 1962, Assistant Secretary of Defense for International Security Affairs Paul H. Nitze was particularly interested in getting high caliber military and naval officers into other agencies of the government, particularly the State Department. A dozen years earlier, Nitze had headed the Policy Planning Council and knew well its importance and its role. The Navy had never sent an officer to the Policy Planning council, but Nitze's assistant, Captain Elmo R. Zumwalt, Jr., USN, shared Nitze's view and also wanted to see the Navy increase its influence. Both Zumwalt and Nitze believed that an assignment to the State Department would be career broadening. Colbert, too, shared this belief, but the detailing officers in the Bureau of Naval Personnel consistently told him that such an assignment would irreparably damage his career. Colbert's ability obviously impressed Rostow, while within the Department of Defense, Zumwalt as Nitze's aide "pulled the necessary levers" and got Colbert the assignment he wanted.[37]

Colbert's work ranged widely and deeply in foreign policy issues during his two years with the Policy Planning Council, including work on topics such as multilateral forces, Vietnam, the Inter-

American Military Force, a U.S.-Australian squadron, and nuclear arrangements cast of Suez in the face of a Chinese communist nuclear threat.[38] The Inter-American Military Force was an idea which specifically reflected Colbert's ideas; it was a subject on which he wrote a number of papers. Colbert had in mind a force that, though primarily naval, included army and air components. As he visualized it, the force would be of modest size involving a few thousand people drawn from seven or eight countries in Latin America, with United States participation limited to no more that 15–20 percent of the total force. In Colbert's view "it would be important that the U.S. not be any more than just a partner in the project."[39] Colbert envisaged that its primary mission would be ocean surveillance and sea control, but it could also be a peacekeeping force, thus providing a place for the participation of armies. An important aspect of this force was its training; significantly, Colbert believed that it would be provided by the force itself at a base set up in some convenient place in Latin America. This would have an advantage in keeping the force's training independent of the United States and limiting the number of officers who would be brought into the United States for training.[40]

In 1964, at the end of his State Department duty, Colbert began to be involved in developing the concept for the multilateral Force, a concept which he believed might be attractive to NATO countries whose navies had surface ships but no aircraft carriers. Colbert believed it would form a much less costly alternative to American nuclear submarines, by placing Polaris missiles in merchant ships, manned by mixed NATO crews with joint responsibility among all NATO nations for nuclear deterrence. This proposal, which implied that the nuclear nations would delegate a certain amount of their sovereignty to an Allied committee, was never implemented.

The idea of mixed manning was tried out. Colbert was one of the small group with Rostow that recommended to Secretary Nitze that the U.S. Navy demonstrate the feasibility of manning a single ship with officers and men from different nations. The short-term experiment was successfully carried out by the USS *Claude V. Ricketts* in 1964–5.[41]

Reflecting on their time together in the State Department, Colbert and his colleague Colonel Robert N. Ginsburg, USAF, wrote:

> To participate in the work of the Council . . . can be an exhilarating experience for the military man who follows the path and precepts of George C. Marshall. For the Council's work is almost daily vindication of the dedicated military officers' unuttered creed. It is not, he knows, the man that is important, nor is it the idea, nor the military service or branch of gov-

ernment, nor the government itself. It is only the Republic and its per-
petuation that really matter.[42]

While Colbert was off in the depths of the State Department, some
of his fellow officers thought he had been forgotten by the Navy, but
it was not so. In May 1964, he was one of five of his classmates selected for rear admiral. And to show the importance of his work, the
Navy promoted him while still on the Policy Planning Council rather
than waiting for him to assume his naval command.

Then in June 1964, he reported as Commander, Cruiser-Destroyer
Flotilla, Six, based at Charleston, South Carolina. The fifty or so
ships under his command gave him the responsibility, as one friend
commented, equivalent to the commander-in-chief of a smaller navy.
A year later, Colbert became deputy chief of staff and assistant chief
of staff for policy, plans, and operations to the Supreme Allied Commander, Atlantic (SACLANT), Admiral Thomas H. Moorer.

Colbert's first assignment after he reported to SACLANT was to
establish the Iberian-Atlantic Command. When Moorer became
SACLANT in April 1965, he had pointed out that NATO had agreed
several years before to establish a command covering the sea approaches to the Straits of Gibraltar, but that neither the money nor
the men necessary to carry this task out had been authorized.
Moorer told the NATO Military Committee that he wished either to
have the directive cancelled or receive the resources necessary to do
the job. The committee agreed to provide what was needed and this
task, in turn, was given to Colbert. In short order, Colbert brought
IBERLANT (Iberian Atlantic) into being. In Moorer's words, "this action not only significantly enhanced the capability of NATO to deal
with naval operations in the area, but also significantly increased
the morale, prestige an overall interest of the Portuguese allies. I
give Admiral Colbert all of the credit for this important move."[43]

Simultaneously, Colbert began to develop a proposal to create a
Standing Naval Force, Atlantic. For three years NATO had run an
operation called Matchmaker in which ships of various allied navies
joined in an exercise for a six-month period. In late November 1966,
Colbert, as a result of a discussion with Admiral Moorer, prepared a
concept paper which proposed a permanent Matchmaker force that
could serve as a naval contingency force for the Allied Command, Atlantic.[44] In May 1967, the NATO Defense Committee agreed in principle to establish a standing naval force, an this was approved in a
ministerial meeting in December 1967. The force was activated in
January 1968. In Colbert's view, this was only the beginning. He had
already written that:

With this as a prototype conceivably we can follow suit with similar forces in time in the Mediterranean, the Indian Ocean, the Western Pacific, and very importantly Latin American. As the Soviet Union continues to expand its sea power world wide, I can think of no more pragmatic and meaningful counter to their activities than the U.S. participating as partners with friendly countries in their various areas.[45]

PRESIDENT OF THE NAVAL WAR COLLEGE

After the activation of the Standing Naval Force, Atlantic, and its first visit to the United States in the spring of 1968, Colbert was unexpectedly selected to be President of the Naval War College. Promoted to vice admiral in a sudden jump over some ten of his classmates, Colbert was delighted to be returning to Newport. "It is a dream come true-a dream that I would never have mentioned to anyone, for fear of being precocious,"[47] he remarked.

As President of the Naval War College, Colbert made a remarkable imprint on the institution. He was largely responsible for implementing new plans to expand the scope of the college's academic programs as well as to improve its physical plant. Like other colleges, the Naval War College had several academic chairs named for distinguished naval men in specific subject areas. Colbert continued the policy of that time by inviting distinguished civilian academics to hold these positions for a short time. He also wanted to increase the number of academic areas they represented.

In particular Colbert took special interest in two of the civilian academic chairs which had been proposed by his senior academic advisor, Professor Frederick H. Hartmann. Colbert's interest in these particular positions reflected his deep-seated appreciation for different cultural outlooks. First he brought to fruition the proposal to establish the Claude V. Ricketts Chair of Comparative Cultures. He appointed an anthropologist, John M. Roberts of Cornell University, to hold this chair in 1969–70.[48] Second, and for similar reasons, he supported an unsuccessful proposal to establish a chair in Oriental Studies. Explaining his view, Colbert wrote, "There are some leading contemporary thinkers who believe that the twenty-first century will be the Asian Century." With this increased awareness of the importance of the Far East in world power politics, economically, socially, and strategically, such a scholar "would be able to add perspective to every point on the Asian scene where we as a nation have been and remain very much involved."[49]

Then after expanding the civilian faculty, he and his staff established a number of military chairs which were designed to extend the concept of the civilian academic chairs and ensure that the best qualified officers in each area of professional naval interest were brought to the college as instructors in those areas.

In developing the curriculum, Colbert continued along the lines of his predecessors, but he stressed the historical importance which the Naval War College had placed on international law since its founding in 1885. In the pages of the *Naval War College Review,* Colbert asked rhetorically, "Why should the Naval War College alone amongst service colleges, place such emphasis on the study of international law?" The answer was obvious to Colbert, for at sea, "international law is the only law." But also, "the inter-relationship of legal, political, economic and social factors which are operative on a global scale and increasing significance of our international commitments require a clear understanding of the rules governing the relations between states."[50]

In the specific area of international naval cooperation, Colbert took four major initiatives at the Naval War College. He established the first of several exchange visits between the presidents of the U.S. Naval War College and the Royal Naval College, Greenwich,[51] supplemented by a week-long visit of forty U.S. Naval War College students to Greenwich in 1970. Second, he proposed the establishment of a Naval Staff Course for middle-grade free-world naval officers, complementing the Naval Command Course, but at a lower level and emphasizing the participation of smaller navies, which did not have comparable educational facilities. Colbert particularly had in mind that this course would primarily develop the professional and managerial skills for the student officers to use in their own navies, emphasizing the naval decision-making process, naval planning, and the broad understanding of the roles of sea power. At the same time, it could familiarize the students with the methods, practices, and doctrines of the U.S. Navy while developing an international bond among the graduates.[52]

Third, Colbert built on the long-standing desire of the Naval Command Course graduates to have a reunion in Newport, combining it with the successful rise of so many of them to flag rank. He wished to use it as a means to create at the senior flag officer level "areas of mutual interest, co-ordination, and co-operation that could pay substantial dividends for the future."[53] The result was the International Sea Power Symposium in November 1969, the first in a series of meetings bringing together the chiefs of navies and other naval leaders to discuss, in an academic setting, current naval issues of mutual concern.[54] Out of the conference came much constructive and valuable thinking which led to the development of further regional discussions on the implication of Soviet maritime expansion. But most important for Colbert, senior naval officers at the conference became aware of their common outlook. As Canadian Rear Admiral Harry Porter wrote to Colbert after the meeting, "I have come away from it with an increased realization of the brotherhood of the sea and comforting knowledge that most naval officers share the same problems, the same aspirations, an the same feelings about the importance of sea power on countries and mankind as a whole."[55]

The last of Colbert's contributions at the Naval War College consisted of projects which he designed as practical contributions to promote international naval cooperation. For example, he gave to the students in the Naval Command Course the mission of designing a "Free World Frigate," a modern, efficient, and economical ship of frigate or corvette size. The basic idea in Colbert's mind was to have officers from a variety of friendly nations "design" a ship that could provide the basis for commonality and standardization in multinational naval forces, such as the Standing Naval Force, Atlantic. Eventually he hoped to see a squadron of such escort ships with the same hull design, using components for many nations, each flying a different national flag. The resulting design found support from key leaders in the United States such as Admirals Elmo Zumwalt and Isaac C. Kidd, Jr., but nothing came of it. Colbert was deeply disappointed that it seemed impossible to break down nationalistic barriers in building warships.[56]

Colbert's final effort at the Naval War College was developed from a point in Zumwalt's "Project Sixty," the action plan for his term as Chief of Naval Operations. Colbert created the detailed plan of action Zumwalt used to persuade allied navies to improve and expand their antisubmarine warfare capabilities, better to counter the growing Soviet Navy.[57]

FINAL ASSIGNMENTS

In June 1971, Colbert left the Naval War College to become chief of staff to the Supreme Allied Commander, Atlantic. He was delighted with the prospect of continuing his work with NATO. "It will be like 'going home,'" he wrote.[58] Taking a circuitous route from Newport to Norfolk, Colbert prepared himself for his new position and laid the groundwork for the second International Sea Power Symposium in 1971 by visiting the chiefs of navies in Italy, Greece,

Turkey, Belgium, West Germany, the United Kingdom, and Portugal. On this, Colbert acted as Admiral Zumwalt's personal representative as well as the prospective SACLANT chief of staff.[59]

Later at the SACLANT headquarters, Colbert was deeply involved in the daily work of allied naval cooperation. A year later, he was promoted to admiral and appointed Commander-in-Chief, Allied Forces Southern Europe. During his final years as a NATO officer, both in Norfolk and Naples, Colbert rounded out his series of practical initiatives to support international cooperation by recommending additional multilateral naval forces for the Indian Ocean and the Mediterranean. Recognizing, too, the deep expertise needed by naval officers who work within alliances, Colbert drafted a proposal to establish a NATO postgraduate school to train recently commissioned officers under the guidance of the NATO international staff.[60] Within the U.S. Navy, Colbert recommended that a NATO career pattern should be laid out for selected officers, who would then be fully aware of NATO procedures, problems, and programs. His plan was rejected, but too often he believed, U.S. naval officers who came to NATO on short tours of duty without enough international experience were engrossed in the path their careers would take them within the U.S. Navy and lacked much of the expertise, knowledge, and sensitivity to alliance problems which extended experience would bring. "Techniques for dealing with foreign personnel require more thoughtfulness, understanding, and patience," Colbert wrote, characteristically putting the issue in terms of personal relationships. In an international setting, a tactless remark of insensitivity to another viewpoint, he believed, was often far more difficult to repair than they would be within a single nation's staff.[61]

As Commander-in-Chief, Allied Forces Southern Europe in 1972–73, Colbert's principal concern was to reduce the tension between Greece and Turkey. Under his leadership, the Naval On-Call Force, Mediterranean was started and expanded with the hope of developing it into a standing naval force using Greek, Turkish, Italian, British, and U.S. ships. Colbert had more success in his initiatives to develop cooperation between the French navy and NATO, working out a treaty allowing annual exercises. Through the combined efforts of Colbert and French Admiral Jean Guillou, a large Franco-American naval exercise took place off the coast of the United States in 1973.[62]

During Colbert's tenure as Commander-in-Chief, he discovered that he had an incurable case of cancer, but he remained at his post until a week before his death at the age of fifty-eight, on 2 December 1973. As Admiral Giuseppe Pighini, Commander, Allied Naval Forces

Southern Europe under Colbert, put it, he was "a man dedicated to his duty till the last breath of life."[63]

Colbert's highest duty, as he saw it, was clearly revealed in a letter he wrote to Chaplain Henry Duncan, only a few months before he died:

> I am a realist and know that I am on borrowed time. I am convinced that the Lord has decided to give me some extra time to do some things in this, my last command, which might better insure a safer world. That is the gist of my prayers. All I ask is just a bit more time to carry on and establish some concepts-multinational NATO forces which will strengthen our Free World against what I am convinced is a desperate threat, despite all the talk of detente.[64]

REFLECTION ON A CAREER

Richard Colbert's entire naval career was developed around a gradually growing and strengthening commitment to international naval cooperation. He never worked out or developed his thoughts on this subject in any complete way, but as one reflects on his various statements and the innovations he made during his career, one can discern a philosophy that bears much of enuring value. It was a philosophy grounded in a sense of the need for cooperation, close personal ties, loyalty, camaraderie, and social grace in day-to-day life. He was a friendly outgoing man with an understated style—a man who assumed that cordial cooperative behavior was the best way to accomplish things.[65] In the life of a career naval officer, this meant leadership and personal responsibility. Colbert reflected these concepts in a letter he wrote near the end of his career to a young officer just taking up his first command. Referring specifically to Admiral Zumwalt's innovative reforms in the U.S. Navy, Colbert advised:

> Old Navy or New, long hair or short, it seems to me what ultimately makes the difference in readiness and effectiveness is the sense of camaraderie and respect that come from personal involvement and identification on the part of all hands. I fear that a lot of Navy men never got the underpinning message behind many of the recent innovations: the emphasis on personal responsibility.[66]

This point was an essential aspect of his philosophy, not only in shipboard command but also in forming bonds with other countries and other navies. The key was personal responsibility and, through it, personal relationships. In opening the first International Sea

Power Symposium, he stressed "the pure professional naval competence which each of us can bring . . . [to] provide threads of a cloth which might well be woven into a durable and serviceable fabric."[67]

Colbert believed that the highest professional naval competence arose from two equally important sources: practical experience and war college education. "War colleges have always been the storehouses of the military arts," Colbert said, "but nowadays they must prepare officers to function outside the confines of purely operational expertise, in an era of transition, of apparent detente, of new structuring of international politics."[68]

The international courses played an essential role in this. Colbert believed that through such courses which stressed "undiluted, the small, close, intimate nature"[69] of the relationship built during a year's study together. It was nothing that could be mass produced but was created slowly and surely over time by a delicate formula: a small group, one officer only from each country interacting with the entire group of carefully selected students and well-chosen staff, teaching a curriculum that takes into account the foreign officer's diverse backgrounds, and letting them develop together where they would not be overwhelmed or at a disadvantage as they came to understand something of life not only in a foreign country but in one so very different from their own.[70] The result of this, Colbert found, was that it created a bond. "Once one has become part of that special fraternity," he wrote, "neither time nor distance can dissolve the unique ties it forms among its members."[71]

These kinds of ties were the basis, he believed, for the kind of partnership among nations which is urgently needed in the modern world. After the Second World War, the United States responded to the urgent and practical needs of her allies with the Truman Doctrine, the Marshall Plan, and other forms of assistance. But these led to domination. With full economic recovery from the war, these policies were no longer appropriate. "Domination leads to dependence," Colbert believed, "while true "partnership" encourages the independence, pride and dignity of our sovereign allies."[72]

Further developing this idea, Colbert saw that there was an alternative to previous U.S. foreign policy, one which encouraged and supported regional co-operation and partnership in various areas. The growth of Soviet maritime power presented a challenging problem "which no one country is able to resolve itself."[73] In this situation, Colbert saw many advantages in a policy and strategy founded on partnership among allied and friendly nations. This could best be achieved through multilateral naval forces designed for major regions of the globe. The advantages of such forces were clear to him: the cost, financially and politically was low, and they avoided the internal political dissent caused by massive or overwhelming commitment by the United States, while at the same time increasing the effectiveness of such a force by being the symbolic and real expression of several nations united in common effort. Moreover, the general maritime interests of the free world could be served by multilateral naval forces which could give rationale and justification for navies in countries where they were under attack.[74] In all of this, Colbert clearly perceived the forms of naval expertise which regional and small navies provided that complemented the expertise within larger navies concentrating on global-scale naval operations.

In a career intertwined with ideas of international, naval cooperation, Richard Colbert sought to achieve four important objectives"[75]

First, he believed that naval officers were particularly competent in solving international problems. For navies, the sea is the same good friend or cruel foe all over the world. Because of this, naval officers have naturally developed a similar way of thinking and can easily discuss mutual problems, apart from national prejudices. With this in mind, Colbert sought out successful senior naval officers as responsible representatives of different free world societies and tried to motivate them to learn through each other's perspective the value of freedom. He did this in the Naval Command Course by creating an academic environment of mutual respect and candor where the American political system and way of life, and that of each country represented, was openly discussed.[76]

Second, through the International Sea Power Symposium, he sought to establish a forum where the highest naval leaders could exchange with their professional peers knowledge, concepts, views, and opinions about naval technology, tactics, strategy, and the importance of sea power. Through this, he hoped to foster deeper understanding through an appreciation of different national perspectives.[77]

Third, in all his proposals for international cooperation, he hoped to establish among naval officers a deeper awareness of the need for mutual reliance as a key element in every nation's national interest.

Fourth, he sought to establish rapport across cultural boundaries and to develop personal knowledge and understanding for different national views as expressed by naval officers. In doing this, Colbert wanted to create a group of knowledgeable naval leaders who could ensure that the effectiveness of multinational forces would not be jeopardized by any failure to understand one's own ally.

Although Richard Colbert was an officer in the United States

Navy, his vision was clearly wider than the ordinary officer's. His vision has certainly touched the officers and men of all ships who have served in the Standing Naval Force, Atlantic; the senior flag officers who have attended the International Sea Power Symposia, and the faculty and students of the Naval War College.

In all of his objectives, the unifying theme is the mutual experience of the naval profession, which reaches beyond cultures and nations to establish its own fraternity. Few naval officers have seen this vision so clearly as Richard Colbert and few have done so much to foster it. Those who would follow in his wake must share his notion that no measure of international leadership can replace trust and understanding among allies and a sound appreciation of common goals.[78]

NOTES

This is a revised version of an essay that originally appeared in W. A. B. Douglas, ed., *RCN in Transition, 1910–1985*. (Vancouver: University of British Columbia Press, 1988), pp. 233–253. This excerpt is revised and reprinted with permission of the publisher from *RCN in Transition 1910–1985* edited by W.A.B. Douglas © UBC Press 1988 All rights reserved by the publisher.

1. Naval Historical Collection, Naval War College, Manuscript Collection 30: Richard G. Colbert papers (Hereafter, Colbert Papers), Series 2, box 19, folder 62: Concluding Remarks to Sea Power Symposium, 20 November 1969. Printed version in Naval War College brochure "First International Sea Power Symposium," 17–18.
2. Colbert Papers, Series I, box 19, file 382: Commander Falcon Accame, Italian Navy, to Colbert, 10 November 1971.
3. Letter from Captain Henry A. Ceulemans, Belgian Navy (Ret.) to Hattendorf, 27 August 1985.
4. Letter from Admiral Thomas H. Moorer, USN (Ret.) to Hattendorf, 27 August 1985.
5. Letter from Captain Allan P. Slaff, USN (Ret.) to Hattendorf, 6 September 1985; NHC, Oral History 9: Captain Clarence O. Fiske, USN (ret.), 68.
6. Colbert Papers, Series 4, box 21, folder 1: Citation, Honorary Doctor of Education, Salve Regina College, Newport, Rhode Island, 12 September 1970.
7. Elmo R. Zumwalt, Jr., *On Watch* (New York: Quadrangle Books 1976), 141–2.
8. Colbert Papers, Series 1, box 1: "Diary of Richard G. Colbert, SS Robert Luckenbach, NY-Seattle, via Panama Canal," 15 July-8 September 1931.
9. Colbert Papers, Series 1, box 1, folders 1–7.

10. Colbert Papers, Series 1, box 1, file 6: Franklin D. Roosevelt in Charles W. Fling, 25 January 1933.
11. Colbert Papers, Series 1, box 2, file 27: R.G.C. to Charles Colbert, 17 June 1936.
12. Letter from Rear Admiral John R. Wadleigh, USN (Ret.) to Hattendorf, 19 August 1985.
13. Colbert Papers, Series 1, box 1, file 19: R.G.C. to Charles Colbert, 5 March 1935.
14. Colbert Papers, Series 1, box 1, file 18: "The War Peril," speech.
15. Letter from Captain Robert S. Guy, USN (Ret.) to Hattendorf, 27 August 1985. For details of these actions, see F. C. Van Oosten, *The Battle of the Java Sea* (Annapolis, MD: Naval Institute Press 1976, 29–33.
16. R. G. Colbert, "International Co-operation for Peace," *Vital Speeches,* 33, No. 4 (1 December 1966): 127.
17. Colbert Papers, Series 1, box 2, file 43: R.G.C. to Lt.G. W. Beck, Jr., USN, 8 March 1948.
18. Letter from Captain Robert S. Guy, USN (Ret.) to Hattendorf, 20 August 1985.
19. Letter from Mrs. Prudence Colbert Mackall to Hattendorf, 23 September 1985.
20. Letter from Captain Guy to Hattendorf, 27 August 1985.
21. Naval Historical Collection, Oral History Number 1, "The Reminiscences of Vice Admiral Bernard L. Austin, USN (Ret.)," (Annapolis: Naval Institute 1971), 417; Letter from Captain Robert C. Penniston, USN (Ret.) to Hattendorf, 14 August 1985, Colbert's original 1951–2 study has not been found.
22. Letter from Captain Guy to Hattendorf, 27 August 1985.
23. Gaddis Smith, *Dean Acheson* (New York: Cooper Square 1972), 367–9.
24. Clark G. Reynolds, "Forrest Percival Sherman," in Robert M. Love, Jr., *The Chiefs of Naval Operations* (Annapolis: Naval Institute Press 1980), 230–2.
25. Interview with Captain Wilbur Holmes, USN (Ret.) 27 August 1985.
26. Rear Admiral John F. Davidson, USN (Ret.), to Hattendorf, 23 August 1985.
27. Vice Admiral Robert H. Rice, USN (Ret.) to Hattendorf, 27 August 1985.
28. Colbert Papers, Series 1, box 3, file 76: Admiral Richard I. Conolly to Colbert, 12 December 1954.
29. J. B. Hattendorf, B. M. Simpson III, an J. R. Wadleigh, *Sailors and Scholars: The Centennial History of the Naval War College.* (Newport, RI: Naval War College 1984), 230; Conversation: Admiral Arleigh Burke, USN (Ret.) to Hattendorf, 27 September 1985.
30. Letter from Captain Guy to Hattendorf, 27 August 1985.
31. August C. Miller, Jr., "An International Mission for the Naval War College," U.S. Naval Institute *Proceedings* 83, No. 12 (December 1957): 1364.
32. Colbert Papers Series 1, box 4, file 85: R.G.C., to Captain A. O. Vorse, 22 August 1956.
33. Ibid., Series 1, box 7, file 158: Arleigh Burke to R. G. C., 25 July 1967.
34. Ibid. Series 2, box 20, file 69: Draft "Factors bearing on the Proposed U.S. Navy withdrawal from Barcelona, Spain."

35. Letter from Admiral David L. McDonald, USN (Ret.) to Hattendorf, 26 August 1985.
36. Telephone conversation, Walt W. Rostow to Hattendorf, 26 August 1985.
36. Telephone conversation, Walt W. Rostow to Hattendorf, 16 September 1985.
37. Letter from Admiral Elmo R. Zumwalt, Jr., USN to Hattendorf, 27 August 1985.
38. W. W. Rostow, *The Diffusion of Power 1957–1972* (New York: Macmillan 1972), pp. 400, 426–7, 505, 510.
39. Colbert Papers, Series 1, box 6, file 129: R.G.C. to Captain A. B. de Vasconcelles, 4 January 1965.
40. Ibid. file 134: R.G.C. to Commander T. E. Fortson, 4 July 1965; R.G.C. to Colonel R. N. Ginsburgh, 14 July 1985.
41. Letter from Vice Admiral W. W. Behrens, USN (Ret.) to Hattendorf, 20 September 1985 and telephone conversation 12 November 1985.
42. Richard G. Colbert and Robert N. Ginsburgh, "The Policy Planning Council," U.S. Naval Institute *Proceedings*. 92, No. 4 (April 1966): 81.
43. Letter from Admiral Thomas H. Moorer, USN (Ret.) to Hattendorf, 27 August 1985.
44. Colbert Papers, Series 2, box 49: Memo c-3 to c-00, 28 November 1966.
45. Ibid., Series 1, box 7, file 161: R.G.C. to W. W. Rostow, 27 December 1967.
46. Ibid., box 16;, file 365: R. G. C. to Captain W. P. B. Barber, RN, 18 July 1967.
47. Ibid., file 302: R. G. C. to Vice Admiral C. K. Duncan, 2 August 1968.
48. Colbert Papers, Series 2, folders 1–3.
49. Ibid., Series 1, file 312: R.G.C. to "John," 18 June 1971, serial 1855.
50. Richard G. Colbert, "Challenge," *Naval War College Review* (January 19690: 1
51. Colbert Papers, Series 2, box 17, file 375: Admiral F. R. Zumwalt to Rear Admiral Colin C. Dunlap, 8 September 1970.
52. Ibid., Series 1, file 310: President Naval War College to Chief of Naval Operations, 4 February 1971; file 351: R.G.C. to Captain David F. Emerson, 20 December 1971.
53. Letter from Admiral Thomas H. Moorer to Hattendorf, 27 August 1985; Quote from Colbert Papers, Series 2, box 19, file 46: R.G.C. Memo to Captain Stansfield Turner, aide to the Secretary of the Navy.
54. The Fifteenth International Sea Power Symposium met at the Naval War College, 7–10 November 1999.
55. Colbert Papers, Series 2, box 19, file 57: Rear Admiral H. A. Potter to Colbert, 27 November 1969.
56. Ibid., Series 1, box 13, file 265: R.G.C. to Scott Terrill, 10 April 1973. For detailed information on the design, see Naval Historical Collection, Ms Coll. 57: Harrison T. Loeser Papers.
57. President, Naval War College Letter to CNO, 00/rbm, Serial 0015, 2 April 1971 forwarding "The Newport Study: A Plan to Persuade Allies to Improve and Expand Their ASW Capabilities," Love, *Chiefs of Naval Operations,* 372–5.
58. Colbert Papers, Series 1, box 10, file 222: R.G.C. to W. W. Rostow, 12 April 1971.

59. Ibid., file 318: R.G.C. to Zumwalt, 21 December 1971; box 12, file 257: R.G.C. to Vice-Admiral T. Lewin, RN 10 January 1973.
60. Ibid., Box 12, file 250: R.G.C. to Zumwalt, 2 November 1971.
61. Letter from Admiral Giuseppe Pighini, Italian Navy (Ret.) to Hattendorf, 23 September 1985; Admiral J. Guillou, French Navy (Ret.) to Hattendorf, 12 January 1986.
62. Pighini to Hattendorf, 23 September 1985.
63. Captain Henry C. Duncan, USN, "A Tribute to Admiral Richard Colbert," Arlington Cemetery, 5 December 1973.
64. Letter from Professor Vincent Davis to Hattendorf, 28 August 1985.
65. Colbert Papers, Series 1, box 13, file 279: R.G.C. to Commander Spencer Johnson, 3 August 1973.
66. R. G. Colbert, "Address to First International Sea Power Symposium" *Naval War College Review* (February 1970): 2.
67. R. G. Colbert, "War College Education and the Future," U.S. Naval Institute *Proceedings,* 99, No. 11/849 (November 1973): 109.
68. Ibid.
69. Colbert Papers, Series 1, box 13, file 271: R.G.C. to Zumwalt, 14 June 1973.
70. Ibid., file 270: R.G.C. to Lieutenant (jg) August C. Miller, III, 1 June 1973.
71. Colbert papers, Series 2, box 2: "Draft of Remarks Prepared for E. R. Zumwalt at ACLANT Flag Symposium, 3 November 1970" by R. G. C., and Commander McNulty; Series 3, box 21, file 14. "Closing Remarks to R.G.C.," 2 June 1970.
72. Colbert papers, Series 2, box 18, file 41: Unpublished draft article, "The Indian Ocean Enigma."
73. Ibid., Series 3, box 20, file 20: Remarks to R.G.C., not dated.
74. The following is based largely on letter from Commander Humberto Cancio, Jr. Cuban Navy (Ret.) to Hattendorf, 2 October 1985, and letter from Rear Admiral Christer Kirkegaard, Royal Swedish Navy (Ret.) the Hattendorf, 1 October 1985.
75. As of June 1997, 79 countries had sent a total of 1,296 officers to the Naval Command Course, of whom 690 had by that date become flag officers in their country's navy and 135 had risen to be chief of the navy. In June 1997, 19 graduates of the course were simultaneously serving as Chief of a Navy.
76. *International Sea Power Symposium XI* [1991] , *XII* [1993], *XIII* [1995], and *XIV* [1997]: *The Proceedings of the Conference* were edited by Hattendorf and published in separate volumes by the Naval War College Press. Copies are available in some naval and research libraries.
77. For another view of Colbert, see Joel Sokolsky, *The Fraternity of the Blue Uniform: Admiral Richard G. Colbert, U.S. Navy, and Allied Naval Cooperation.* Naval War College Historical Monograph series, vol. 8. (Newport, RI: Naval War College Press, 1991).

11

NATO's Policeman on the Beat: The First Twenty Years of the Standing Naval Force, Atlantic, 1968–1988

A howling gale was blowing along "Q" Pier at Portland, Dorset, on Saturday, 13 January 1968. Four ships, each from a different nation, lay securely moored alongside: The American Fram I destroyer, USS *Holder;* the Dutch "A" class destroyer escort HNLMS *Holland;* the Norwegian Oslo class destroyer escort RNoNS *Narvik* and the British Rothesay class frigate, HMS *Brighton,* flying the Commodore's pennant of Captain Geoffrey C. Mitchell, RN. The high winds and horizontal rain made the NATO flag stand briskly from the mastheads. The weather as well as the flag, with its compass rose within a ring and four rays all in white on a blue background, clearly represented the North Atlantic. Ashore, in the shelter of a hangar, the Commander-in-Chief, Eastern Atlantic Area, Admiral Sir John Bush, RN, spoke to the assembled officers and men and, in a short ceremony, officially formed the four ships from four different nations into the Standing Naval Force, Atlantic. "You will serve, as it were, as a policeman on the beat," Bush told them. "The policeman's task is to keep the peace and deter the troublemakers. And just as a policeman is backed by a greater force, should he be unable to cope with the situation he finds, so you too are backed by the navies of NATO."[1]

For the first time in modern history, a permanent international naval force had been formed in peacetime. The idea of an international naval force is not new in naval history. There are certainly well remembered examples from past wars; for example, the Anglo-Dutch-Swedish naval bombardment of Copenhagen in 1700, and numerous other Anglo-Dutch operations in the late seventeenth and

Ships of the Standing Naval Force, Atlantic

Ships of the Standing Naval Force, Atlantic, in column open order formation and flying the NATO flag on the starboard yard, 22 December 1976. Left to right: the Dutch frigate HNLMS *Tjerk* Hiddes (F-804), the German frigate FGS *Karlsruhe* (F-233), the Canadian helicopter destroyer HMCS *Huron* (DDH-281), and the American frigate USS *Truett* (FF-1095). (*U.S. Naval Institute Photo Archives*) early eighteenth centuries; the ABDA naval command in January-February 1942, and allied naval operations in both World Wars.

What was new in 1968 was the establishment of a permanent force, command of which is rotated among participating navies, under the structure of an alliance, and by which ships of various nationalities operated together on a continuous basis. The ships of each nationality serve on a rotational basis, each vessel being relieved by another. This allows the least disruption to other national operational requirements, training programs and overhaul cycles for the ships involved, while at the same time, assuring participation of the maximum number of ships at the highest level of their readiness.

THE ORIGINS

The idea which lay behind the formation of the Standing Naval Force, Atlantic, on that blustery January day in 1968, did not appear over night. It was the product of long patient negotiations and development. The experience of allied naval cooperation during World War II was clearly in the minds of many naval leaders in the 1950s and early 1960s when the detailed work involving the creation of the various NATO naval command structures had taken place. Exercises had been held and a variety of links between navies had been forged. As early as 1960, a Canadian delegate to a NATO antisubmarine warfare symposium proposed that a NATO ASW Group be formed.

The first positive action came following SHAPEX 63. This was the annual conference held at Supreme Headquarters Allied Powers Europe near Rocquencourt, France, and which brought together the North Atlantic Council, the chiefs of staff of the NATO nations, members of the NATO Standing Group, principal NATO commanders and senior officers of Allied Command Europe to discuss major problems facing the Alliance in the context of the world situation. At this conference in 1963, the newly appointed Commander-in-Chief Eastern Atlantic Area, Admiral Sir Charles Madden, RN, made a speech in which he reasoned that although the allied navies had achieved an agreed communications system and were then well on the way to achieving agreed tactical doctrine, particularly in antisubmarine warfare, they had not yet become in any way mutually supportive in any form of logistics. "The only way to remedy that situation," Madden told his audience, was "to keep a NATO Group together for a longish period of time." When he had finished his speech, Madden recalled, a general sitting behind Madden leaned forward and tapped him on the shoulder, saying "You are much too practical a man for this assembly."[2]

However, by November 1963, the discussion had progressed to the point that Madden formally proposed to the Supreme Allied Commander, Atlantic, Admiral Harold P. Smith, USN, that an extended exercise be conducted for a small NATO task group of four to six frigates. This group would take part in selected NATO exercises, undergo a joint training program and show the NATO flag. In early January 1964, Smith forwarded Madden's proposal. After approval by the NATO Standing Group, member nations were invited to provide ships. Canada, The Netherlands, the United Kingdom, and the United States responded with firm commitments and, on 8 June 1964, SACLANT named the exercise "Matchmaker."[3]

In early 1965, the ships joined for a five-month exercise series. This exercise was experimental and designed to find out what problems were involved in using base and support facilities of several nations for extended periods. The success of the 1965 series of exercises led to another five-month exercise in 1966, "Matchmaker II."[4] This exercise had the purpose of showing goodwill among NATO countries and demonstrating NATO strength an unity through participation in both NATO and national exercises using a variety of support and maintenance facilities from different countries. This was followed in January 1967 by "Matchmaker III," a seven-month long exercise.[5]

Meanwhile, a number of suggestions were put forth for international naval forces. One of these was the mixed-manning demonstration carried out in USS *Claude V. Ricketts*. In the summer of 1963, the U.S. Navy proposed placing a destroyer at the disposal of interested NATO countries to test the practicality of an internationally manned ship. The offer was accepted and Great Britain, Greece, Italy, The Netherlands, Turkey, and West Germany agreed to participate, and the United States selected the USS *Biddle* (DDG-5) to be the test ship. At a ceremony on 28 July 1964, *Biddle* was renamed the USS *Claude V. Ricketts* in honor of the late Vice Chief of Naval Operations. For 18 months, including a five month deployment to the Mediterranean, the ship operated successfully with a crew which was half-American and half from six other nations.[6]

Other ideas which were under discussion at the same time were the Multilateral Force, a mixed manned force of merchant-type ships which would carry Polaris missiles and serve as a less costly alternative to the use of nuclear submarines as a deterrent. This surface, nuclear deterrent was to have been a joint responsibility of all NATO nations, under the direct command of NATO. Another idea was a proposal for a Maritime Contingency Force, which could be activated and deployed in a period of tension to deal with the situation of that moment. In November 1966, at the earliest stage of its development, the concept for a permanent "Matchmaker" squadron and Standing Naval Force to be an operational rather than an exercise force and to serve as the nucleus upon which a larger Maritime Contingency Force could be built.

The key person who developed the early plans at the Norfolk Headquarters of the Allied Command, Atlantic, was Rear Admiral G. Colbert, USN, who from June 1966 to August 1968 was the Deputy Chief of Staff and Assistant Chief of Staff for Policy, Plans, Operations to the Supreme Allied Commander Atlantic, Admiral Thomas H. Moorer. Colbert had a deep interest in promoting international naval cooperation which continued throughout his career.[7] Well versed in the issues, Colbert had been the first director of the Naval Command course for free world officers at the Naval War College in 1957, and later served under Dr. W. W. Rostow on the State Department's Policy Planning Council. In Norfolk, Colbert successfully advanced the idea of a permanent Matchmaker squadron, despite lack of support from Army an Air Force staff members. With strong staff support from Colbert, Admiral Moorer carried the proposal forward.[8] With the additional support of the Allied Commander-in-Chief Eastern Atlantic, Admiral Sir John B. Frewen, RN, the proposal was submitted to NATO's Military Committee. On 9 May 1967, the Military Committee, in Chiefs of Staff session, agreed in principle to the concept. After obtaining the opinions of the defense ministries of all the nations involved, Moorer's successor as SACLANT, Admiral Ephraim P. Holmes, USN, submitted the final proposal in November 1967. This was approved on 13–14 December at the first ministerial meeting of the North Atlantic Council to be held at the new Brussels headquarters.

GROWTH AND DEVELOPMENT 1968–1988

The proposed Maritime Contingency Force, to which the Standing Naval Force had originally been connected, was set aside for the time being. Despite this, immediate directives were issued for The Standing Naval Force proposal to be implemented on 11 January 1968, or as early as practicable thereafter, using the staff and ships which had already been committed for use in "Matchmaker IV." The actual formation of the Force on 13 January at Portland, thus, directly carried on the "Matchmaker" series on a permanent basis.[9]

The goals of the newly formed peacetime force were clear from the outset:

- to maintain the naval art within NATO at a high level, by providing squadron experience and training for units and their staffs on a multi- national basis;
- to provide continuous and visible evidence of the solidarity and unity of NATO, by showing the flags of the various member navies work- ing closely together;
- to be available, at the first threat of a challenge, for immediate deployment to the scene; and
- to provide an initial element around which a more powerful NATO naval force could be formed.[10]

In peacetime, the Standing Naval Force was formed as a squadron—eight to ten ships—of destroyer and frigate types. The ships themselves were assigned to the force for a minimum of four months, preferably for longer periods, on a rotating basis. Units of one nationality do not necessarily relieve units from the same nation. To provide for continuity, the force commander and his staff are appointed on a more permanent basis, the post of Force Commander rotating annually among the participating countries. The tours of duty for his staff are so arranged as to be consistent with national policies and to maintain a balance of representation among member nations.

In normal peacetime operations, the Force operates primarily in the Eastern Atlantic, that being the most probable area of operation. For this reason, operational command of the Force is held by the Supreme Allied Commander, Atlantic, and administrative control is delegated to the Allied Commander in Chief, Eastern Atlantic. SACLANT delegates operational control to the subordinate area commander where the force is operating. This may be the Western Atlantic Headquarters at Norfolk, the Eastern Atlantic Headquarters at Northwood near London, or the Iberian Atlantic Headquarters at Lisbon.

In terms of its specific and continuing tasks, the Standing Naval Force, Atlantic conducted squadron training exercises, cooperating with other national forces to make the optimum use of available training and support facilities. In the course of this work, the Force participated in major exercises at sea, and played an important part in the evolution of new NATO naval tactics. Second, the Force visited various ports, including those of non-NATO countries, to show itself as a visible symbol of naval solidarity and through its various social and athletic activities during in-port periods, demonstrates, to an additional degree, the intangible qualities inherent in multinational cooperation, showing that the working relationships of NATO was a reality.

One of the great attractions to many member nations of NATO for the Standing Naval Force was its establishment—without significant cost implications—on the basis of equality with other member states, regardless of the size of the navy involved. The ships themselves were assigned from national forces already in commission and their training in the Force, as well as some of the schedules ports visits, substituted for those carried out on a national basis. At the same time, the operations of the Force provided an effective means and opportunity for each participant to keep up to date and to test the latest weapons systems and techniques within the context of realistic exercise and full participation in the integrated NATO defense system.

After its initial formation in 1968 at Portland, the four ships from Britain, The Netherlands, Norway, and the United States were joined within weeks by the Canadian destroyer escort HMCS *Gatineau* and the West German fast frigate *Köln*. In 1969, Portugal provided a ship for the first time and, in 1970, Denmark provided a ship for the first time. Since that time, each of the participating NATO navies has regularly contributed a ship to the Force. Five countries, Canada, Germany, The Netherlands, the United Kingdom, and the United States provided ships continuously and rotated the command of the squadron among them. Other countries, Belgium, Denmark, Norway, and Portugal, participated as regularly as national priorities have permitted. In any one year, some nations have contributed up to three ships on a rotating basis, or if necessary, limited their participation to periods when the Standing Naval Force was operating in waters relatively close to their homeland. This method has allowed flexibility to meet national priorities and needs while maintaining a continuously high level of readiness that would not be possible if ships were assigned on a permanent basis to NATO.

During the Cold War years, the Standing Naval Force was often used in direct surveillance operations of Soviet naval forces at sea. As the Supreme Allied Commander, Atlantic, Admiral Wesley L. McDonald told the Force in 1983, "To my mind one of the most important things you have done for the Alliance this year is to have seen and *been seen* by the Warsaw Pact . . . This is where deterrence really begins, and the Navy should be as fully involved in it as any of the other military arms." Although the Standing Naval Force was not used directly as a contingency force in any crisis situation during its first twenty years, it came very close to it in 1980 when its potential use was reaffirmed.[11]

In early December 1980, international affairs had grown tense as troop movements near the eastern border of Poland suggested that the Soviet Union might intervene in response to the general strike that had been threatened by the leaders of the *Solidarity* movement. NATO defense and foreign ministers met in Brussels to consider the situation and they warned that Soviet military intervention in Poland would alter the entire international situation, threatening detente.[12] On 9 December, the Chairman of the NATO Military Committee, Admiral Robert H. Falls of Canada, announced at a news conference that the Standing Naval Force had not been dispersed for the Christmas holiday that year, as routinely planned, "because NATO wanted to signal the Soviet Union that we do not think we should go on with business as usual." Admiral Falls said, "to disband the STANAVFORLANT might have said to the Soviet Union that what you are doing on the eastern border of Poland is not terribly important." With that in mind, he announced that the destroyer and frigates of the Force "would remain on readiness for the foreseeable future." As Admiral Falls later recalled, "Both the Council and Military Committee were very supportive of the Standing Naval Force Atlantic. . . . It was positive, physical evidence of those most important characteristics of NATO: Solidarity and Cohesiveness."[13]

A byword in NATO has always been "Standardization," and while some in NATO have felt it has only been given lipservice, the issues are met from the moment that the Standing Naval Force ships join one another. There are obvious differences in standards caused by differing ages of ships and their equipment. It has been a mix of modern and elderly ships. Important progress has been made over the years as new procedures are tested out in practical circumstances and ships with sophisticated data-link procedures, equipped with satellite communications, operate together with others, using voice procedures to keep noncomputerized ships in the picture. This has tended to allow the most effective use of the available ships and equipment, using similar tactics and procedures rather than using identical ships and capabilities. The differences among ships have been compensated for by the challenge of close, friendly international cooperation. As Commodore F. J. Haver Droeze of the Royal Netherlands Navy who commanded the Force in 1986–87 commented, "No sailor of any of the nations wants to be second to any of the others and I have continuously witnessed the crews of less modern ships work their __ off to show that they could cope with modern warfare just as well as the 'Rolls Royces'!"[14]

Over the past twenty years, ships assigned to the Standing Naval Force have shown an increased commonality in ammunition is improving, but slower to come due to specific national regulations. Other systems have become more complex and there is a tendency to repair failures by "black box" replacements that are tied to a variety of different equipment. Despite the diversity, there is an advantage in that the new material has a longer period of time between failures. These factors have combined to make a more readily supported force using common logistics channels. The recent and regular assignment of underway replenishment vessels to support the Force has increased its sustainability. In recent years, the new destroyers and frigates which have been assigned are more capable and better armed. The trend has been toward a Force that has a great capacity to survive in a modern wartime situation.[15]

One of the clear developments that has occurred over the years has been the obvious, natural cohesion. From the very beginning, Admiral Richard Colbert stressed the importance of the fraternal bond that forms from the common experience of operating at sea. As the first Commodore, Rear-Admiral Geoffrey Mitchell, RN, recalled, "no newly formed and vital group of ships, speaking four languages could have encountered more violent weather in their first few hours together. Maybe though, it was the dragging anchors in our first night at Lamlash during what proved to be the worst storm that the Clyde had had for fifty years that helped bond us. We were certainly relieved to have survived that night intact while the nearby city of Glasgow suffered tremendous and unprecedented damage."[16]

Language, of course, is a difficulty, and although French and English are the official NATO languages, there are a number of enlisted men in each national ship who speak only their own language. A Force chaplain recalled that he regularly provided Sunday worship services in six different languages. Ambiguity in discussion of operational issues in English, a foreign language to many, becomes an issue. As one Commodore recalled:

> Very severe weather had made the continuation of screening of the convoy quite impracticable. I therefore sent a message to the forces under my command as follows: 'Ships are to maintain station as far as possible during the night and are to rendezvous in position . . . at 0700 tomorrow! We soon became somewhat perturbed to see the entire force of 10 escorts on our radar dispersing like the expanding universe and realized that the

ambiguity of the message would have to be corrected in a hurry before contact was totally lost.[17]

Over the years, the officers and men of different nations have developed a strong sense of belonging to the Force. Despite the fact that they come from a variety of nations, use a variety of languages, and follow a variety of customs, the Standing Naval Force has become a workable system. Vice Admiral Daniel Mainguy, Canadian Forces, who commanded the Force in 1975 remarked recently, "it is difficult to express to those who have not been intimately involved with the evolution of international naval cooperation over the past two decades, just how far we have come. In 1968, conducting cooperative operations was very difficult technically at the individual ship level, although it could be done reasonably well at battle group level. . . . By the time I got in command of the Force, we could operate as a really well-oiled machine-and I like to think we did!"[18]

Rev. Peter P. Ball, Force Chaplain in 1971–72, explained that the Standing Naval Force became an entity of its own, both at sea and shore. The fact that all the ships flew the NATO flag and that all members of each ship's company wore the Standing Naval Force badge on their uniforms contributed to a sense of belonging. The exchange of up to 10 percent of a ship's company during period of transits developed close contacts, as did friendly rivalry in sports ashore, and exercises and contests between ships at sea. In port, sailors from different ships went ashore together and in case of problems, 'STANAVFORLANT'" became a rallying cry that usually brought help when needed.[19]

Such exchanges brought a vast repertoire of stories. For example, in 1978–79 during a bicycle race in Rotterdam, when teams got prizes for the best costume, one of the tasks en route was to get the daily exchange rate of yen into guilders. "When the team went into a local bank dressed in Mickey Mouse outfits, it wasn't surprising that the door clanged shut, and they were arrested!," Rear Admiral Gordon Edwards recalled.[20] In this flexible, intensely competitive, hard working, hard playing environment, professional performance has flourished. The regular appearances and departures of participating ships from different nations has become routine. As Commodore Haver Droeze pointed out in 1987, "it is amazing and heartening to witness newly joined ships melt into the Force within two weeks, very often within a couple of days. This really proves that nineteen years of SNFL is richly bearing fruit."

PRESENT AND FUTURE PROSPECTS

There were some differing views, to be sure, but on the balance the positive outweighed the negative. It was significant that Dr. J. M. A. H. Luns wrote, "As Secretary General of NATO, I never had to deal with any problems or misunderstandings within STANAVFOR-LANT."[22] There have been debates over how the Force should be used and in what waters it should operate. Many repeatedly debated whether it should operate South of the Tropic of Cancer, further than 18° East longitude in the Baltic, or be used in out-of-area crises, in the Middle East, Persian Gulf, West Indies or South America. Some suggested that the ships should be standardized, through the development of a "Free World Frigate."

There have been occasional difficulties in visiting specific ports or operating in specific areas that raise issues touching individual, national sensitivities. At an operational level, there have been stresses caused by ships being not properly prepared for a climate different from her home waters, ships which have had shortages in certain ratings, ships withdrawing from events at awkward moments for the Force, and by consideration of individual, national budgets which limit the number of hours a ship of its Navy may steam.[23]

Any alliance is subject to its internal and external strains, but nearly all who have been closely connected with the Standing Naval Force, Atlantic, see it as an effective, means of cementing potentially divisive situations. After twenty years, the Force has become so much a part of the established scene that the concept of national forces under international command no longer seems a novelty, but a positive reason to expand on, as future opportunities provide. This has already seen fruit in the establishment of the Standing Naval Force, Channel, in 1969, the Mediterranean On-Call Force in 1973, and in proposals for a Standing Naval Force, Pacific.

All agreed that

- The crews of the ships assigned to grow into an effective, homogeneous team with those from other nations would develop personal friendships.
- There is an exchange of professional experience which greatly improves the status of training in each ship, as well as by the group as a whole.
- The officers and men who serve together broaden their own horizons as they come to appreciate the professional expertise and national outlook of their colleagues.

COMMANDERS
STANDING NAVAL FORCE ATLANTIC
1968–1988

Rear Admiral		
G. C. Mitchell	United Kingdom	1968–69
Vice Admiral		
B. Veldkamp	The Netherlands	1969–70
Vice Admiral		
D. S. Boyle	Canada	1970–71
Captain		
R. W. Allen	United States	1971–72
Admiral of the Fleet		
Sir John Fieldhouse	United Kingdom	1972–73
Rear Admiral		
J. W. E. Wevers	The Netherlands	1973–74
Commodore		
G. M. de Rosenroll	Canada	1974
Vice Admiral		
D. N. Mainguy	Canada	1975
Captain		
A. C. A. Sigmond	United States	1975–76
Vice Admiral		
Sir John Cox	United Kingdom	1976–77
Rear Admiral		
K. J. L. Gerretse	The Netherlands	1977–78
Rear Admiral		
G. L. Edwards	Canada	1978–79
Captain		
G. M. Carter	United States	1979–80
Commodore		
D. G. Armytage	United Kingdom	1980–81
Rear Admiral		
J. J. Leeflang	The Netherlands	1981–82
Rear Admiral		
H. M. D. MacNeil	Canada	1982–83
Captain		
G. F. Streeter	United States	1983–84
Captain		
Klaus Schwabe	Germany	1984–85
Captain		
A. B. Richardson	United Kingdom	1985–86
Vice Admiral		
F. J. Haver Droeze	The Netherlands	1986–87
Vice Admiral		
L. G. Mason	Canada	1987–88

As Captain Klaus Schwabe, the first German commander of the Force noted at the end of his command period in 1985, "the Force indisputably is a spearhead of NATO and one of NATO's show windows at the same time. The spearhead must be kept sharp without fail-and in our show window we must display the best we have."[24]

During the first two decades of its existence, the Standing Naval Force, Atlantic, provided an innovative and increasingly effective means by which allied navies, small and large, operated together side by side. As it slowly worked out procedures for mutual communications, cooperative operations, and logistical supply, its effectiveness lay in the growth of mutual operating familiarity as a team, at a level of significance proportional to its capability. This capacity for international cooperation became the hallmark of NATO and a model for other regions of the world.

NOTES

A shorter version of this essay originally appeared as John B. Hattendorf and Commander Stan Weeks, "NATO's Policeman on the Beat," U.S. Naval Institute *Proceedings,* (September 1988), pp. 66–71.

The authors acknowledge with great appreciation the advice and suggestions provided by Rear Admiral Warren E. Aut, USN; Captain Raymond W. Allen, USN (Ret.); Rev. Peter P. Ball, RN (Ret.); Vice Admiral D. S. Boyle, CF (Ret.); Admiral Sir John Bush, RN (Ret.); Carl A. Christie; Admiral C. K. Duncan, USN (Ret.); Admiral Sir James Eberle, RN (Ret.); Rear Admiral Gordon L. Edwards, CF (Ret.); Admiral Robert H. Falls, CF (Ret.); Admiral of the Fleet Sir John Fieldhouse, RN; Captain Herbert Graubohm, FRGN; Commodore F. J. Haver Droeze, RNLN; Admiral of the Fleet the Lord Hill-Norton, RN (Ret.); Dr. Morris Honick: Admiral Isaac Kidd, Jr, USN (Ret.); LCDR Philip Kenny, CF; Professor Robert S. Jordan; Captain J. A. King, CF; Captain David Kirkpatrick, USN; Captain Krancke, FRGN; Admiral of the Fleet Sir Henry Leach, RN (Ret.); Rear Admiral J. J. Leeflang, RNLN (Ret.); Admiral Sir Charles Madden, RN (Ret.); Vice Admiral D. N. Mainguy, CF (Ret.); Rear Admiral Geoffrey C. Mitchell, RN (Ret.); Captain A. B. Richardson, RN; Captain Klaus Schwabe, FRGN; Mr. Paul Stillwell; Commander W. F. L. Van Leeuwen, RNLN; LCDR P. H. Whalley, RN.

1. Letter from Vice-Admiral Daniel N. Mainguy, CF, to Hattendorf 15 June 1987; Daniel N. Mainguy, "The Standing Naval Force Atlantic, *Canadian Forces Sentinel,* vol. 5, no. 1 (January 1969), pp. 27–28. Naval Historical Collection, Naval War College: Manuscript Collection 30: Admiral R. G. Colbert Papers. Series 2, subject files, folder 51: STANAVFORLANT. Hereinafter cited as Colbert Papers. Admiral Sir John Busch, RN. Speech to Standing Naval Force, Atlantic, 13 January; Letter from Admiral Sir John Busch to Hattendorf 4 September 1987.

2. Letter from Sir Charles Madden to Hattendorf, 6 June 1967.
3. Ibid.
4. SACLANT Staff, "Analysis of the Operations of the Standing Naval Forces, Atlantic, 1968-1978, pp. 1–2.
5. Colbert Papers, file 51: STANAVORLANT File Notes.
6. Toby Marquez, "The Mixed-Manning Demonstration," U.S. Naval Institute *Proceedings* 91 (July 1965), pp. 87–102; "Notebook: *Ricketts* Skipper Hails 6-Nation Crew," Ibid., 91 (October 1965), p. 144.
7. On Colbert, see chapter 10 above.
8. Letter from Admiral Thomas H. Moorer to Hattendorf. 27 August 1985.
9. Colbert Papers, file 54: Script for unclassified briefing on STANAVFORLANT, 1968, p. 8.
10. Ibid. Pp. 9–13.
11. Admiral Wesley L. McDonald, USN, speech to Standing Naval Force, Atlantic, Mess Night, Charleston, SC, 10 November 1983.
12. SACLANT Message 102205Z DEC 1980.
13. Letter from Admiral Robert H. Falls, CF, to Hattendorf, 26 June 1987.
14. Ibid., and letter from Rear Admiral J. J. Leeflang, RNLN to Hattendorf, 3 September 1987, and Commodore F. J. Haver Droeze RNLN to Hattendorf, 22 August 1987.
15. Interview with Captain R. W. Allen, USN, June 1987; Letter from Admiral C. K. Duncan, USN (Ret.) to Hattendorf 4 July 1987; SACLANT News release 13 July 1987; "Standing Naval Force, Atlantic: Some trends in ship assignments."
16. Letter from Rear Admiral G. C. Mitchell, CB, RN (Ret.), to Hattendorf, 21 August 1987.
17. Ibid.
18. Letter from Daniel N. Mainguy to Hattendorf, 15 June 1987.
19. Letter from Rev. Peter P. Ball RN (Ret.), to Hattendorf, 29 August 1987.
20. Letter from Rear Admiral Gordon L. Edwards, CF, to Hattendorf, 9 June 1987.
21. Letter from Commodore F. J. Haver Droeze RNLN, to Hattendorf, 22 August 1987.
22. Letter from Dr. J. M. A. H. Luns to Hattendorf, 16 June 1987.
23. Letter from Rear Admiral G. C. Marshall, RN, to Hattendorf, 21 August 1987.
24. Captain Klaus Schwabe, FGN, "Remarks at Change of Command Ceremony, April 1985," enclosed in letter from Schwabe to Hattendorf, 30 June 1987.

12

The Evolution of the U.S. Navy's "Maritime Strategy," 1977–1987

The American system of strategic planning is pluralistic, whereby statements of strategy are made at four levels:

1. High policy is established at the level of the President and modified or supported by Congress.
2. War planning, the general conceptual planning for war, originates with the Joint Chiefs of Staff.
3. Program planning, the system of coordinating weapons procurement, is accompanied by statements of strategy that define the rationale for the weapons involved. The programs are designed by each service and coordinated by the Secretary of Defense.
4. Operational planning, the preparation of precise plans for wartime operations, is done by the various unified and specified commanders in chief.

In theory, the four levels of strategy making should directly complement one another. High policy establishes the goals and objectives for both war planning and program planning. They, in turn, reflect operational planning. Some academics argue that, in practice, the theory is rarely, if ever, achieved. Each level of strategy making has its own set of requirements and constraints, resulting from the nature of the system, thereby creating the possibility for contradictions and disjunctions. Every decision-making element within each of the various levels of strategy making is the result of a strictly rational calculation of strategy.[1] This is caused by the practical necessity to simplify complex issues. It involves a high degree of uncertainty and motivated bias created through the interaction of bureaucratic interests. These factors, present in nearly every system of governmental machinery, need constant reevaluation and adjustment in order to reach a rational application of strategy. That rational calculus is forever changing as political events and technological developments alter the situation on the global stage. Thus, the development of strategy is a perpetual process of questioning, application, and reexamination. Within this context, one can profitably examine the U.S. Navy's development of the Maritime Strategy during the period 1977 to 1987.

THE EVOLUTION OF NAVAL THINKING IN THE 1970s

Following the U.S. withdrawal from Vietnam, events in Ethiopia, Angola, Afghanistan, and Iran clearly demonstrated that the American position in international politics was not faring well, while the Soviet Union seemed to be having great success. This situation, following the stabilizing influence of Gerald Ford's presidency, evoked a changing mood among leaders within the U.S. government. Beginning with the Carter administration, the United States began to move outward again, using her armed forces to complement her foreign policy and establishing a clear trend in the use of U.S. naval and military forces as a political instrument. Simultaneously, strategic nuclear forces seemed to play a declining and less obvious role, while conventional forces become much more important.

These trends in American foreign policy paralleled a number of other apparently separate but, in fact, interlocking developments. First, there were indications that the confusion that had evolved about naval theory was coming to an end. Second, there was a clear resurgence in general strategic thinking in many areas of the U.S. armed forces as well as in the academic world. Third, the U.S. Navy was engaged in rebuilding its forces to modernize about half of the U.S. surface fleet. Finally, while these developments progressed, the Soviet navy demonstrated new capabilities in its own dramatic development that had begun in 1962, culminating with the capacity of a global naval power. The consequence of these trends provided the central features of ambience in which new American naval thinking began to take shape.

NAVAL THEORY REFINED

Theory has never been an attractive area of study for naval officers, yet naval theorists do work in an important area, one that can both reflect and inform those whose concerns are strictly practical. In America, the most widely read theoretical works written in the postwar period were devoted to the political uses of navies short of war. The most prominent writers were academics such as Lawrence W. Martin, Edward Luttwak, and Ken Booth, as well as the diplomat Sir James Cable.

A small, but less well-known, group of thinkers centered at the Naval War College consistently devoted their efforts to creating a thoroughly modern synthesis of major strategic ideas for wartime. The dominant figure in this work was Rear Admiral Henry E. Eccles, joined by Dr. Herbert Rosinski and Dr. William Reitzel, among others. They tried to define, with semantic precision, the nature of naval strategy in modern warfare. At the same time, they wrote a basic description of what senior naval officers should understand intuitively and be prepared to develop into practical, operationally sound strategic plans for naval forces.[2] Eccles expanded on Rosinski's definition that strategy is the comprehensive direction of power to control situations and areas in order to attain broad objectives. As Eccles so succinctly defined the matter in practical terms:

A strategic concept is a verbal statement of:

- What to control
- For what purpose
- To what degree
- When to initiate control
- How long to control and, in general,
- How to control in order to achieve the strategic objective.[3]

Another naval officer, Rear Admiral Joseph C. Wylie, took this concept one step further. For him, the common factor in all power struggles is the concept of control. "Military control, or military affairs in the broad sense, can seldom be taken up in isolation," Wylie wrote. "Military matters are inextricably woven into the whole social fabric. And that is why a general theory of strategy must, I believe, be a theory of power in all its forms, not just a theory of military power."[4]

Naval theorists within the U.S. Navy initially concentrated on the uses of the Navy in wartime and then extended their thinking to include peacetime political applications of naval strategy in relation to the broader aspects of maritime and national power. There was a clear realization within the Navy that naval force is related to other aspects of national power. Among the most important aspects of this thinking was the perception that conventional naval forces had a role to be played in a world of nuclear deterrence and parity of forces.

This general trend in thinking augured a significant alteration in the American viewpoint. Conventional force seemed to gain utility, not only in its relation to the nuclear balance and deterrence, but also as an increment of escalation. It contributed to the threat of a prolonged conventional war whereby economic and industrial strength would be the decisive factor.[5]

THE RESURGENCE OF STRATEGIC THINKING IN THE U.S. NAVY

The development of strategic thinking within the U.S. Navy goes back more than a century. For most of that time, the Navy had its contingency plans and analyzed ways in which to use naval power in future wars. Despite this planning, there has never been a clearly identified cadre of officers who have been given specific responsibility for developing naval strategy. Over the years, senior officials in Washington and scattered groups of more or less intellectually inclined naval officers working at the Naval War College, in the Office of the Chief of Naval Operations (OpNav), and on the staffs of fleet commanders have dealt with strategic ideas and issues. The entire history of the Naval War College, in fact, has been a chronicle of repeated efforts to promote broad strategic thinking within the naval officer corps to complement the routine emphasis on technological developments and new weapons.

In the 1960s and 1970s, the official Department of Defense statement on naval missions did not change, yet, within that same time frame, the long-term naval force goals which the Navy used did change. In 1975, the goal for 575 ships was set by Secretary of Defense James Schlesinger; in 1976 Secretary Donald Rumsfeld set it for 600; in 1977–78, Secretary Harold Brown set it for 425–500 ships. The variance in these numbers reflected the differences in judgment regarding prudent planning for facing the uncertainties of the future. The high numbers reflected estimates that focused on a future world war involving the Soviet Union. The low numbers, particularly the 400-ship figures used by the Carter administration in its 1977 Department of Defense Consolidated Guidance, reflected the idea that the U.S. Navy's surface fleet was designed for peacekeeping operations and for conflicts in which the Soviet Union would choose not to be involved. In contrast to this view, the U.S. Navy wanted to maintain an edge of naval superiority over the Soviets.

The Navy's staff, under Admiral James L. Holloway, III, Chief of Naval Operations in the period between 1974 and 1978, considered the question of "how to size a navy." Studies were conducted for various naval force levels: 500, 600, 700, and 800 ships. Both the Atlantic and Pacific Fleets required a balanced force of combatant ships, amphibious assault lift capabilities, support ships, and appropriate aircraft. The plan for a 500-ship navy was designed to retain the then current fleet size with a reduction to 40 SSBNs and 12 carriers. The 800-ship figure corresponded to the 1984 fiscal year force objective recommended by the Joint Chiefs of Staff, while the 600 and 700-ship fleets were intermediate alternatives. The Five-Year Defense Plan, already in use, corresponded to a 588-ship fleet by fiscal year 1983. When extrapolated to fiscal year 1985, it would be a 600-ship navy.

During the late 1970s, several changes occurred which had an impact on the transition to widespread offensive thinking within the naval officer corps. Admiral Holloway's emphasis on carrier battle groups and surface action groups became the operational basis upon which later strategic concepts were formed. There were two important early ideas in the area of strategic thinking, and though sharing some qualities, their origins were different. One was the "Sea Strike Strategy" project developed by Admiral Thomas B. Hayward as Commander in Chief, Pacific Fleet, 1977–78. The other was "Sea Plan 2000," which began in the office of the Secretary of the Navy in Washington.

"Sea Strike" and the parallel work on "Sea Plan 2000" were key components in the Navy's opposition to the Carter administration's defense policy. Carter called for greater emphasis on the central front in a NATO-Warsaw Pact war, but a more constrained role for naval forces. The focal point of the Navy's criticism was the thought that the central front could not be isolated from the European flanks or from other theaters of war.

Leaders such as Secretary of the Navy Graham Claytor, Under Secretary James Woolsey, and Admiral James L. Holloway clearly established a consensus within the Navy's Washington leadership that the service should strive for superiority at sea against the Soviets and, when examining the variety of possible wartime operations against the Soviet navy, think in terms of forward, offensive operations as the most effective means for employing the Navy to achieve the nation's broad defense policies. In promoting this perspective the Navy was reasserting a traditional view of its strategic role. It reflected the strategic ideas which lay behind the establishment of

NATO in the late 1940s and the long tradition of naval thinking embodied in the classic works of Alfred Thayer Mahan and Sir Julian Corbett.

THINKING ABOUT THE SOVIET NAVY, 1967–1981

Any serious thinking about strategy must necessarily deal with the effect that one's forces will have on an opponent. How an enemy will use its forces is a critical factor in any strategic evaluation. Thus, when determining how forces might be deployed for achieving broad future goals in a war, one must also assess the probability of how an enemy might act and react. One must examine everything that an enemy can do which may materially influence one's own courses of action.

From the early 1960s, when the growth of Soviet naval power became apparent, the predominant perception in America was one that contemplated the Soviets building a naval force with many capabilities-many of them similar to those which the U.S. Navy had already developed. The existence of a blue-water Soviet navy seemed to emphasize, in American minds, the capability for peacetime power projection and for wartime attack on United States and other Western naval forces and sea lines of communication, as well as a capacity for strategic nuclear strikes from the sea. Increasingly, Americans worried about the Soviet navy as a sea-denial force that could deprive the West of the free use of the sea, thereby creating political, economic, and miliary disaster. In short, many Americans viewed the Soviet naval capability by mirror-imaging and refighting World War II.

The public discussion of the issue in Congress and the press, as well as in the statements of senior naval officers, stressed this interpretation. But at the same time, specialists on Soviet affairs began to develop an interpretation that tried to move away from an American, ethnocentric view of the Soviets. The soil in which this interpretation grew consisted of the Soviet Union's values and the views, aims, and objectives of its leaders. The first widely read book in America on this subject was Robert W. Herrick's *Soviet Naval Strategy: Fifty Years of Theory and Practice,* published by the U.S. Naval Institute in 1968. Herrick wrote much of the book while serving as staff intelligence officer at the Naval War College in 1963–64. He based his study on his own detailed reading of Soviet literature and many years of experience as an intelligence specialist in Soviet affairs. Herrick concluded that Soviet naval strategy, like tsarist

Russian naval strategy before it, was essentially defensive. This view was so different from the commonly held official viewpoint that the publisher added a preface to the volume and enclosed a printed bookmark which drew attention to this fact. The publisher called for comments and articles expressing alternative views to be published in the U.S. Naval Institute's *Proceedings.*

It took a long time for Herrick's interpretation to prevail within the U.S. Navy. This change did occur, however, at about the same time that the Maritime Strategy was formulated in the later 1970s and early 1980s. The process by which the U.S. Navy changed its views appeared clearly in two places: in the work of the Center for Naval Analyses (CNA) during the period 1967–1981 and within the official, naval intelligence community.

CNA's conclusions were quite different from those made at that time in the classified intelligence literature being prepared at the Pentagon. While some on the Navy staff endorsed the CNA conclusion, they were obliged to add qualifying language, anticipating objections from some quarters of the intelligence community.[6]

Continuing this work in the following years, CNA analyst James M. McConnell made a crucial contribution in 1977 in a draft, first chapter of *Soviet Naval Diplomacy,* which corroborated earlier interpretations of Soviet intentions to withhold their SLBMs. Developing evidence that the Soviet Union's SSBNs were under the direct control of the highest political leaders, and those forces would be used mainly in later periods of war, McConnell wrote, "Wars might be won by other branches of the armed forces, Gorshkov seems to be saying, but surrenders and armistices are arranged from the sea; and beyond that, navies have a value in influencing the course of actual peacemaking."[7]

In an October 1977 contribution to James L. George's volume, *Problems of Sea Power As We Approach the Twenty-first Century,* McConnell went further. He suggested that Soviet SSBNs would operate in defended, local sanctuaries in home waters such as the Barents Sea for the Northern Fleet and the Sea of Okhotsk for the Pacific Ocean Fleet. They would be heavily guarded by mines and fixed underwater acoustic surveillance systems. In addition, the Soviets would continue to emphasize the use of flight-deck cruisers which could provide air defense and intercepter cover for submarines, surface ships, and aircraft engaged in barrier operations.[8]

Throughout the late 1970s, CNA analysts expressed growing concern that U.S. Navy plans were giving insufficient attention to the implications inherent in the Soviet adoption of a withholding strat-

egy for their SLBM force and the assignment of their general purpose navy to a protective mission for their SSBN force.[9] In March
1980, Bradford Dismukes reported the results of an initial investigation of possible war termination missions for the U.S. Navy. This
new topic arose from an attempt to assess the implication of the Soviet withholding strategy. In a briefing reflecting seminal ideas by
James McConnell, Dismukes declared that "our nation's strategies
require adjustment in reaction to a fundamental change that has occurred in maritime affairs."[10]

Reflecting on this dilemma for analysts of Soviet strategy, Captain
W. H. J. Manthorpe, Jr. suggested that those who would try to predict whether the changes suggested by theory would actually occur
are as likely to be wrong as they are to be right. In the U.S.S.R., the
transformation of military science into doctrine is as much a function of party and bureaucratic internal politics as are other factors.
However, those who wait for the hard evidence from fleet exercises
that Soviet strategy actually has changed are likely to be the last to
recognize when that change has taken place. "The moral is," Manthorpe wrote, "if you want to be early you may be wrong, but if you
want to be right you'll surely be late in recognizing changes to Soviet
strategy."[11]

With this in mind, official analysts in the Office of Naval Intelligence proceeded to evaluate the original contributions made by the
Center for Naval Analyses, expanding and modifying them in the
process. The essential point in this intelligence work involved
changing the perception that, in case of a war, the Soviet navy intended to attack NATO's sea lines of communication supporting the
Central Front in Europe. This long-standing view had led many,
particularly in the Carter administration, to focus on antisubmarine warfare in the open Atlantic and to favor construction of
smaller frigates and patrol aircraft over larger ships. The new intelligence showed that the Soviet Union had quite different objectives and the United States needed a much different mix of naval
forces to counter the threat. In March 1983, the Central Intelligence
Agency's National Intelligence Estimate on "Soviet Naval Strategy
and Programs through the 1990s" summarized the key judgments
in these new findings:

> Within the Soviet's overall wartime strategy, however, the primary initial
> tasks of the Navy remain:
> —To deploy and provide protection for ballistic missile submarines in
> preparation for and conduct of strategic and theater nuclear strikes.

—To defend the USSR and its allies by enemy ballistic missile submarines and aircraft carriers.

Accomplishment of these tasks would entail attempts to control all or portions of the Kara, Barents, and Norwegian and Greenland Seas, the Seas of Japan and Okhotsk, and the Northwest Pacific Basin, and to conduct sea denial operations beyond those areas to about 2,000 kilometers from Soviet territory. We believe that virtually all of the Northern and Pacific Fleet's available major surface combatants and some three-quarters of their available attack submarines would be initially committed to operations in these waters. Other initial naval wartime tasks are: support of ground force operations in the land theaters of military operations (including countering naval support to enemy operations in peripheral areas such as Norway), and some interdiction of Western sea lines of communication.[12]

Intelligence analysts believed that these basic strategic and defensive tasks would guide the Soviet navy's growth in the coming decade, as it sought to maintain a fleet of about sixty modern, ballistic missile submarines, develop a long-range nuclear-armed land attack cruise missiles to be launched from a variety of naval vessels and bring into service a new class of nuclear-powered aircraft carriers. At the same time, they estimated that the Soviets would decrease the size of their surface ship fleet, while they moved toward larger-sized ships with more sophisticated weapons. While these changes were taking place, they expected that the conventional submarine force would decrease in size and the amphibious force ships would increase in number. They expected that major technical improvements would take place in Soviet naval aviation as the Soviet navy focused on sea control and sea denial efforts against Western forces in nearby ocean areas and on fleet air defence. Turning to operations other than war, the intelligence analysts concluded,

the Soviet Navy will continue to play important peacetime roles, ranging from routine show-the-flag port visits to support for distant-area client states during crisis situations and limited wars. Given the likelihood of continued instability in the Third World, the use of such naval diplomacy and power projection techniques probably will increase during the 1980s and 1990s.[13]

The intelligence assessments clearly showed that the United States Navy faced quite a different threat than it had previously imagined that it faced. The Navy's senior leadership clearly understood that it needed to develop new approaches to thinking about future warfare and to plan for a different type of naval force to meet the Soviet challenge that the new intelligence estimates portrayed. This involved a wide range of initiatives in a variety of areas, involving trends and developments that were already taken place for other reasons.

FROM THE CNO STRATEGIC CONCEPTS TO THE WORK OF THE CNO'S STRATEGIC STUDIES GROUP, 1978–1986

The appointment of Admiral Thomas B. Hayward as the 21st Chief of Naval Operations in June 1978 marked an important stage in the transition of thinking within the U.S. Navy's officer corps. It won an affirmation of the strategic thinking which Hayward had done for the Pacific Fleet in 1976–78, and it marked the change in approach to strategic problems within the Navy. Up to this point, much of the debate about naval issues centered around the Navy's budget. The complicated explanation of costs and program alternatives were often confused with strategy. Some critics charged that unrealistic strategies were occasionally employed for no other reason than to justify larger shares of money for one program or another. In this way the budget tended to drive strategic concepts. "This is why," Hayward explained, "academics and others say the Navy doesn't have a strategy."[14] To combat this problem and to remove the misperception, Hayward sought to change the terms of the debate from a budget battle to an analysis of the strategic issues for a global maritime power. Under Hayward, the Navy's leadership agreed not to fight for particular force levels. Instead, they began to work for a highly ready navy with adequate manning and let Congress worry about how big that navy should be. In order to increase readiness, Hayward put his priority on spare parts, ammunition, pay, and benefits. Then he went on to point out that the central front in Europe was not the only problem for the United States. The country needed a war-winning strategy.[15]

Hayward gave briefings to Congress, to the Joint Chiefs of Staff, the Defense Science Board, the CNO Executive Panel, as well as other groups. He used the concepts which he developed in these briefings as the basis for the first part of his Annual Posture Statement to Congress. An unclassified version was published in the U.S. Naval Institute's *Naval Review 1979* in an article by Hayward entitled, "The Future of U.S. Sea Power."[16] Drafted for Hayward by Captain William Cockell, the article cast Hayward's unclassified Congressional testimony in a new format. It was, as Cockell later described it, "some simply stated principles . . . simple, not simplistic, and simple, by design."[17] It lacked the sophistication of the classified version, but the article expressed Hayward's basic concepts on how to think about naval force. For the readers of the *Naval Review,* Hayward made his point clear: classical naval theory is still valid.[18]

BUREAUCRATIC REFINEMENTS

While people began to discuss Hayward's strategic concepts, the Chief of Naval Operations was directly concerned with making some organizational changes within the Navy. In particular, he wanted to assist the Navy's leaders in thinking about strategy. First, he wanted to establish a focal point within the Navy staff for discussions on the broad aspects of naval warfare. In order to do this, in mid-January 1980 Hayward changed Op-095 from the Anti-Submarine Warfare Directorate to the Directorate of Naval Warfare. His idea was to create a directorate which could coordinate the work of the various platform sponsors-the Deputy CNOs for Air, Submarine, and Surface Warfare. This office was to be sympathetic to them while at the same time being the primary contact point for the fleet commanders and their concerns for future war-fighting developments.

Second, Hayward wanted to create a means within the bureaucracy to evaluate the new intelligence information and to ensure that it received proper attention, in a situation when some elements within the Navy seemed tied to older interpretations and unwilling to change views. In organizing this effort, Hayward's executive assistant, Captain William Cockell, and the Director of Naval Intelligence, Rear Admiral Sumner Shapiro, played key roles. To deal with this issue, Hayward organized teams to analyze the intelligence and all its implications for the U.S. Navy. The Director of Naval Intelligence brought a civilian, Richard Haver, then Technical Director of the Naval Fleet Operational Intelligence Office to head a special section (Op-009J), directly under Rear Admiral Shapiro and his successor, Rear Admiral John Butts. After 1981, the intelligence information coming from this office was shared with a newly established team of flag officers called the Advanced Technology Panel, established by the Vice Chief of Naval Operations, Admiral William N. Small, and this continued under Hayward's successor, Admiral James Watkins. A working group headed by Rear Admirals Bell and Bacon, along with a group of knowledgeable captains and commanders including Captains Linton Brooks and William Studeman, actively worked on new ideas and approaches for the U.S. Navy. Working closely with this, Vice Admiral Kinnaird McKee, the Director of

Naval Warfare, established "Team Charlie," headed by his technical director, Dr. Alfred Andreassen, to examine the implications of the intelligence for fighting a future war.[19]

Hayward saw another need within the Navy staff. For many years the Navy had undertaken long-range planning, and the various groups which had done this work had varying degrees of success and influence on naval policy.[20] In January 1980, Hayward established the Long Range Planning Group (Op-00X) under Rear Admiral Charles R. Larson. Consisting of a small group of highly qualified officers, the mission of Op-00X was to assess resource limitations on future naval capabilities and analyze alternative strategies for achieving long-range goals. The Long Range Planning Group had an important area to consider, but Hayward also wanted to examine another aspect of strategic thinking: the interplay between strategy and tactics.

At the same time, Hayward had two parallel interests. He wanted to create a core of future naval leaders who would be well-versed in the role of naval forces in national policy and strategy. He also wanted to reestablish the Naval War College as the pinnacle for education in naval strategic thinking.

As Hayward told the Current Strategy Forum at the Naval War College in April 1981, "there is no dearth of strategic thinking going on these days in your Navy. What is lacking is a more useful way to capitalize upon that abundant talent with more alacrity."[21] As a step in this direction, Hayward established "a prestigious Center for Naval Warfare Studies" at the Naval War College. Along with this, he announced "the creation of a small, but impressive cell . . . a group of the best and brightest of our military officers, "what was to become known as the CNO's Strategic Studies Group. Making his point clear, Hayward declared,

> Our objective is to make this Naval War College respected around the globe as the residence of the finest maritime strategic logic of our time. A related objective is to provide the Chief of Naval Operations and our senior military officers with stimuli relative to strategy and tactics in order to make certain that regardless of the perception of those less informed, our Navy will never, never be found "sailing backwards."[22]

Although the Strategic Studies Group (SSG) reports directly to the CNO, it is based in Newport to take advantage of the academic atmosphere and resources available at the Naval War College and to use the distance from Washington as insulation from the bureaucratic traumas of Pentagon life.

THE AMBIENCE FOR STRATEGIC THINKING IN 1981

The Strategic Studies Group did not operate in a vacuum. Its first mission was to educate itself in the strategic thinking of the day and to move forward, unencumbered by the friction of bureaucracy, in an effort to stimulate flag officers who held positions of responsibility for executing strategy in wartime. In the 1970s, one of the characteristic problems of the naval bureaucracy was the way in which it tended to isolate thought in certain communities within the Navy, preventing the exchange of views necessary for cultivating commonly shared opinions. Like the Naval Warfare Directorate on the Navy staff, the Strategic Studies Group tried to surmount the natural and artificial barriers to a free exchange of thinking which had developed over the years. In many ways the SSG acted like a small swarm of honeybees, migrating from one flag officer to another, discussing issues, exchanging views, and carrying the pollen of stimulating thought from one command to another. Charged as they were with thinking in global terms about how to win a future conventional war with the Soviet Union, he viewpoints they expressed were so different that they shocked some listeners. As Captain Sam Leeds recalled, "the first reaction was to shoot the messenger."[23] However, once the initial defensive reaction was overcome, a fruitful exchange of opinion developed which was both educational and constructive.

At the Naval War College, each Strategic Studies Group was given one entire academic year for its work. As each succeeding group of officers worked on their project, they developed and refined a progressively better statement of the nature of the Soviet threat and a more coherent approach for using naval forces to achieve national aims. Each group found it necessary to examine the best use of all national resources in order to understand the role of naval forces. In so doing, they elevated the Navy to the forefront of thinking in terms of joint and combined strategy. The first SSG established the basic tenets and conceptual feasibility of a forward maritime strategy. They focused on Soviet missions and sensitivities and used a theater-wide combined arms approach to exploit Western advantages.

Upon completion of the second group's work, SSG Director Robert J. Murray summarized the outlook that had been developed in the two previous years:

> The principles espoused here cut across the bow of prevailing opinion in some instances, but the strategy is not radically different from long-held conceptions of the proper employment of naval forces. The principles

would not be unfamiliar to Mahan. In particular, our work confirms the value for national strategy of naval forces designed, trained and intended for offensive operations, and rejects as impractical and undesirable the notion, sometimes espoused outside the Navy Department, of a defensively organized and equipped Navy. It is clear to us that the best defense remains a good offense.[24]

The concept of forward defense, adopted as NATO strategy and already applied to land and air forces, is equally applicable to naval forces. Continuing, Murray said "it adds much to deterrence and places naval forces in preferred positions if deterrence fails." Going further, Murray noted that the SSG found no instance where it was necessary for U.S. naval forces to employ nuclear weapons to achieve their objective. "While it is necessary to understand how to operate in a nuclear environment," Murray concluded, "it is not necessary to take the initiative in using nuclear weapons for naval purposes; on the contrary, the use of nuclear weapons at sea appears to be to our clear disadvantage."[25]

Thus, in the five years of evolutionary development between Admiral Hayward's announcement of his strategic concepts in 1978, through the cumulative work of the first two CNO Strategic Studies Groups, American naval strategic thinkers had revived and modified classical naval theory and placed it clearly within the context of both the peacetime use of naval force and the context of the nuclear age. In the process, a common approach and view was developing at the highest levels of the Navy's leadership, leaving room for future modifications and evolution to this firm conceptual foundation.

THE WORK OF THE STRATEGIC CONCEPTS BRANCH (OP-603), 1982–1986

The publication entitled *The Maritime Strategy,*[26] prepared in the Office of the Chief of Naval Operations, is the official statement of what is sometimes called the "Forward Maritime Strategy" or "The Maritime Component of National Military Strategy." The immediate origins of this booklet are clearly definable and lead directly from three memoranda written by the Vice Chief of Naval Operations, Admiral William N. Small.

In December 1981, Small wrote a memo to the Director of Navy Program Planning in which he said: "I think it is high time we take a formal, critical look at how we do the analysis that leads to our appraisals of Navy programs and strategy, but even within the Navy where we are professionally misled by both the scenario displayed and the conclusion which may logically be drawn therefrom."[27] Small objected to the typical thinking within the Navy staff in Washington. He saw that strategy was ignored in program discussions for ship and weapon construction. He thought that the programs often seemed to drive the strategy. He wanted to reverse this situation so that serious and responsible thought about the naval aspect of national strategy would eventually become the basis upon which the United States built its future Navy.[28] In Small's view, a major deficiency in naval thinking was a worst-case mentality. "We assign the best capabilities to the enemy and the worst to our own forces," he wrote. In analyzing engagements, we put our forces "into tactical situations which no prudent planner or responsible commander would countenance. Moreover, the U.S. Navy seemed to have adopted a defensive outlook, not an offensive one. "Naval forces are intended to seek out and destroy the enemy," Small declared, "not defend themselves."[29]

Within the Pentagon's naval staff, Small saw the parochialism of each of the platform sponsors and the failure of the OpNav staff to integrate the analyses, appraisals, requirements, and programs with strategic planning. "None of the characteristics of a naval engagement are played in isolation from each other in the real world, as they seem to be in our current methods of analysis," Small declared. "If affordability were injected early into analysis, which is itself based on national forces employment against realistic threats, we would have fewer and better supported combat systems."[30] Small believed that the practices which were then current in the Pentagon led to exotic responses to extreme requirements, resulting in insufficient forces for real needs.

Although a consensus had been formed by Small's first two memos, the document which actually triggered the immediate action to prepare the briefing that eventually became the Chief of Naval Operations and Secretary of the Navy approved Maritime Strategy booklet was a memo written for Small's signature by Rear Admiral John A. Baldwin, Director of the Systems Analysis Division (Op-96). This memo expressed what many people on the Navy staff believed was necessary to tie strategy to force development and fiscal responsibility. As Vice Admiral Carlisle Trost wrote on the cover sheet for the memo as it went along the clearance ladder for Small's signature, "We really need this to get the entire OpNav staff moving in the same direction."[31]

Small signed the memo on 2 August 1982 and sent it to all four flag officers directly concerned with the preparation of the upcoming annual Program Objective Memorandum (POM). The POM is a complete line-by-line list of every appropriation item that the Navy requires for the next five years, within fiscal limits. Each service submits comparable memoranda in May of every year to the Department of Defense, and they become the basis for the budget request to Congress. The POM ties the multiple planning functions together in a single document and serves as the foundation upon which a budget can be constructed in support of the defined goals and objectives of the Navy. In starting the annual process which would lead to the submission of the POM in May 1983, Admiral Small repeated his view that a strategy appraisal was needed "at the outset of the POM process with respect to how naval forces will be employed in wartime and their disposition both in the sense of our CINC war plans and in the DG [Defense Guidance] scenario." The Strategic Concepts Group (Op-603), then headed by Captain Elizabeth Wylie, took action on Admiral Small's memo. Within that office, Captain Wylie selected an action officer, Lieutenant Commander Stan Weeks, to carry out the required work. When Weeks was given this task, it seemed only another routine chore in Op-603; neither he nor others realized how quick or extensive would be the success of their project.

As the scope of the work became plain, Commander W. Spencer Johnson was assigned to join Weeks in the project to produce a draft as soon as possible, focusing his efforts on the "front end" connection of national strategy and defense programming.[32] Within three weeks, these two officers, Johnson and Weeks, pieced together a secret draft briefing which answered Admiral Small's request. In developing their initial briefing, they turned immediately to some of the work which was already in progress. The key sources were the work being done in Newport by the Strategic Studies Group; the analyses of the Soviet Navy by the Center for Naval Analyses and the Office of Naval Intelligence; and the basic ideas that Admiral Hayward had developed for the Pacific Fleet and elaborated upon for the entire Navy as Chief of Naval Operations.[33]

In 1982, the first version of the CNO/SECAV approved statement of the Maritime Strategy began as an internal OpNav effort to state clearly the strategic background for naval force planning and budget decisions. Almost immediately, the Weeks-Johnson Maritime Strategy began to develop a wider significance. By late September 1982, the new Deputy CNO for Plans, Policy and Operations (Op-06), Vice Admiral Arthur Moreau, had reported and immediately approved the basic Weeks-Johnson Maritime Strategy briefing, deleting only one backup paper.

The next step was to begin the process of review. The statement of the strategy, as well as the entire Program Objective Memorandum, would normally pass through three phases of review by three different oversight committees. These committees, from junior to senior, are The Program Development Review Committee, chaired by the Director, General Planning and Programming Division, (Op-90); The Program Review Committee, chaired by the Director of Navy Program Planning (Op-090); and The CNO Executive Board, chaired by the Vice Chief of Naval Operations. In early October, the Op-603 officers presented the briefing to the Program Development Review Committee, the most junior of the three. This committee of rear admirals, chaired by Rear Admiral Joseph Metcalf, III, decided that the Maritime Strategy briefing should be presented "as is." Within a week, Weeks and Johnson presented it to the CNO Executive Board, consisting of the CNO and all his deputy CNOs and principal assistants. When Weeks and Johnson made this presentation to their most senior audience, the new Chief of Naval Operations, Admiral Watkins, and the other senior flag officers reacted positively. In the discussion following the briefing, Watkins emphasized the need to keep the Maritime Strategy focused on cooperation with allies and with other services, particularly with the U.S. Air Force.

On 7 October, Admiral Watkins issued a message to the Fleet CINCs reviewing his first ninety days as Chief of Naval Operations and identified the areas on which he wanted to focus. Among those areas were war-fighting readiness, the revitalization of the Naval War College as the crucible for strategic and tactical thinking, integration of the Naval Reserve into our war-fighting thinking, and improvement of interservice cooperation and mutual understanding.[34] His design was to unify the work of the CINCs, bringing their collective knowledge and understanding to bear on the broad issues facing the Navy and particularly on the use of naval forces for deterrence. The briefing which Weeks and Johnson had developed during August and September 1982 to help decision makers in the budgetary process played into Watkins's broader goals.[35] It quickly took on a larger significance, building on the wide range of thinking within the Navy.

What had begun only two short months before as Lieutenant Commander Weeks and Commander Johnson's briefing was now the official statement of the Navy's maritime strategy. The transition has been rapid, but the concepts which Weeks and Johnson had used and coordinated were firmly based in a line of thinking that had developed over a much longer period. They used ideas that had emerged in the 1970s and had been refined in the Office of Naval Intelligence, the Strategic Studies Groups, and on the staffs of the unified and fleet commanders.

During the winter and spring of 1982–83, the officers in the Strategic Concepts Branch gave the Maritime Strategy briefing widely. In February 1983, it figured largely in Admiral Watkins's Posture Statement before the House Armed Services Committee. Watkins's own concept of how strategic and tactical thinking was being improved within the Navy was important and reflected the emphasis he placed on certain organizations and their work. Emphasizing some long-term work which was already in progress, he mentioned in his Posture Statement four key elements in his thinking:[36]

- The effort to develop a better understanding of the Soviet thought processes and inherent strengths and weaknesses in order to counter and exploit them.
- The revitalization of the Naval War College as a crucible for strategic and tactical thinking; the parallel effort to expose the finest, tactically proven professionals to strategic thinking as a means of testing professional thought; as well as creating a cadre for sound-thinking, educated commanders ready for key assignments.
- The use of combined arms war games which were explicitly designed to avoid a parochial, Navy-only point of view.
- The use of the semiannual Navy Commanders-in-Chief's conference as a forum for discussing national strategy and the Maritime Strategy flowing from it; using this conference to help establish the basis for organizing fiscal programming considerations related to the CINCs' employment plans.

The new emphasis was on a wider role and wider audiences for the strategy briefing. The departure of Weeks for duty as a shipboard executive officer and the subsequent assignment of Commander Peter Swartz as replacement for both Weeks and Johnson coincided with the appointment of Captain Roger Barnett as the new Branch Head in Op-603. These changes marked the beginning of the next step in conceptual development of the strategy as well as the next phase of staff work in support of the POM-86 testimony on Navy budget and programs, along with joint and allied cooperative planning efforts. The key actors this time were Barnett and Swartz.

Vice Admiral Moreau took a great personal interest in the plans for the new revision, although he himself would be transferred shortly. In all his years in the Navy, until 1982, he had not known of an American naval strategy for global warfare. He felt that the Navy had not thought through all the time-tested theories nor examined their applicability to the present. Moreau spent a great deal of time with Barnett, working directly with him on evenings and Saturdays, and also with Swartz. Moreau saw the first version of a maritime strategy briefing as a categorization of the priorities of naval tasks in global warfare. Through it, the Navy portrayed the relative importance of tasks and began to see that there was a problem in positioning the fleet during a crisis between the great alliances. "In every scenario, there is always a set of naval tasks to accomplish with competing assets," he said. "Fundamentally, naval tasks are a given, beyond that it is a question of recognizing Soviet strategy and tactics and dealing with them."[37] Captain Roger Barnett echoed the same point when he said "strategy is not a game of solitaire."[38]

For Moreau, it was important to take the conceptual underpinnings of the first version and begin the process of advancing them step-by-step, prioritizing, and then going on to examine the most probable course of action within this analysis. However, he saw there was a danger in this which could lead to an absolute vision of strategy unless the concepts were continually open to challenge.[39] Many naval staff officers believed at the time that the Maritime Strategy should not become dogma.

Moreau discussed the substance of the strategy directly with Barnett and Swartz and directed them to build upon the first version and develop an architecture on which to expand and provide depth. In essence, he felt that the strategy needed attention given to naval forces other than the carrier battle groups, to the allied navies and air forces, and to joint U.S. Army and U.S. Air Force strategy. It needed clear and in-depth connection with our understanding of Soviet naval strategy in both crises and wars. This kind of thinking carried with it the need to look carefully at Norway and its adjacent waters, the subject of the Strategic Studies Group's first analysis; the question of naval support to the central front; and the issues of the sea lines of communication in both the Atlantic and the Pacific.

As action officer for the Maritime Strategy briefing, Commander Swartz undertook his task with the strong belief that it should not be the product of some brilliant, ethereal strategic thinker, but rather the collective thought of the high command of the entire Navy. Influenced in his general approach by Rear Admiral Joseph C. Wylie's book, *Military Strategy*,[40] Swartz strived to employ Wylie's basic thesis that strategy is a form of control that is not isolated from other factors. In developing further the Weeks-Johnson statement of the strategy, he endeavored to use this concept to apply a wide variety of sources to the issue, including the global war games at the Naval War College; the thinking of the Strategic Studies Groups; the speeches of Secretary of the Navy John Lehman: NATO's war plans; and the CINCs' current concepts of operations. As he studied these various sources, he found that they were, for the most part, mutually reinforcing and reflected the "operate well forward in an offensive stance" atmosphere that seemed attractive to naval officers at that time.[41]

Working to establish a broad statement of this approach, he saw clearly that the different and separate branches of thinking within the Navy fundamentally complemented one another. Swartz saw his basic task as one that would bring these lines of thinking together in a way that would be acceptable to all interest groups within the Navy. Having become thoroughly acquainted with strategic thinking throughout the Navy, Swartz concluded that the Pacific Command Campaign Plan formulated under Admiral Robert Long as Commander in Chief, Pacific, provided the basic model to apply globally. Long's briefing to the Joint Chiefs of Staff, which had been used by Weeks and Johnson, reflected some of the earlier thinking in Hayward's Sea Strike study and was compatible with the first version of the Maritime Strategy. For Swartz, this was the "main recent antecedent" to his work as the action officer on the Maritime Strategy.[42]

Swartz wanted to co-opt as many key officers on the Navy staff as he could, reflecting many different interests and perspectives. His purpose was "to partake of their knowledge and not get knifed later" as well as "to make sure of a baseline that would last."[43] To achieve these goals, he focused on the working-level of captains and commanders rather than flag officers, trying out his ideas and modifying his approach in the summer and fall of 1983 through many informal, off-the-record "murder board" sessions. During these meetings a variety of strategically minded officers and civilians gave Swartz their constructive criticisms and helped him to refine his synthesis. Following these sessions, Swartz's briefing was widely presented, gaining clarity in its concepts and precision in its phraseology as a result of nearly every session.[44]

Between October 1983, when the first full draft briefing was given, and May 1984 when the CNO signed the final version, some seventy-five briefings had been given to audiences ranging from OpNav officers to students at the various U.S. war colleges, allied chiefs of naval staff, representatives of other services, and members of Congress.[45] Nearly every meeting had produced a nuance that led to further polishing and clarification. This very process bothered some observers. As one officer harshly wrote, "My frank view is that the Maritime Strategy brief basically reflects the lowest common denominator approach commonly developed through a committee effort. . . . My reaction to the brief—and the strategy it proposes to develop—is that we genuinely expect the Soviets to do exactly what we want them to do, and that somehow 'Right will make Might' enabling us to carry out our plans successfully despite severe undernourishment in such areas as sustainability, sea-lift, and dare I say it—strategic thought."[46] Such criticism touched on an essential aspect of the Maritime Strategy: it was a commonly held view of strategy in the process of development. As an officer in the Strategic Concepts Branch (Op-603) commented, "The Maritime Strategy has a lowest common denominator problem. But it has to be agreed upon." Moreover, the National Intelligence Estimate, which at that time was the view that all agencies within the U.S. government had agreed upon, presented the same interpretation that the Maritime Strategy presented of the Soviet Navy.[47]

FURTHER DEVELOPMENTS, 1984–1986

The distribution of *The Maritime Strategy* during the summer of 1984, as a classified document within the Navy, was a major step in the effort to educate naval officers in the various considerations involved in thinking about a future war with the Soviet Union. It opened a new series of developments for further refinement and examination of the Navy's strategic ideas. Most important, many officers were being educated in current strategic concepts. Ideas about strategy were widely exchanged, both inside and outside the Navy. Using the central focus of *The Maritime Strategy*, officers throughout the naval service were beginning to ask the essential question: What must the Navy accomplish in wartime, and how does it use its forces to achieve those ends?

Through the widespread dissemination of the basic concepts involved in *The Maritime Strategy*, a broad variety of contributions were made to its further development, while the Strategic Studies Group at Newport and the Strategic Concepts Branch in OpNav continued their work. The staffs of the various commanders in chief continued to reexamine and refine their war plans. Discussions were held with the other services and with the allied forces. New campaign concepts were examined at the Center for Naval Warfare Studies at the Naval War College, at the Center for Naval Analyses, and at other institutions. In short, there was a blossoming of maritime and naval thinking in a variety of ways and places. In the years before the collapse of the Soviet Union in 1989, these concepts became guiding thoughts as naval officers continue to develop and refine their thinking about strategy. The general trends of development between 1983 and 1987, however, were quickly reflected in the work of Op-603 and the successive Strategic Studies Groups, while an increasing number of other staffs and individuals also became involved in the process.

By August 1984, following the publications of the first Maritime Strategy booklet, a new team of officers arrived in Op-06 and determined that it was time to begin again the cycle of reflection and revision. With the booklet in hand, Admiral Watkins looked for further, more detailed development of the strategy. He directed the Strategic Studies Group to explore further insights into the peacetime uses of navies, emphasizing that the Maritime strategy was a deterrent strategy whose purpose was to help prevent war. Its effectiveness for such a task, of course, derives from the U.S. Navy's ability to be ready for war should deterrence fail and then to fight and to help win such a war.

It became obvious during discussions that some officers questioned the propriety of the CNO's role in creating a strategy. For some who served on CINC staffs, the CNO appeared to be interfering with the prerogatives of the CINC and with his chain of command to the Joint Chiefs of Staff.[48] For those who shared such views, the concepts of the CNO/SECNAV Maritime Strategy were appropriate as plausible arguments to present in the procurement process, but not as an actual, operational strategy.

The officers in the Strategic Concepts Branch of OpNav concentrated their efforts on combating that criticism and pointed out that the Maritime Strategy filled a gap in the American system of strategic planning. The CINCs' strategies reflected only regional strategies and the national strategy was not tied to the procurement planning process. The Op-603 officers worked to explain the Maritime Strategy as the fully developed maritime component of a national strategy which no CINC was in a position to develop alone, but through the CNO's position as a member of the Joint Chiefs of Staff he could serve to coordinate and reflect the broad aspects of the strategy and naval campaign options available to the various Navy CINCs. At the same time, the CNO's role in the procurement and budget process under the Secretary of the Navy allowed him to link these additional matters to planning for future operations, thus filling the missing part of the strategy process.

There had been widespread criticism of the Maritime Strategy outside the Navy, and in Congress, as one Op-603 officer remarked, "we took on some of our most ardent critics head to head."[49] Despite fears, the briefings before Senate and House committees were very successful. In the report of the House Subcommittee on Seapower and Strategic and Critical Materials, Congressman Charles E. Bennett wrote, "The subcommittee finds that the maritime strategy is, in fact, a proper naval component to national level military strategy, and that the 600-ship Navy as currently described is a reasonable and balanced approach to meeting the force structure requirements of that strategy."[50]

Throughout the work of explaining the idea of the Maritime Strategy as a strategic concept rather than just a budgetary argument, Admiral Watkins frequently became personally involved. From January to June 1985, Watkins was most actively involved with the further development and "selling" of the strategy. It was during this period that the Navy staff developed the idea to publish an unclassified article on "The Maritime Strategy." A first draft was written, but it was not until more than six months later, in January 1986, that Watkins's article appeared as a special supplement to the U.S. Naval Institute *Proceedings*.

By the end of 1986, there had been considerable discussion, not only in the *Proceedings* and in the *Naval War College Review,* but in Newspapers, magazines, and journals. Important comments were made by John J. Mearsheimer in *International Security* which were paired with an article by Captain Linton Brooks.[51] Additionally, in his *Maritime Strategy, Geopolitics and the Defense of the West,*[52] Dr. Colin S. Gray made some interesting comments about Ambassador Robert Komer's criticisms of the Maritime Strategy. As the public debate widened, it became the basis of discussion in university lecture courses, such as that offered by Professor Paul M. Kennedy at Yale, "Seapower Past and Present,"[53] and even in Tom Clancy's best-selling novel, *Red Storm Rising.*

In January 1987, President Reagan delivered to Congress a public and unclassified statement of the *National Security Strategy of the United States.* Although it swept widely across the spectrum of American strategy, a few paragraphs clearly reflected the development of the Maritime Strategy that for a decade had been the focus of effort by naval strategists. Most significantly, the report states: "Maritime superiority enables us to capitalize on Soviet geographical vulnerabilities and to pose a global threat to the Soviets' interests. It plays a key role in plans for the defense of NATO allies on the European flanks. It also permits the United States to tie down Soviet naval forces in a defensive posture protecting Soviet ballistic missile submarines and the seaward approaches to the Soviet homeland, and thereby to minimize the wartime threat to the reinforcement and resupply of Europe by sea."[54]

A careful examination of the evolution of the Maritime Strategy reveals the confluence of several streams of development. First there is the revival of classical naval thought and its modification for use in the nuclear age. Second, there is the development of a new American interpretation of Soviet naval intentions that contrasted sharply with that held in the 1960s and 1970s. Third, there is the development of institutional procedures to break down the parochialism of the various parts of the U.S. Navy and to develop a consensus. Fourth, there is the development of a means to rationalize and to coordinate procurement of new equipment. The Maritime Strategy reflects the confluence of these developments as a statement of a broad, national maritime strategy with a range of campaign options for use in the event of war with the Soviet Union. This statement is designed to be the link which unifies the Navy's procurement policy with operations and training, reflecting the war plans of the Joint Chiefs of Staff and the operational plans of their regional commanders in chief. Along with it, the Navy attempted to provide a realistic assessment of Soviet capabilities and intentions in a war with the United States.

The Maritime Strategy, as it evolved in the decade between 1977 and 1987, was an attempt to coordinate the pluralistic system of American strategic planning for the Navy. By 1987, the public and professional discussion of the issues surrounding the Maritime Strategy had taken a sophisticated form. The issues of naval strategy could be, and were, understood and debated widely. This contrasted starkly with the absence of such discussion a decade earlier and, at the same time, demonstrated a widespread revitalization of strategic thinking within the naval officer corps.

For the first time in many decades, the U.S. Navy's leaders in the 1980s had developed a concept of a national maritime strategy which, they agreed, was a reasonable basis upon which to plan and to prepare for a possible future war with the Soviet Union, the basis to work with allies, and at the same time, to serve as a deterrent to such a war.

The U.S. Navy's Maritime Strategy in the 1980s is an illustrative example of a long-term approach for a future naval war that was clearly based on intelligence information and integrated with changes in bureaucratic structures, force planning, strategical and tactical concepts, while at the same time, it was closely tied to key personalities, issues of public debate, and national politics. The practice of naval affairs in the late twentieth century can no longer be described and analyzed merely in terms of dramatic actions at sea, or simply in terms of abstract and isolated strategic concepts. As the story of naval planning in the ten years between 1977 and 1987 shows, strategic calculation must include the complex interaction of the many broad forces that have not often been previosuly accepted as part of that story.[55] What many called "the maritime strategy" was a plan that included strategic thinking, but, more precisely, it was not strategy. Rather, it was a reflection of practical naval contingency planning that, for a time, integrated the varied elements of a complex naval bureacracy. It clearly created a general approach to the most effective use of American naval forces, in the context of a range of specific naval situations that planners considered the most likely they would expect to face, had a major war with the Soviet Union occurred in the 1980s.

NOTES

This is a revised version of an essay that first appeared in *The Naval War College Review*, XLI (Summer 1988), pp. 7–28.

1. Jack Snyder, *The Ideology of the Offensive: Military Decision Making and the Disasters of 1914* (Ithaca, NY: Cornell University Press 1984), pp. 19–34; and David Alan Rosenberg, "Reality and Responsibility: Power and Process in the Making of United States Nuclear Strategy, 1945–68," *The Journal of Strategic Studies,* (March 1986), pp. 36–38.

2. A summary of the basic concepts may be found in H. E. Eccles, "Strategy—The Theory and Application," *Naval War College Review,* XXXII (May-June 1979), pp. 11–21. The key works of Herbert Rosinski and William Reitzel prepared at the Naval War College are reprinted in B. Mitchell Simpson III, ed., *War, Strategy and Maritime Power* (New Brunswick, NJ: Rutgers University Press), 1967), p. 110.

3. Eccles, p. 13.

4. J. C. Wylie, *Maritime Strategy: A General Theory of Power Control.* (New Brunswick, NJ: Rutgers University Press, 1967), p. 110.

5. Samuel P. Huntington, "The Defense Policy 1981–82," in Fred I. Greenstein, *The Reagan Presidency: An Early Assessment* (Baltimore, MD.: Johns Hopkins University Press, 1983), pp. 101. For the relationships to naval thinking in the immediate post-World War II war period, see Michael A. Palmer, *Origins of the Maritime Strategy:American Naval Strategy in the First Postwar Decade.* (Washington: GPO, 1988).

6. The bulk of this section is based on Robert B. Pirie, Jr., Director, Naval Strategy Program, Center for Naval Analyses (CNA), Memorandum for Director, Strategic and Theater Nuclear Warfare Division (Op-60). Subj: Revised "Audit Trail" on Pro-SSBN/Strategic Reserve Missions of the Soviet Navy (U). (CNA) 82–0762, 10/22, June 1983. This is a series of photocopied excerpts from earlier CNA studies gathered on the suggestion from Admiral W. Small, Jr., USN, 20 May 1982. Hereinafter, reference to the excerpts from this document will be made by citing the original document, followed by the note: "Excerpt in CNA 82–0762."
7. Excerpt from first draft of James M. McConnell, Doctrine, Missions, and Capabilities, (U) Chapter 1, in Bradford Dismukes and James M. McConnell, eds., *Soviet Naval Diplomacy*. (New York: Pergamon Press, 1979), pp. 1–49, 50. Unclassified, May 1977. Excerpt in CNA 82–0762.
8. James McConnell, "Strategy and Missions of the Soviet Navy in the Year 2000" in James L. George, ed., *Problems of Sea Power as We Approach the Twenty-first Century*. (Washington, DC: American Enterprise Institute for Public Policy Research, 1978), pp. 61–62.
9. Bradford Dismukes, *Implications of Soviet Naval Strategy* (U), CNA 77–0902, 16 June 1977.
10. Bradford Dismukes, *The War Termination Mission of the U.S. Navy: A Briefing*, CNA 80–0412.00, 31 March 1980, p. 1.
11. Letter from Captain W. H. J. Manthorpe, Jr., USN (Ret.) to Hattendorf, 31 December 1986; see Dismukes and McConnell, eds.
12. Director of Central Intelligence, *National Intelligence Estimate: Soviet Naval Strategy and Programs Through the 1990s*. NIE 11–15-82D, March 1983, p. 5. See also, RADM Tom Brooks, USN (Ret.) and CAPT Bill Manthorpe, USN (Ret.), "Setting the Record Straight: A Critical Review of Gregory Vistica's *Fall from Glory* (New York: Simon & Schuster, 1995), *Naval Intelligence Professional's Quarterly*, XII, number 2, April 1996), p. 2. I am grateful to Professor David Alan Rosenberg for providing me with copies of this review and this declassified document.
13. NIE 11–15-82D, March 1983, pp. 6–7.
14. Hattendorf interview with Admiral Thomas B. Hayward, USN, The Pentagon: 17 April 1985.
15. Ibid.
16. Thomas B. Hayward, "The Future of U.S. Sea Power," in *Naval Review*, (1979), pp. 66–71.
17. Hattendorf interview with Rear Admiral William A. Cockell, Jr., USN, San Diego, CA: 5 April 1985.
18. Ibid.
19. RADM Tom Brooks, USN (Ret.) and CAPT Bill Manthorpe, USN (Ret.), "Setting the Record Straight", p. 2.
20. For the history of this, see David A. Rosenberg, *U.S. Navy Long-Range Planning: A Historical Perspective*, Washington: Naval Research Advisory Committee, 1980). Released September 1981.
21. CNO address to Current Strategy Forum, Newport, Rhode Island, 8 April 1981.
22. Ibid.
23. Captain R. Leeds, USN, conversation with Hattendorf, August 1986.
24. Robert J. Murray letter to Admiral William N. Small, USN, 1 September 1983.

25. Ibid.
26. *The Maritime Strategy*. (U). Opnav 60 P-1–84. Distributed under CNO letter 00–45300236 dated 4 May 1984.
27. Office files of the action officer for the Maritime Strategy, Strategic Concepts Group (Op-603). The Pentagon, Room 4E486 (Hereinafter, Op-603 Files). VCNO Memo N-1241 dated 18 December 1981 to Director, Navy Program Planning, Subj: Program Appraisals and Analysis.
28. Interview with Admiral William M. Small, USN, Commander in Chief, Allied Forces Southern Europe, in Naples, Italy: 11 April 1985.
29. Op-603 Files. VCNO Memo N-1241 of 18 December 1981.
30. Ibid.
31. Op-603 Files: VCNO memo ser 09/300636, 2 August 1982. Memo for Director, Navy Program Planning (Op-090); director, Office of Naval Warfare (Op-095); DCNO (Manpower, Personnel and Training)/Chief of Naval Personnel (Op-01); DCNO (Plans, Policy and Operation (Op-06); Subj: POM-85 CPAM/Warfare Appraisals.
32. Interview with Commander Stanley B. Weeks, USN: 12 December 1985 and letter from Captain W. Spencer Johnson, USN to Hattendorf, 5 September 1985. See also Spencer Johnson's comments in James Goldrick and Hattendorf, eds, *Mahan is Not Enough:The Proceedings of a Conference on the Works of Sir Julian Corbett and Admiral Sir Herbert Richmond.* (Newport, RI: Naval War College Press, 1993), pp. 202–204.
33. Interview with Commander Weeks: 12 December 1985; Commander Weeks's Briefing script B06249–05G:MH, 3 September 1982.
34. CNO Message 071841Z October 82, Personal for Admirals Crowe, Williams, Foley, McDonald, Vice Admiral Hays, Info: Vice Admiral Carroll; Rear Admirals Shugart, Palmer, Horne, Dillingham, from Watkins.
35. Interview with Admiral James Watkins, USN: 12 December 1985.
36. A Report by Admiral James D. Watkins, USN, Chief of Naval Operations on the "Posture of the U.S. Navy for the Fiscal Year 1984," in Department of the Navy, *Fiscal Year 1984 Report to Congress* (Alexandria, VA: Naval Internal Relations Activity, 1984), pp. 15-31.
37. Interview with Vice Admiral Arthur Moreau, USN: 18 April 1985.
38. Interview with Captain Roger Barnett, USN, (Ret.): 17 January 1985. See also, Captain Roger Barnett, USN (Ret.), "The Origin of the U.S. Maritime Strategy," Parts I and II, *Naval Forces.* vol. X, no. 4, pp. 52–57; vol. X, no. 5, pp. 58–62.
39. Interview with Vice Admiral Moreau, USN, Op-603 Files. Critique of POM-85 CPAM.
40. See Wylie.
41. Interview with Captain Peter Swartz, USN: 25 March 1985.
42. Ibid.
43. Ibid.
44. Ibid.
45. Op-603 Files. "The Maritime Strategy Development/Presentation/Publication Schedule," B08447: 061:HCB. Op-60317. September 1984.
46. Op-603 Files. Commander Bruce Valley, USN, CSIS Navy Fellow at Georgetown Univ. to Commander Peter Swartz, USN, 4 April 1984.
47. Op-603 Files. Commander J. R. Stark, Comments on Valley's Critique. Op-603J. B10282: 05J: bms of 1 May 1984.

48. Captain Peter Rice comments on draft, January 1988; Hattendorf interview with CINCPAC Staff: 23 April 1985.
49. Letter from Commander T. Wood Parker, USN to Hattendorf, 14 August 1986.
50. Bennett to Aspin, 18 November 1985. Letter of transmittal in U.S. House of Representatives, 99th Congress, 1st Session, Committee Print No. 11. *600-ship Navy: Report of the Sea Power and Strategic and Critical Materials Subcommittee of the Committee on Armed Services,* p. iii.
51. John J. Mearsheimer, "A Strategic Misstep: The Maritime Strategy and Deterrence in Europe," *International Security,* 11 (Fall 1986), pp. 3–7; and Linton F. Brooks, "Naval Power and National Security: The Case for the Maritime Strategy," in Ibid., pp. 58–88. A detailed listing of the literature involved in this discussion may be found in Peter M. Swartz, *The Maritime Strategy Debates: A Guide to the Renaissance of U.S. Naval Strategy Thinking in the 1980s.* Report Prepared for the Strategic Concepts Branch (Op-603), Office of the Chief of Naval Operations. (Monterey, CA: Naval Postgraduate School, 24 February 1988). NPS-56–88-009. This updated three earlier listings, published in the U.S. Naval Institute *Proceedings* in 1986 and 1987. Further references and insights may be found in John Lehman, *Command of the Sea.* (New York: Scribners, 1988) and Frederick H. Hartmann, *Naval Renaissance: The U.S. Navy in the 1980s.* (Annapolis, MD: Naval Institute Press, 1990).
52. Published by National Strategy Information Center, New York, 1986.
53. Professor Kennedy's lecture series ran from September to December 1986, and included guest speakers whose subjects ranged from ancient history to the examples of failed sea powers, Germany, Japan, and Italy in World War II. It concluded with lectures by Michael MccGwire on current Soviet seapower, and John Mearsheimer and Secretary Lehman on the Maritime Strategy. Selected papers were published in *The International History Review,* (February 1988).
54. The White House, *National Security Strategy of the United States,* January 1987, pp. 29–30.
55. See David Alan Rosenberg, "Process; The Realties of Forming Modern Naval Strategy" in Goldrick and Hattendorf, eds., *Mahan is Not Enough,* pp. 141–175; Jon Tetsuro Sumida and David Alan Rosenberg, "Machines, Men, Manufacturing, Management, and Money: The Study of Navies as Complex Organizations and the Transformation of Twentieth Century Naval History," in Hattendorf, ed., *Doing Naval History.* (Newport, RI: Naval War College Press, 1995).

13

What is a Maritime Strategy?

What is a maritime strategy? The question is a simple and direct one, but the answers are complex. To add to the complexity on this occasion, we are looking at history to enlighten us on some current issues in defense strategy. First, we must remind ourselves something about the basic problems of studying maritime strategy in history and along with them we must know about the actual practice of maritime strategy in the past. Second, we should think about the history of maritime strategic thought and the way it has changed and developed. Finally, with those basic thoughts in mind, one can say something about the way in which we currently understand maritime strategy.

MARITIME STRATEGY IN HISTORY

History has much to tell us about maritime strategy; indeed, some of the most important works on the subject of maritime strategy are analyses of history. The study of history certainly broadens our perspective and gives us deeper insight into the reasons why we have become what we have become. To study strategy in history, one must be alert to different times, different outlooks, different ideas, different problems, different mind-sets, different capabilities, different decision-making structures, and different technologies. All of these dissimilarities show us that the past is often not a precise model to follow in the present or in the future. Despite the contrasts, however, one can perceive some broad, recurring characteristics, issues, and problems that arise for maritime strategists in the range of action and roles that they consider. From these, one can outline a broad concept of maritime strategy, but such a concept is highly influenced, if not entirely determined, by the historical examples from which it is derived.

One's own national history and experience in maritime strategy can help to identify continuing national interests and priorities, but

over time, there are changes in the structure of international relations and changes in the role that a particular nation plays within
that structure. Thus, in order to understand the full range of problems in maritime strategy, one's own historical experience needs to be
supplemented by an understanding of other nations' experiences, in
various time periods and in differing situations. Let me try to clarify
this point in the context of twentieth-century maritime strategies.

TWENTIETH-CENTURY MARITIME
STRATEGIES

Over the past century, a variety of maritime strategies have been
at work. Most recently, in the regional crises in the Adriatic, in the
Gulf War, and in the blockade off Haiti, as well as in both the Vietnam and Korean Wars, maritime nations concentrated on using the
sea for their own purposes. They supported and carried out military
actions while also imposing blockades against enemy shipping, without having to devote their full energies to countering a concerted enemy attempt to seize control of the sea for its own uses. Thus, the
maritime strategy of these more recent wars are different from the
two World Wars as well as different from the maritime strategies of
the Cold War.

In the Cold War, the NATO and the Warsaw Pact nations developed opposing maritime strategies centered around two superpower
navies, both armed with submarines carrying nuclear missiles,
while many small- and medium-sized countries tailored their maritime contributions to fit broad alliance strategies through specialized functions such as mine-sweeping, air defense, or antisubmarine
warfare.

By contrast, during the Second World War, the Allied nations faced
the Axis powers, who posed a very serious threat as they sought to
dominate large portions of the Mediterranean, the Atlantic, and the
Pacific. Allied maritime strategy was characterized by the struggle
to oppose the nearly successful strategy of the Axis U-boats against
vital merchant shipping in the Atlantic, by the great island-hopping
amphibious campaigns in the Southwest and Central Pacific, as well
as by the carrier-to-carrier air battles in mid-ocean and by coordinated surface, air, and submarine actions.

In both the First and the Second World Wars, the Allies shared
similar maritime strategies that required providing critical logistical support for armies by carrying vast amounts of men and materiel
from one continent to another through contested waters. Similarly,

the Allies enforced long and tedious economic blockades in the face of determined opposition at sea.

More prominent in the popular memory of the First World War, the naval battle of Jutland brought back memories of the great sea battles of the seventeenth and eighteenth centuries. While naval officers of the day saw the connections to a great naval tradition, many others had expected a different kind of war from that which had emerged in 1914. They had incorrectly predicted that their immediate future would hold no world-engulfing war, but rather the confined crises and limited warfare that they had seen in the Spanish-American War in 1898, the Anglo-Boer War of 1899–1902, or the Russo-Japanese War of 1904–1905. All of these wars required major navies to move men and equipment great distances and to fight or support wars for limited objectives and to deal with crises in distant waters.

Such thoughts seem to resonate with current American thinking. Perhaps, the experience and ideas of that time contain some valuable maritime lessons and insights for the major naval powers in the present and the future.[1] Today, we all share an interest in the general problems of limited wars and regional crises. We also share an interest with another set of problems that maritime nations faced in both sets of peacetime years, 1898–1914 and 1919–1939: The challenge of developing adequate naval forces and maintaining them while costs rise, technology changes rapidly, and international law increasingly imposes restraint on the use of force. Here, the identification, selection, and development of new technology is interwoven with complex issues of national finance, bureaucratic decision making, personalities, and legislative politics.[2]

Despite such similarities, we must also remember the differences. The period leading up to World War One was quite different from ours. It was a world of imperial rivalry and colonial expansion, a time of rising military and naval budgets, and a period in which regional tensions in Europe had immediate and worldwide impact. The period leading up to the Second World War, a time of unresolved issues left from the First War, was equally different from ours.

In searching for provocative ideas, studies of the maritime experience of Great Britain in the years between 1815 to 1851 might, for the moment, be more useful to American naval thinking today, while America's own experience in the period after 1815 might even be useful to some countries today.

In the decades following the long and exhausting Napoleonic wars, nearly all nations reduced their armaments. Among them,

Great Britain retained a relatively large navy, although it was, in fact, drastically reduced from what it had been. In this period, there was a tendency to deal with conflict through collective security and various national navies found themselves operating in multilateral actions.

However instructive this period can be, one can not press the parallels too far. The Congress system for collective security and the multilateral naval actions of the period, such as those at Navarino in 1827, at Acre in 1840, and even the Black Sea operations in the Crimean War at mid-century, were far less sophisticated than the approaches available today.

We can deepen our understanding of the problems involved in multilateral naval operations by studying these events, but the experience of the twentieth century has already shown us that the additional technical aspects of logistics, communications, command and control as well as detailed planning and standardized procedures are central to success in modern multilateral operations. The failure of the Australian-British-Dutch-American (ABDA) squadron in the Java Sea in 1942 provided a salutary lesson that was not lost on the survivors. By 1943–44, the Allied landings in North Africa and in Italy were remarkable feats of international and inter-service cooperation. With further insights from the experience of the war in the Pacific, only the success at Normandy in June 1944 surpassed these achievements. After months of detailed planning, British and American admirals commanded a fleet that included not only vessels of the Royal Navy, the U.S. Navy, and Commonwealth navies, but also Polish, Norwegian, and Free French ships.

In spite of these remarkable successes, some naval leaders in the postwar period were naturally doubtful about the prospects for peacetime, multilateral naval cooperation. Much of the doubt came from ingrained habits of thought, not from a dispassionate examination of historical experience. The major stumbling block came from the fact that navies are nearly always thought of in national terms. We all tell our citizens and our sailors that the Navy represents the nation. Everything about navies are organized in national terms. We have fought on the decks of our ships for our own nation. For this, we fly our national flag and our ships often carry evocative national names: the names of heroes, battles, symbols, or places that link our ships and sailors to our national heritage. Sometimes it can seem improper, even sacrilegious, to think of our Navy operating in another context.

In the mid-1960s, when some naval officers in NATO first suggested the idea of the Standing Naval Force, Atlantic, senior NATO leaders were extremely skeptical that it could succeed. Yet, thirty years later, STANAVFORLANT or SNFL as it is alternatively known, has shown itself to be a model multilateral force, with command rotating among all national participants, each on an equal footing with ships and shipmates from other countries; the smaller countries' contributions not being dominated by the larger. Over the years, within the context of NATO, the Standing Naval Force has developed common naval tactics, publications, communications equipment, and procedures while working toward greater standardization in logistics and repair parts. While the Standing Naval Force went on to see its first combat action in the Adriatic, NATO maritime procedures also became models for maritime operations in the Persian Gulf and off Haiti. These wider experiences in the early 1990s showed that multilateral naval operations could effectively take place outside a strongly structured alliance through the use of the United Nations, regional organizations and even ad hoc arrangements.

As defense budgets decline and navies grow smaller, the range of their responsibilities remain unchanged and may even grow. One effective way of dealing with these facts is to develop multinational maritime strategies. In 1995, to meet requests from many parts of the world, the U.S. Naval Doctrine Command distributed a draft manual to facilitate multilateral naval operations for this purpose in various parts of the world.

The experiences of the twentieth century clearly show that there is no one maritime strategy that is valid for all situations. Maritime strategy changes with the context, structure, purposes, technologies, and equipment available. Our abstract understanding of maritime strategy has also changed. As we examine strategy in history, particularly for the twentieth century, one needs to be aware of these changes and know that the theory of maritime strategy has been evolving over time, even if the actors in history may or may not be aware of the changes.

THE DEVELOPMENT OF MARITIME
STRATEGIC THOUGHT

Nations have practiced maritime strategy for centuries, but historians, political scientists, and theoreticians have only examined it analytically for a relatively short period of time. It was only a century ago that Alfred Thayer Mahan pointed out the role of sea power in wartime national policy,[3] and it has only been eighty-five years since Sir Julian Corbett first provided a more complete theoretical statement of the principles for establishing control of the sea in wartime.[4] During the period of the naval wars in the age of sail, few people looked at any kind of strategy as a separate concept or area of practice; together, admirals and statesmen practiced the craft of maritime strategy as if it were part of one great continuum, rarely putting the reasons for their actions on paper.

Although some historians have objected that leaders in this period did not think strategically, but certainly, we can counter that point by showing that they acted strategically. At the very end of the period of naval wars under sail, only a very few people, men such as Karl von Clausewitz and Henri Jomini, were just beginning to think more abstractly about military strategy[5]—although not maritime strategy. Sailors continued to practice the craft of maritime strategy pragmatically until the last quarter of the nineteenth century without worrying about this subject. Both seamen and statesmen knew from long practice the characteristics and capabilities of their ships and men; with that knowledge, they could easily calculate a maritime strategy.

In the 1870s and 1880s, something happened in navies. Suddenly, the maritime world seemed different. Over the previous half century, ships, weapons, and propulsion systems had changed. These innovations changed the capabilities and characteristics of ships so dramatically that people began to think that the old ways of practice had no relevance at all. Soon people saw that maritime technology had not just changed once, but was changing continually.

The maritime world of the late nineteenth century was at the beginning of the phenomenon of technological change that we have come to experience every day. As people came to grips with this phenomenon, many argued that the best choice was to run with the change, go wholeheartedly for the new technology and the new capabilities. The reactionaries, of course, dreamed of a return to the old days and dug in their heels to resist change of any kind. Pragmatic naval officers, however, began to struggle with the same issues that we deal with today, asking the pertinent questions: Do we really need the new equipment? What new and essential capabilities will it give us? How much will it cost? How much is enough?

To provide a firm basis to answer this range of questions, some insightful naval men began to ask a series of even deeper questions: What are the functions of a navy? What are the requirements for maritime power? What is the relationship between a navy and other aspects of national power?

The pioneer thinkers in this area, men such as Sir John Knox Laughton, Vice-Admiral Sir Philip Colomb, and Sir Julian Corbett in Britain with Rear Admiral Stephen B. Luce and Captain Alfred Thayer Mahan in the United States, turned to two areas of established thought to begin to work out their answers: military theory and historical study. This effort paralleled the spread of ideas and procedures used by the German General Staff in developing war plans and training staff officers to prepare them and to advise senior military commanders. This was the foundation of modern maritime strategic theory.

Initially, maritime strategic theory focused largely on the role of the navy in wartime. In the first stages, several of the pioneer writers turned to the historical example of the Anglo-French naval wars in the years 1660–1815, seeing in that period some parallels to the imperial rivalry and great power clashes in that period with those of the late nineteenth century.

Since that time, both the practice and the theory of naval and maritime strategy has progressed, widening perceptions. Today, there is a much larger theoretical understanding that builds, expands, and modifies these earlier ideas for wartime strategy. New technologies, new situations and new experiences brought wider practice, and stimulated further development of theory. The Second World War, for example, brought home the need for the navy, and for all the separate armed services, to work together more closely. Among theorists, Rear Admiral J. C. Wylie was the first to attempt to integrate the main, service-oriented theories into a general theory of power control.[6] Additionally, the Cold War stimulated extensive thinking about the uses of military power for deterrence, in particular, and a navy's diplomatic and persuasive uses in peacetime. These broadened perspectives have extended the foundations of theory for modern and peacetime, maritime strategies.[7]

What, then, is our understanding of maritime strategy today?

MODERN MARITIME STRATEGY

Both our experience of practicing maritime strategy and our historical examination of other maritime strategies during the last hundred years show that maritime strategy is a kind of subset of national grand strategy that touches on the whole range of a nation's activities and interests at sea. In its broadest sense, grand strategy is the comprehensive direction of power to achieve particular national goals. Within those terms, maritime strategy is the direction of all aspects of national power that relate to a nation's interests at sea. The Navy serves this purpose, but maritime strategy is not purely a naval preserve. Maritime strategy involves the other functions of state power that include diplomacy, the safety and defense of merchant trade at sea, fishing, the exploitation, conservation, regulation and defense of the exclusive economic zone at sea, coastal defense, security of national borders, the protection of offshore islands as well as participation in regional and worldwide concerns relating to the use of oceans, the skies over the oceans and the land under the seas. Such issues include expanding the scientific and technological understanding of the entire maritime environment, working with the full range of national organizations, (the navy, the army, the air force, customs, coast guard, commerce and trade, to name but a few of the ministries, bureaus, and departments that touch on these issues) in order to bring forth a truly national concept and plan for the maritime aspects of national life.

The fundamental focus of the military element in maritime strategy centers on the control of human activity at sea through the use of armed force in order to contribute to the broad ends established in a national maritime policy. The are two parts to this: (1) establishing control and (2) using control, once it has been established.

In the effort to establish control and, along with it, to deny control to an enemy, there are gradations that range from an abstract ideal to that which is practical, possible, or merely desirable. In this, one can consider whether control is to be general or limited, absolute or merely governing, widespread or local, permanent or temporary.

Following the establishment of control is the use of the control in order to achieve specific ends. The effort to achieve control, by itself, means nothing unless that control has an effect. In the wide spectrum of activity that this can involve, the most important aspect is the use of maritime control to influence, and, ultimately, to assist in controlling events on land. In this, the fundamental key is to have an effect on those places, times, or routes of travel to which an adversary is sensitive, and which are critical and essential enough to move an adversary to alter plans or actions so as to accommodate one's own objectives.

The fundamental characteristics of these two, broad elements of maritime strategy stress the sequential and cumulative relationship between them. One needs to obtain some degree of control at sea before being able to use it to obtain the important ends that one seeks. This sequential nature does not exclude the possibility of simultaneously pursuing these objects, but whatever the nature of the relative and temporal control that is achieved, it affects the nature of the result that is attained.

In many past wars, fighting decisive battles between great opposing fleets or blockading an enemy battle fleet in port to prevent it from getting to sea were the two principal means by which one nation prevented an enemy from establishing maritime control or from interfering with one's own use of the sea. In these ways, one navy could remove another as a threat. Today, there are additional mean to achieve these wartime objects: submarine attack, missiles, mines, and air attack.

In examining the role of navies in maritime strategy, many people tend to over-emphasize the effort to achieve control, focussing particularly on battles, and to ignore the less glamorous, but far more important, ways in which maritime forces use the control they obtain. After obtaining some degree of control in wartime, the most important wartime functions of naval forces are as follows:[8]

- Protecting and facilitating one's own and allied merchant shipping and military supplies at sea.
- Maintaining safe passage for shipping through restricted waters and access to ports and harbours.
- Denying commercial shipping to an enemy.
- Protecting the coast and offshore resources.
- Acquiring advanced bases.
- Moving and supporting troops and advanced bases.
- Gaining and maintaining local air and sea control in support of air and land operations.

From a narrow perspective, all of these seem to describe a navy operating in its own unique element—the sea—using its specialized skills and equipment in a special way. But, in a wider understanding, all of these functions are closely related to other aspects of national power. In many cases, they are also parallel and complementary to the wartime functions of the other armed services.

Maritime strategy prescribes a wide variety of other considerations for navies in peacetime, in naval operations short of open warfare, and in the non-war functions of naval power that continue even during wartime. One theorist, Ken Booth, has placed these under three general categories:[9]

1. the diplomatic role;
2. the policing role;
3. the military role.

The military capacity of a navy to use force in the event of war is the foundation upon which the diplomatic and the policing role rest. However, there are additional features of the military role in peacetime. These include both nuclear and conventional deterrence to prevent war. The military role also includes development of the necessary and basic shore facilities and procedures that are prudent to develop in peacetime, in case war should break out. Additionally, the military role involves protecting the lives, the property, and the interests of one's national citizens on the high seas, in distant waters, and on offshore possessions in time of natural disaster. Most important for all of us in the coming century, the military role includes compliance with and active assertion of the international law of the sea regime.

Based on its military capability, navies have a *policing function* within a maritime strategy. A large country, with wide geographical scope and responsibility in this function, might choose to centralize these functions and assign them to a separate and specialized coast guard service. Other states, by tradition or for other reasons, may choose to share these activities among several governmental agencies. Since the policing role involves military force, it is logically a naval role. Nevertheless, it is one that involves a whole range of civil responsibilities which extend it to a different realm, often involving specialized procedures and legal knowledge. This can be one reason for exercising such a naval role through agencies other than the Navy, itself. Conversely, in a period of extended peace and international stability, when legislatures will not provide for a war fleet, the agency that exercises the policing role is the one through which wartime capabilities and seagoing experience can be preserved in a contingency force while, at the same time, performing an important naval task.

In another role related to the policing function in a maritime strategy, navies can contribute to internal stability and development. This type of peaceful use of naval force is limited by geography for most countries, but can be considerable in nations made up of island groups. In case of emergencies, navies can, sometimes more readily than other agencies, supply electrical power, provide hospital facilities, and transport heavy equipment to communities on islands, along navigable rivers, and in distant coastal regions where other types of transportation are limited. In addition to ship-visits, the presence of naval shore facilities and active bases in distant areas serve as symbols of a nation for the peoples of those regions, contributing to local solidarity as well as to the local economy.

The third peacetime role for navies within a maritime strategy is the *diplomatic and international role*. In this role, navies can play an important part to reassure and to strengthen bilateral alliances, regional and worldwide international organizations through mutually supportive cooperation. From a position of moderate naval strength, nations can in this way contribute to international stability and maintain a nation's presence and prestige on the international stage, while at the same time cooperating with others to achieve collective security. Building upon the natural links and mutual experience that bind professional seamen of all nations together, naval men and women can create ties between navies, even though they serve under different flags. Through such ties—nurtured through personnel exchanges, language, and cultural training as well as operational exercises—navies can help to reduce tensions and avoid misunderstandings.

Unlike other types of military forces, navies offer a quality that is not apparent in an army, an air force, or a marine assault force. While soldiers and warplanes always appear to be menacing, ships and seamen can appear in ports around the world in ways that easily allow them to be ambassadors and diplomats—or even benign helpers in times of catastrophe.[10] The traditional and fundamental relationship of navies to national economies, through the international freedom of the seas and its common heritage, gives maritime forces a unique character that distinguishes them from other types of forces. Traditionally, navies have found their capabilities and functions derive from two complementary, but quite different spheres of tradition, one civil and one military, providing important resources for contributing to maritime strategies in both peace and war.

In conclusion, one must underscore the point that a maritime strategy involves much more than a navy. Although the terms "naval" and "maritime" are not synonymous, navies are very clearly an integral part of the maritime world. Within it, their work is linked in two directions. On the one hand, the Navy is linked to the full range of activities in national defense; on the other, it is tied to the entire spectrum of civil activities relating to the sea. A maritime strategy is the comprehensive direction of all aspects of national power to achieve policy goals by exercising some degree and some type of control at sea. In understanding the general concepts underlying maritime strategy, there are no absolute dicta, only a constantly evolving theory that is ever in need of modification and correction through our understanding of maritime history, our changing experiences and challenges, and our own reflective analysis on history in the light of those experiences.

NOTES

This was the keynote address at the Royal Australian Navy's 1996 Naval History Seminar, held in Canberra, 20 August 1996. It was first published in David Stevens, ed., *In Search of a Maritime Strategy: The Maritime Element in Australian Defence Planning Since 1901.* Canberra Papers on Strategy and Defence, no. 119. (Canberra: Strategic and Defence Studies Centre, The Australian National University, 1997), pp. 5–18.

1. See for example, Sir Julian S. Corbett, *Maritime Strategy in the Russo-Japanese War, 1904–1905.* Introduction by John B. Hattendorf and Donald M. Schurman. (Annapolis, MD: Naval Institute Press, 1995), volume 1, p. 41.
2. See Jon T. Sumida, *In Defence of Naval Supremacy: Finance, Technology, and British Naval Policy, 1889–1914.* (Boston: Unwin and Hyman, 1989).
3. A. T. Mahan, *The Influence of Sea Power Upon History, 1660–1783.* (Boston: Little Brown, 1890). His related ideas on naval strategy are summarized in John B. Hattendorf. ed., *Mahan on Naval Strategy.* Classics of Sea Power series. (Annapolis, MD: Naval Institute Press, 1991).
4. A. T. Mahan, *The Influence of Sea Power Upon History, 1660–1783.* (Boston: Little, Brown, 1890). His related ideas on naval strategy are summarized in John B. Hattendorf. ed., *Mahan on Naval Strategy.* Classics of Sea Power series. (Annapolis, MD: Naval Institute Press, 1991).
5. See Azar Gat, *The Origins of Military Thought: From the Enlightenment to Clausewitz.* (Oxford: Oxford University Press, 1989).
6. J. C. Wylie, *Military Strategy: A General Theory of Power Control.* Classics of Sea Power Series, with an introduction by John B. Hattendorf and an postscript by J. C. Wylie. (Annapolis, MD: Naval Institute Press, 1989).
7. See the more detailed outline of these and the following developments in John B. Hattendorf and Robert S. Jordan, eds., *Maritime Strategy and the Balance of Power: Britain and America in the 20th Century.* (London: Macmillan, 1989), Part II: Theory.
8. Frank Uhlig, Jr., *How Navies Fight, 1775–1991.* (Annapolis, MD: Naval Institute Press, 1994), summary of chart on pp. 416–417.
9. Ken Booth, *Navies and Foreign Policy.* (London: Croom Helm, 1977).
10. J. C. Wylie, "Mahan: Then and Now," in John B. Hattendorf. ed., *The Influence of History on Mahan.* (Newport, RI: Naval War College Press, 1991), p. 41.

14

Naval Doctrine

Navies have never been entirely happy with the idea of doctrine. For many a sailor, it reeks too much of the land and of rigid ideas. In recent years, to make the problem even more difficult, observers have too often interpreted doctrine as a political statement or, alternatively at the opposite end of the scale, as a hard and fast directive that must always be obeyed in every circumstance. While these definitions may be appropriate in other contexts, there is such a thing as naval doctrine. It is an important topic, and one that has become increasingly important as the different branches of the armed services work closely together in joint operations and different navies work more closely together with one another in combined operations. There are, in fact, different levels of doctrine, ranging from the political and the strategic to the operational and the tactical. Although the two ends of the spectrum are related, they should not be confused with one another. In this brief chapter, the subject is operational and tactical doctrine.

At the operational and tactical level, naval doctrine is a general statement of procedures. This becomes clearer and more useful when we see that it arises most dominantly from the principles of seamanship and not the principles of war. Seamanship includes everything that one must know in order to handle ships safely at sea. It is a learned body of knowledge that involves application of all sorts of specific, practical skills, but it is not a rigid set of rules. Seamanship is filled with standard routines and procedures that require careful and scrupulous attention to detail, but, more important, it is an art that demands the ability to be alert to changing conditions at sea and requires readiness to cope with unexpected emergencies. The characteristics of a good seaman are initiative, foresight, reliability, and the ability to improvise with superior judgment in dealing with the unpredictable. "Because the sea is neither predictable nor tolerant of human mistakes," one writer has succinctly explained to a literary audience, "the practice of seamanship is often complex, demanding imagination and discrimination more than adherence to fixed rules of procedure."[1]

Both seamanship and naval doctrine contain rules and procedures, but they are rules that merely provide for the routine. They let other seaman know what to expect and what to do at the opportune time, without having to wait to be told at every move in the pattern. They establish a normal way of thinking and an approach that is both a standard and a necessary basis for seaman to work together efficiently in their unpredictable environment. Yet, there is a dividing line between good discipline in following the rules and superior judgment in meeting a crisis. There is always a place and an appropriate time for a seaman to put the telescope to a blind eye, ignoring the standard signal, using imagination and initiative to meet an unusual challenge effectively.

✓ NAVAL DOCTRINE IN HISTORY

There is a long history to the evolution of tactical and operational naval doctrine. In the age of sail, we see it in the early stages in the Baltic with operations of ships of the Hanseatic League,[2] followed by the development of the line of battle in the mid-seventeenth century Anglo-Dutch Wars and the Royal Navy's inseparable *Sailing and Fighting Instructions*.[3] Simultaneously, there is a long and parallel history in the French Navy. This is one of practice by admirals in the various battle fleets. Only later and occasionally can one find theoretical studies reflecting these changes, new approaches, and new ideas for consideration. Here the great writers are Père Paul Hoste,[4] Grenier,[5] Ramatuelle,[6] and John Clerk of Eldin.[7]

As steam supplanted sail, some of the old ideas of tactics were incorporated, but the freedom of maneuverability that steam power allowed gave rise to a whole range of new ideas. There was a fundamental feeling that a new approach was necessary. Some naval officers turned to ancient history for inspiration, and led ship designers of some late nineteenth-century warships to fit rams, following the classical examples of the ancient galley warfare. As the work of naval officers came to recognized as a profession in the second half of the nineteenth-century, a range of professional literature arose. In this new field, tactics was a popular theme and some of the influential and leading authors here were General Sir Howard Douglas,[8] Commodore Foxhall Parker of the U.S. Navy,[9] Admiral Bouët-Willaumez,[10] and Edward Freemantle.[11]

While the leading naval powers in Europe were following their own course, American naval officers observing the scene found the developments unsatisfactory for their own uses.[12] As Rear Admiral Stephen B. Luce, the President of the U.S. Naval War College, noted in 1885, "The conclusion forced upon is inevitable—that we must begin *de novo* and build up this science for ourselves."[13] It was this conclusion that led Luce to establish at Newport, along side the broader historical work of A. T. Mahan, the use of naval war-gaming as tool to achieve this end. Here, the key man in the American Navy was Lieutenant William McCarty Little, who guided this development for nearly thirty years.

The situation for the United States Navy had been different from that of the major naval powers. In the late nineteenth-century, there was no tradition of using battle fleets. In the sailing ship era, its most memorable sea actions were the single-ship, frigate actions of the War of 1812 period. Even in the Civil War, when the new age of steam had already dawned, interest focused largely on the cruise of the Confederate raider *Alabama* and the action between the two iron clads, *Monitor* and *Merrimack*.

It was only in 1873, at the time of the *Virginius* crisis, that the U.S. Navy first attempted to mobilize quickly and to operate together as a squadron in combined operations. The American Navy's failure to effectively do this, in response to Spain's execution of the crew of a vessel running arms to insurgents in Cuba, was not only an embarrassment that showed that the Navy was unprepared, but it was a spur that led to improvement. The incident drove home the fact that the U.S. Navy had no effective means to communicate or to exercise command and control with a squadron of ships, raising serious questions about tactics, the roles of ship types and war readiness that occupied naval officers for two decades to come.

The first notable step forward for the U.S Navy came in August 1884 with the Atlantic Fleet's first attempt to exercise a "squadron of evolution" in order to teach the practical aspects of seamanship and tactics in squadron maneuvers, the different roles of ship types in conjunction with amphibious landings. This was followed in November 1887, with the second major fleet exercise in the U.S. Navy's history.

In the 1890s, these trends to develop fleet exercises continues and were merged with other aspects of the U.S. Naval War College's work. On the one hand, naval war gaming continued to be used while new elements were added, adapting military ideas from German experience and applying those approaches to naval opera-

tions.[14] This brought with it the concepts of staff planning, the interrelationships of logistics with operations, and the development of
contingency war plans. It was at this point, exactly one hundred
years ago in June through September 1894, that the first European
officers came to the United States to participate in these early developments at the Naval War College. They were, of course, from
Sweden: Carl-Gustaf Flach and Gösta af Ugglas, who made a contribution to this work in America and brought home additional new
ideas for the Swedish Navy.[15]

The ideas that were developing at the turn of the century in the
United States Navy took many years to gestate and to become accepted widely within the service. By 1915, they were only just being
fully appreciated when Lieutenant Commander Dudley W. Knox
wrote his important essay on "The Rôle of Doctrine in Naval Warfare."[16] Knox's argument was important:

> before the ships are ready to go into action, no matter how efficient indi-
> vidually, they must be welded into a body, whose various members can be
> well controlled from a single source and can act collectively as a unit free
> from embarrassing internal friction.[17]

Knox brushed over the point that effective seamanship is the pre-
requisite upon which naval doctrine can be developed, but it is clear
that without first establishing the fundamental means of joining
ships together in operation, one can go no further to develop it. He
touched on a related point, however, when he clearly argued that the
principles of war are very different from doctrine. The object of doctrine, he wrote, is

> to furnish a basis for prompt and harmonious conduct by subordinate
> commanders of a large military force, in accordance with the intentions of
> the commander-in-chief, but without the necessity of referring each deci-
> sion to superior authority before action is required. . . . The object is to pro-
> vide a foundation for mutual understanding. . . .[18]

In this sense, then, the meaning of doctrine is that it provides a practical basis for coordination in the difficult conditions of warfare, providing the basis for harmonized methods, rules and actions. Interestingly, Knox's essay on the subject of naval doctrine appeared in
the same year that Congress established the office of the chief of
naval operations, thereby creating a staff system for the Navy.

In the years that followed, the U.S. Navy continued to develop its
ideas along these lines, culminating in 1942 with the most detailed

statement of this tradition: *Sound Military Decision.*[19] This manual
expressed the fundamental thought patterns of American naval officers up through the end of World War II. Derived from the German
military concepts of "Estimate of the Situation" and the "Formulation of Orders" that had been introduced to the U.S. Navy in 1910,
Sound Military Decision—or "The Green Hornet" as it was popularly
known among fleet staff officers—avoided stressing the principles of
war. Instead, it provided an outline for a logical thought process for
a naval commander to arrive at a sound decision that could be translated into successful action. The idea behind the manual was to focus the mind in a way that allowed a commander to consider all factors in a complex situation, mentally "war-gaming" each move one
might take against enemy capabilities and considering alternative
courses of action for carrying out a mission.

Closely tied to this was the establishment of the "order form," pre-
scribing standardized operation orders that grouped tasks at various
levels of command and allowed subordinate commanders appropriate levels of initiative and freedom of action.

Much of this fundamental thinking remains at the heart of modern American naval operational thinking, but there has been one
fundamental change to this. By the end of World War II, there was a
split in opinion among naval officers regarding the utility of *Sound
Military Decision.* Although nearly every one of the successful staff
officers resounded their praise for the manual, some of the senior
commanders disagreed. Most prominent among them, Admiral Raymond Spruance, thought the book far too complicated and too dense
for practical use, insisting instead upon a short summary of ideas. In
1948, Spruance's *Naval Manual of Operational Planning*[20] super-
seded *Sound Military Decision.* By 1953, this new manual became,
with minor changes, the standard Naval Warfare Publication for
naval warfare, *NWP-11,* and was revised six times up to 1991.

While moving toward clarity and simplicity in thought, Spruance's
manual brought with it much more fundamental change for the U.S.
Navy, reflecting his own frustration with the earlier manual's lack of
emphasis on the principles of war. Spruance's new manual was an
important force that served to help revive these ideas in naval thinking. Traditionally, naval thinkers had always shied away from
stressing these principles, believing them to be overly simplistic and
tending to obscure the fundamental issues that were intended to be
brought to mind.[21]

One may obviously trace this basic change in naval thinking to the
experience of World War II, yet the exact influences involved remain

obscure. One can speculate on some of major factors involved. Certainly, one of the great lessons of World War II was to stress the importance of joint operations and the need to coordinate land, sea, and air forces into unified operations. This, in itself, raised a force that encouraged the navy to accept an approach that the other armed services commonly used. Eying this trend with suspicion, Rear Admiral J. C. Wylie cautioned in 1967:

> At the risk of treading on the toes of sincere and able men, I suggest that worship of any such patter as the "principles of war" is an unaware substitution of slogan for thought, probably brought about by the intellectual formlessness that must inevitably exist when there is no orderly and disciplined pattern of fundamental theory from which one consciously or unconsciously takes departure.[22]

Reflecting another aspect of the lessons of World War II, Wylie pointed out the principles of war did not apply to strategy, which is more fruitfully derived from an understanding of the broad environment within which armed force operates, including the social, political and economic dimensions of that environment.

Despite the recurrence of fundamental objections, the 1986 Goldwater-Nicholas Defense Department Reorganization Act has required all the armed services in the United States to develop complementary, basic approaches. Thus, in accordance with this requirement, official statements of American naval doctrine, published in the summer of 1994, stresses the traditional nine principles of war.[23] The new manual notes that

> The principles of war have proven effective in preparing for combat, but the complexities and disorder of war preclude their use as a simple checklist. Instead, we must be able to apply these principles in war's turbulent environment, to promote initiative, supplement professional judgement, and serve as the conceptual framework in which we evaluate the choices available in battle. These principles provide a solid basis for our warfighting doctrine.[24]

While it is, therefore, necessary to relate the principles of war to American naval doctrine, that doctrine still finds its primary basis in the principles of seamanship through which vessels operate at sea. The main purpose of naval operations remains to gain control of activity at sea so that one can use the sea as a means to effect events ashore. The nine principles of war (Objective, Mass, Maneuver, Offensive, Economy of Force, Unity of Command, Simplicity, Surprise, and Security) may play a role in aspects of combat operations, but they fail to incorporate fully the wider understanding of naval and maritime power that is inherent in the use of maritime power for both war and peace. The principles of war stress only the battle function of armed force, and ignore the function of maritime power in its broader diplomatic, economic, and logistical roles.[25]

DOCTRINE FOR MULTINATIONAL NAVAL OPERATIONS

Naval doctrine for multinational naval operations should and must provide a standard approach for many different navies to work together effectively. Multilateral naval operations are nothing new.

The Dutch and the English navies operated together very successfully in wartime during the late seventeenth and early eighteenth centuries. The French and the Spanish navies fought together in a number of wars during the same period. In the nineteenth century, well known naval actions were fought with ships of various navies working together at Navarino in 1827, at Acre in 1840 and in Black Sea operations in the Crimean War as well as other operations. In the twentieth century, there were successful examples of multilateral naval cooperation in World war I. During the Second World War, the failures of the Australian-British-Dutch-American squadron in southeast Asia in 1942 provided worthwhile lessons that were not lost on the survivors. By 1943–44, the Allied landings in North Africa and Italy were remarkable feats of international cooperation, the experience of which culminated in the Normandy landings. There, British and American admirals commanded a fleet that included not only their own naval vessels, but also British Commonwealth, Polish, Norwegian, and Free French ships.

Despite this successful experience, naval leaders are naturally doubtful about the prospects for multilateral operations. In the first place, we nearly always think of navies in national terms. We all have been taught that our navy represents our nation. Everything about navies is organized in national terms. We fight on the decks of our ships for our own nation. For this, we fly our national flag and our ships often carry evocative national names: the names of heroes, battles, symbols or places that are part of our heritage and that we value as a united people. To think of navies in other terms somehow feels improper, even sacrilegious. These feelings come from ingrained habits of thought, not from a dispassionate examination of the facts. In the mid-1960s, when the idea of the Standing Naval Force, Atlantic was first suggested, NATO leaders were extremely

skeptical that it could succeed. Yet, many years later, STANAVFOR-
LANT has shown itself to be a model for a successful multinational
naval force, with command rotating among all the national participants, each on equal footing with ships and colleagues from other
countries; the smaller countries' contributions not being dominated
by the larger.

Some of the more advanced, cooperative initiatives surrounding
this Force have yet to be implemented. Among them, for example, is
the idea from the 1970s of the "Free World Frigate," a proposal to
share standardization in design and supply through a ship-type built
with components from all participating countries.[26] In recent years,
the fundamental problems in trying to adapt the concept of multinational naval forces to other parts of the world outside NATO have
been threefold: first, the need to provide a workable system for command and control; second, the need to provide standardized procedures; third, the need to establish common communications methods
and equipment.

The experience of the early 1990s in the Persian Gulf War, the
operations in the Adriatic and those off Haiti have each provided
some alternative models, and each with its own drawbacks.[27] In
these situations, we have seen a variety of arrangements used,
from ad hoc cooperation to the use of regional organizations and
the United Nations.

The very practical area of naval doctrine for multinational naval
operations remains a key area that has been worked on more firmly
in the closing years of the twentieth century, so that navies can develop some higher concepts for maritime strategies in the twenty-
first century. As a contribution toward that NATO has recently
published an unclassified version of its tactical manual, ATP-1. Nevertheless, the problem of multinational naval doctrine has remained
a very difficult one, even for fairly routine operations. There is always a lingering fear that it is potentially dangerous to share standard operating procedures. Yet, if multilateral naval operations are
going to be needed much more commonly in the twenty-first century,
as one suspects they will be with all navies facing the need to do more
with less by combining efforts, this is an area that will require much
cooperative effort before international naval forces can operate together more flexibly and more effectively in facing the challenges of
the future. Doctrine for international naval cooperation needs to be
developed to deal with the wide range of new operational problems
that may well become much more common in the new century.

In these new situations, the idea of control at sea paralleled with the principles of seamanship will be the most important considerations in directing the peacetime uses of navies as they deal with the new threats presented by drug-traffickers, environmental pollution, collective security operations, and enforcement of the regime of the Law of the Sea.

NOTES

This is a revised version of a lecture delivered at the Seminar on Doctrines held at the Militärhögskolan [The Swedish Armed Forces Staff and War College], Stockholm, on 18 August 1994.

1. Robert Foulke, "Conrad and the Power of Seamanship," *The Great Circle: Journal of the Australian Association for Maritime History,* 11 (1989), p. 15.

2. See Paul Heinsius, "Zur Entwicklung der Seetaktik und des Seekriegswesens im Ostseeraum während des 13. Jahrhunderts," in Otto Brunner und Hermann Kellenbenz, eds., *Festschrift für Hermann Aubin zum 80. Geburtstag.* (Wiesbaden, 1965).

3. For recent studies on the history of this, see R. E. J. Weber, *De seinboeken voor Nederlandse oorlogsvloten en konvooien tot 1690* (Amsterdam, 1982); Brian Tunstall, *Naval Warfare in the Age of Sail,* Edited by Nicholas Tracy (Annapolis, MD: Naval Institutions 1989); the introductions and documents in the tactics sections of Hattendorf and Knight, et al. *British Naval Documents 1203–1960* (London: Navy Records Society, 1993); Michel Depeyre, *Tactiques et Stratégies Navales de la France et du Royaume-Uni de 1690 à 1815* (Paris: Economica, 1998).

4. Père Paul Hoste, *L'art des armées navales* (Toulon, 1697 and Lyon 1727). For a broad survey of doctrinal thinking, see James J. Tritten and Vice Admiral Luigi Donolo, *A Doctrine Reader: The Navies of United States, Great Britain, France, Italy, and Spain.* The Newport Papers, no. 9 (Newport, RI: Naval War College Press, 1995) and most important,a variety of relevant essays in the series of volumes edited by Hervé Coutau-Bégarie, *L'Evolution de la Pensée Navale.* (Paris: Economica, 1990—in progress). Six volumes published to 1997.

5. Jacques-Raymond Grenier, *L'Art de la Guerre sur Mer* (1787).

6. Audibert Ramatuelle, *Cours Élémentaire de Tactique Navale* (Paris, 1802).

7. John Clerk, *Essay on Naval Tactics,* first published privately in 1782, then publicly in 1790.

8. Sir Howard Douglas, *On Naval Warfare Under Steam* (London, 1858).

9. Foxhall Parker, *Fleet Tactics Under Steam.* (New York, 1879).

10. Louis Edouard Bouët-Willaumez, *Tactique supplementaire à l'usage d'une flotte cuirassee . . . ler août 1864.* Extrait de la *Revue Maritime et Coloniale.* (Paris: A. Bertrand, 1868).

11. E. R. Freemantle, "Naval Tactics on the Open Sea with the existing Types of Vessels and Weapons," *Journal of the Royal United Services Institution* XXIV (1880), pp. 1–60.

12. William Bainbridge-Hoff, *Examples, Conclusions and Maxims of Modern Naval Tactics.* Office of Naval Intelligence, Bureau of Navigation, Navy Department, General Information series, no. III. (Washington, 1884).

13. Stephen B. Luce, "On the Study of Naval History (Grand Tactics)" U.S. Naval Institute *Proceedings* (1887) reprinted in John D. Hayes and Hattendorf, eds., *The Writings of Stephen B. Luce* (Newport, RI: Naval War College Press, 1975), p. 95.

14. For this and the following, see Hattendorf, et al., *Sailors and Scholars: The Centennial History of the Naval War College* (Newport, RI: Naval War College Press, 1984, chapter 3.

15. See Hattendorf and Gunnar Sundell, "Med Sjövinden till Newport: De första svenskarna vid U.S. Naval War College," *Forum Navale,* 41 (1986), pp. 31–75.

16. Lieutenant Commander Dudley W. Knox, "The Rôle of Doctrine in Naval Warfare," U.S. Naval Institute *Proceedings,* 41 (March-April 1915), pp. 325–365.

17. Ibid., p. 325.

18. Ibid., p. 334.

19. U.S. Naval War College, *Sound Military Decision,* with an introduction by Captain Frank M. Snyder, USN (Ret.). Classics of Sea Power series (Annapolis, MD: Naval Institute Press, 1992).

20. *Naval Manual of Operational Planning* (Washington: Office of the Chief of Naval Operations, 1948).

21. This view is succinctly stated in *Sound Military Decision,* pp. 25–28.

22. J. C. Wylie, *Military Theory: A General Theory of Power Control* With an introduction by John B. Hattendorf and a Postscript by J. C. Wylie. Classics of Sea Power series. (Annapolis, MD: Naval Institute Press, 1989), p. 20.

23. *Naval Warfare,* Naval Doctrine Publication 1 (Washington: Department of the Navy, Office of the Chief of Naval, Operations and Headquarters U.S. Marine Corps, 28 March 1994), pp. 43–50.

24. Ibid., p. 50.

25. See my "Maritime Strategy for the 21st Century," in Greg Mills, ed., *Maritime Strategy for Developing Countries.* (Johannesburg: South African Institute of International Affairs and Lancaster, UK: University of Lancaster Centre for Defence and International Security Studies, 1995), chapter 2, pp. 38–48.

26. More detailed information on this proposal may be found at the Naval War College, Newport, Rhode Island: Naval Historical Collection, manuscript collection.

27. For reflections on international cooperation in these events, see *Eleventh International Sea Power Symposium: Report of the Proceedings.* (Newport, RI: Naval War College Press, 1991) and *Twelfth International Sea Power Symposium: Report of the Proceedings.* (Newport, RI: Naval War College Press, 1994). More recent developments can be found in Michael Johnson, Peter Swartz, and Patrick Roth, *Doctrine for Partnership: A Framework for U.S. Multinational Naval Doctrine.* CMB 95–202/March 1996 (Alexandria, VA: Center for Naval Analyses, 1996); Michael Johnson with Richard Kohout and Peter Swartz, *Guidelines*

for the World's Maritime Forces in Conducting Multinational Operations: An Analytic Framework. CRM 95–119/March 1996. (Alexandria, VA: Center for Naval Analyses, 1996) and Robert H. Thomas, *Multinational Naval Cooperation.* Maritime Security, Occasional Paper No. 3. (Halifax, Nova Scotia: Dalhousie University Centre for Foreign Policy Studies, 1996).

15

Sea Power and Sea Control in Contemporary Times

Today, sea power and sea control have a new context. Like so much in the era in which we live, everything seems to have changed. Navies, themselves, have changed. Compared to the situation a mere fifty years ago, ships look different and have different propulsion systems; aircraft are faster and have a wider variety of capabilities. Naval weapons are much more accurate and more devastating in their effects. Communications have proliferated in every imaginable way. Each of us now can have global communications through the Internet, while navies have vastly more complex means to obtain, share, store, sort, and present information to decision makers at various levels of command. The art of navigation and our very understanding of "the way of a ship" have changed through the use of satellites and global positioning systems.

The pace of change in navies is remarkable. Virtually every day, navies are faced with some new technological innovation. Everyday, a new technology seems to overtake an old. One of the most difficult and fundamental questions for naval leaders is how to deal with the this type of change. Although new technological ideas appear every day, it takes time to bring them to fruition—time during which a whole range of other ideas could appear. The practical problem involves identifying the most important new technologies, selecting appropriate ones for testing and developing, and then, with some confidence that they have not inadvertently excluded something critical for future conditions, deciding which new technologies to distribute to the fleet.

Because of the widespread technological nature of navies, there has been a fundamental change among sailors. We can no longer personify them by the bluff and hearty line-haulers who were so essential to the sailing-ship navy. Today, men and women in navies around the world are sophisticated in science and thoroughly educated in technology.

In this environment of ever more rapidly increasing technological change, navies around the world are faced with developing adequate naval force and maintaining it while costs rise and budgets decrease. It is more than a question of new technologies, it is further complicated by questions of national finance, bureaucratic decision making, the personalities of leaders, and legislative understanding of and support for navies.

Navies were once separate, autonomous entities within a government structure; they are no longer so today. One of the most telling lessons of the Second World War was the need to coordinate more closely the joint operations of all the armed services. Throughout the world, over the past half century, ministries of defense have slowly unified admiralties and naval ministries with war departments, ministries of the army, and air ministries, often adding to them in the same defense ministry or department, the munitions and logistics support agencies involved with armed forces. Moreover, naval officers have had to learn to talk with colleagues in other armed forces using the same terms, the same approaches to planning and budgeting, and sharing the same appropriations of tax dollars. Each of the services is increasingly becoming part of this same process, dependant upon one another and essential to one another in planning, budgeting, and operations.

At the same time that this lengthy process of unifying armed forces is occurring within nations, another process of integration is developing beyond and across national borders. While once we could think of a navy entirely in terms of one country and one country's maritime concerns, today we are learning to think of navies operating as part of United Nations forces, in terms of regional alliances, or even in terms of ad hoc coalitions gathered together to undertake some particular, mutually agreed upon task. One is no longer just concerned about coordinating the ships and air craft of a single country, but now increasingly in finding ways by which the forces of an individual country can operate effectively with those from another country. This is an immensely difficult task that involves not only the obvious differences in language, culture, and tradition, but also the basic patterns of solving problems and carrying out routine tasks. Moreover, it means sharing a certain number of procedures and certain types of information that were once state secrets.

In recent years, ships of various navies have operated together very successfully under the United Nations as well as under NATO and under other regional organizations and agreements. We have seen them during the Gulf War, in Somalia, in the Adriatic, and off Haiti. Our recent experience with such multilateral naval forces has emphasized the common concerns and natural ties that exist among sailors around the world.

It was these fundamental ties, found in the shared heritage of centuries of naval tradition and the mutual understanding of ships and the sea, that NATO built upon in the late 1940s in bringing together the naval forces of many European countries. It was the fundamental basis that helped to form the still-continuing Inter-American Naval Symposia in 1959. It was the initial starting point for the successful initiative in 1967 to create the NATO Standing Naval Force, Atlantic, and, in 1969 to establish the first worldwide gathering of chiefs of navies at the International Sea power Symposium.

In subsequent years, the Standing Naval Force has become a model for several other multinational naval forces. The International Sea Power Symposium continues to meet each odd-numbered and has proliferated into regional meetings, in the even-numbered years, with the Western Pacific Naval Symposium in 1988, and the West African Naval Symposium in 1992. Further initiatives along these lines continue to develop.

Old ideas seem to be disappearing. Among them are the traditional view that navies are a nation's "first line of defense", that a navy and its battle fleet exists to fight a huge battle with a similar kind of enemy battle fleet, that a navy is somehow always connected to the growth of imperial power.

In large countries, some citizens wonder why they need naval forces at all, when there is no huge naval force threatening them. Large navies are becoming much smaller. In terms of its ships, the U.S. Navy is 40 percent of what it was five years ago; the Royal Navy, today, is one-tenth of the size of the U.S. Navy. Yet, at the same time, small- and medium-sized naval forces are proliferating. There are more countries in the world today and there are more naval forces in the world today. In 1946, the editor of authoritative reference work, *Jane's Fighting Ships,* listed 52 navies,[1] fifty years later in 1996, there were 166 listed.[2] What is the role of a navy today and what is the purpose of sea power and sea control in the contemporary world?

The fundamental answer to this question lies in the fact that navies operate, not only in the context of national defense, but also in the context of the broad scope of general, maritime affairs. One can not separate the traditional roles of naval force from its wartime uses. Certainly, it derives its strength for peacetime applications from its military potential in the event of war. Today, we understand that, in addition to fighting, navies also have policing and international diplomatic roles to play.

When we think about strategies for a navy, we are thinking of ways of using a navy that will achieve particular ends. Strategy is not something limited to battles and conflict, but to achieving specific goals in any interaction with another power. It is something that is inextricably bound up within the broad context of a situation. This means that navies are not only part of the broader context of national defense issues, but also part of the much broader maritime world and its issues. Thus, navies are inextricably connected with two traditions and two lines of thought which, in modern thinking, are often separate from one another. Maritime affairs are essentially peacetime and civilian activities that range from fishing to ship-building, from activities in ports and harbors to long sea passages across the ocean. A navy does not normally dominate or overwhelm such maritime activities, but it is fundamentally connected with them as part of its own basic nature. Thus, navies need to understand themselves as part of a wider, maritime strategy.

Maritime strategy is a kind of subset of national grand strategy that touches on the whole range of a nation's activities and interests at sea. In its broadest sense, grand strategy is the comprehensive direction of power to achieve particular national goals, within it maritime strategy is the comprehensive direction of all aspects of national power that relate to a nation's interests at sea. The Navy serves this purpose, but maritime strategy is not purely a naval preserve.

Maritime strategy involves the other functions of state power that include diplomacy, the safety and defense of merchant trade at sea, fishing, the exploitation, conservation, regulation and defense of the exclusive economic zone at sea, coastal defense, security of national borders, the protection of offshore islands as well as participation in regional and worldwide concerns relating to the use of oceans, the skies over the oceans and the land under the seas. Such issues include expanding scientific and technological understanding of the entire maritime environment, working with the full range of national organizations, (navy, army, air force, customs, coast guard, commerce and trade, to name but a few of the ministries, bureaus, and departments that touch on these issues) in order to bring forth a truly national concept and plan for the maritime aspects of national life.

This broader understanding emphasizes that different nations have forms and types of interests in maritime affairs. Thus, their strategies and approaches to the use of national power in the maritime environment are different. Maritime powers, continental states, and coastal states, each use and value navies for different functions, some navies playing a relatively more important role in the exercise of national power than in others. For maritime nations, the navy is traditionally its main arm with an offensive strategic stance on the open ocean. Continental powers have depended mainly on armies and land-based air forces, using its navy to complement and enhance the army's and the air force's role as part of a generally defensive strategic stance. Traditionally, small states have had to rely on alliances and have had to adjust their stance according to the capabilities of their larger partners.[3]

Today, one can detect some new differences in the way that a major maritime power and the way that a coastal state think about contemporary sea power and sea control.

For a major maritime power, the fundamental focus of the military element in maritime strategy centers on the control of human activity at sea through the use of armed force in order to contribute to the broad ends established in a national maritime policy. The are two parts to this: (1) establishing control and (2) using control, once it has been established.

In the effort to establish control and, along with it, to deny control to an enemy, there are gradations that range from an abstract ideal to that which is practical, possible, or merely desirable. In this, one can consider whether control is to be general or limited, absolute or merely governing, widespread or local, permanent or temporary. Generally speaking, it is not practically possible to have direct control for an indefinite period of time. The normal situation is a kind of equilibrium that has been set in some previous period of control. When any degree of control is exercised, whether it be through gentle influence or aggressive seizure, it is exercised with a specified amount of force, for some discrete period of time, and to achieve a specific object.

Following the establishment of control is the use of the situation that has been created in order to achieve further goals. The effort to achieve control, by itself, means nothing unless that control has an effect. In the wide spectrum of activity that this can involve, the most important aspect is the use of maritime control to influence, and, ultimately, to assist in controlling events on land. In this, the fundamental key is to have an effect on those places, times, or routes of travel to which an adversary is sensitive, and which are critical and essential enough to move an adversary to alter plans or actions so as to accommodate one's own objectives.

In wartime, a nation can seek a degree of control at sea that will allow it to carry on its merchant shipping and fishing, to secure its coastline and offshore resources, to move troops, and to support air and land operations.

The manner in which a navy seeks this control and handles its forces today has changed in the last fifty years.[4] The way that naval forces form themselves and the effectiveness of their weapons are an integral considerations to new methods to search for and detect enemy forces and countermeasures that can neutralize an enemy. The most important naval weapon today is the missile designed to sink enemy ships. Below it in effectiveness come torpedoes, mines, gunfire, and bombs from aircraft.

Throughout naval history, naval battles have mainly taken place close to land. The only major exception to that has been in World War II the mid-ocean struggle against Axis U-boats in the Atlantic and the battles between opposing carrier air forces in the Pacific. In the past fifty years, the U.S. Navy has supported air and land operations and also carried out a variety of amphibious landings and coastal blockades. In the past few years, these traditional types of naval operations have come to be called "littoral warfare," and renewed emphasis has been placed on the way in which such military operations in coastal areas are carried out as joint-service operations.

The use of highly effective missile weapons in areas close to land creates a tactical environment for navies that reinforces the tendency in both grand strategy and in defense management for close interaction between land, sea, and air forces. In the environment of "littoral warfare" the distinctions between individual armed services quickly blur as all engage in complementary activities to achieve a shared object.

Today, high-speed and maneuverability characterize operations. Fast, small vessels operating in coastal waters have the ability to put much larger warships out of action. Amphibious assaults are made with high-speed surface effect vessels and armed helicopters launched from large ships off-shore. High-speed missiles can be launched from great distances with great effect. Detecting such attacks is particularly important today, as the range and power of weapons have increased. Today, some equipment can detect ships and air craft at ranges of thousands of miles, merging strategic and tactical considerations. In this, the uses and the analysis of the full range of the electromagnetic spectrum have become as important in modern warfare as the weapons that electronics control and guide. In facing a difficult, fast-moving environment, responsible commanders in maritime areas depend upon fast and reliable transmission of large amounts of information. Today, a key issue is the domination and control of information and the interaction of information networks. Although essential to one's own exercise of command and control over forces, the situation also provides another area for manipulation, blocking, and interfering with an enemy's essential needs. In short, warfare in coastal areas requires the close interaction and interdependence of army, air force, and amphibious landing forces. The interaction of different types of forces with the intensity and speed of operations have shifted emphasis from the craft carrying weapons and the color of the uniform behind them to the effectiveness and countering of the weapon itself.

This change in the character and in the focus of contemporary naval warfare is paralleled by a larger matter of maritime interest that also emphasizes coastal regions. The 1982 United Nations Convention on the Law of the Sea has now come into effect and has been ratified by the majority of the world's states. This development in international law has granted coastal states specific rights and responsibilities in offshore waters.

These changes include the extension of territorial seas to twelve nautical miles and the extension of some rights to an Exclusive Economic Zone out to 200 nautical miles and on the continental shelf. These responsibilities and rights in these areas include such matters as the establishment of artificial islands, the conduct of maritime scientific research, and the protection and conservation of the natural marine environment, including controlling the catch of fish and exploiting other natural underwater resources on and under continental shelf.

The extension of a coastal state's jurisdiction at sea has placed certain limitations on the freedom that the great naval powers have traditionally and exclusively exercised and transferred them, in many cases, to small- and medium-sized coastal states just at a time when those offshore resources are becoming increasingly important, both economically and politically. The situation demands that coastal states have adequate power to manage their responsibilities. This fact, combined with the capabilities of modern naval weapons, has made small- and medium-sized navies into major actors. This position is enhanced even further as the world's major naval powers reduce their size. Today, we must take seriously an entirely new dimension in naval affairs: the sea power of the coastal state.[5]

Coastal states exercise their naval power in a different manner and with a different concept than navies that focus on the high seas. The coastal environment provides an advantage that an approaching naval power does not have. One's home waters provide protection to defending forces, particularly when they are intimately acquainted with them and specifically trained to deal with them. At the time, such coastal naval forces can be directly supported by land-based aircraft and coastal defenses, including missile defenses, mines, and torpedoes, and will be able to employ their entire range of armed services to support their navy. From the point of view of force development, a coastal state can most advantageously share roles and missions with its other uniformed services. Coastal navies have their secure support facilities nearby, designed directly to support them in a full range of combat conditions, as they meet any threat. With supplies so close, a coastal navy is not so concerned about onboard supplies and the logistics involved in their more limited radii of action.

Small coastal states use their armed forces in a more restricted manner than those of much larger powers. By their very size, their limited industrial and economic base, and their smaller military capacity, small- and medium-sized countries often cannot maintain all their interests by themselves. Small states can rarely hope to defeat completely a larger power. They can, however, use their armed forces to control an enemy's actions in a way that will shape the outcome of a conflict or a crisis.

Coastal naval forces exercise national sovereignty over offshore areas and enforce national jurisdiction and management over maritime resources. Their capacity for wartime operations allows them to serve as a deterrent to others who might wish to seize or dispute sovereignty. In war, the coastal navy continues to serve a deterrent purpose as its very presence raises the stakes of a foreign navy operating in those waters. It can be a delaying, an increasingly costly and distracting, obstacle to another power. From the smaller, coastal state's point of view, the objective is to preserve its own identity and sovereignty when the struggle is over. In this, there are alternative courses of action that a small coastal state can choose. It can seek direct opposition on its own, it can align itself with other states, or it can even acquiesce with an opposing power, allowing the opposition to take certain actions as long as it does not fundamentally alter the fundamental national interests of the coastal state.

The power of coastal states' objectives and rights lies fundamentally in maintaining and carrying out the guiding spirit of international law. Thus, many of them agree that the United Nations Law of the Sea regime and the Geneva Conventions on the conduct of war are currently the essential criteria for determining a favorable conclusion to any conflict and for guiding peacetime policy.

Emphasis on international law is particularly important to states that focus on the quality of their position after a war is over. By adhering to international law, they would hope to secure both popular support at home as well as international support for their position, while also avoiding recriminating penalties in a postwar era Among other things, this leads to focusing one's military and naval forces and one's military objectives in terms of an enemy's armed forces, not the civil sector of any enemy's society. In following this policy, a coastal state would not want to initiate attacks on a belligerent's merchant shipping. Without a seagoing force, a coastal state could do relatively little harm to a major maritime power's merchant shipping and would probably suffer more from retaliatory attacks on its own civilian maritime activities. The coastal state's primary naval objective in war will be to deter a belligerent's naval attack by having forces that are so effective that it would make such an attack too costly to risk. Should the attack be made, however, the coastal's state's objective is only to stop the attack, to force the enemy away from its own waters, and to prevent an enemy from attaining his goals. With such objectives. it is unnecessary for a coastal state to destroy the enemy naval force when the primary object is merely to disable it.

In preparing maritime defenses, a coastal state may develop a highly specialized naval force that is designed to deal with one particular dimension of defense, leaving other aspects to its other armed services or its allies. Taking such a choice, a country might choose to rely on a relatively large force of sophisticated shallow water, defensive submarines, or alternatively it might choose to invest in a large number of highly sophisticated sea mines, to prevent an enemy seaborne attack.

In its fundamental interest to avoid military conflict, a coastal state has an obligation to exercise its sovereignty in the appropriate areas designated by International Law. Maintenance of appropriately firm and consistent authority in the maritime Exclusive Economic Zone will help to reduce conflict among nations and prevent the problems that arise from other nations unilaterally assuming control of an area outside its own jurisdiction or when an area is left in anarchic conditions. International Law does not yet provide for all situations; variations in practice may arise as nations take up their responsibilities in these new areas and changes may be necessary in the future. This situation, however, is better than one of neglect. In the current situation, effective surveillance and control of sea areas are positive means that can assist to control a crisis and are useful means to help avert war.

If we look at this new development from another perspective, however, it suggests new possibilities that could spark a crisis or even a war. As coastal states expend their sovereignty outward on the open sea, they may easily create friction with their neighbors, who have conflicting interpretations of the facts or overlapping claims in a region. Additionally, the new interest of coastal states in maintaining control in offshore areas puts them potentially in opposition to large naval powers who have traditionally maintained the right of warships to pass on the high seas. It creates potential restrictions for major maritime powers who would like to use their navies as direct adjuncts to diplomacy. At the very least, it moves a coastal state's naval forces further offshore, into positions where a misunderstanding could take place and create a conflict or a crisis.

Here, we see the possibility of a major problem for contemporary sea power and sea control. The very enlargement in areas under sovereign control, the extension in range and capabilities of naval armaments, and the proliferation in the number of nations with navies heightens the potential for conflict.

The parallel rise in the use of multinational naval forces, however, suggests one possible antidote to the situation. While multinational naval cooperation is a very practical means to augment limited resources, by complementing a single nation's naval capabilities with those of another, it also requires close cooperation and interaction among the participating navies. This interaction builds understanding among nations, providing direct links of communication and discussion.

Through such multilateral cooperation, neighboring navies in a particular region can join forces and share responsibilities costs for surveillance, and control of maritime regions. These shared duties could prevent conflict that could arise from neglect. The very means by which such cooperation takes place is also a major avenue to prevent misunderstanding. It builds the connections that could provide mutual solutions to problems and be essential to defusing a crisis. Through such connections, one side could explain to another the rationale for actions that might otherwise appear threatening. In the context of contemporary sea power and sea control, multilateral cooperation can be a positive influence in three ways: (1) helping to maintain lower defense costs, and (2) at the same time making it unnecessary to increase naval armaments, while also (3) lowering tensions.

Looking toward the future, it appears that international cooperation among naval forces is quickly becoming a key issue.[6] It is useful, therefore, to think more precisely about it. Of course, it will never be possible for all navies to cooperate all of the time on every matter. It is a matter of great political sensitivity, involving very expensive forces and highly trained sailors. No nation can afford to use them indiscriminately or wastefully.

To avoid this, one naval leader has suggested three criteria for naval cooperation. The first is to cooperate with those countries who share fundamental values. These values could be the shared concepts of democracy, human rights, free market exchanges, and recognition of the fundamental importance of the United Nations Charter.

A second criterion is to cooperate with neighboring navies in geographical proximity of one another. In practical terms, it is easiest to start cooperation on a subregional basis and to expand gradually. Yet, there is a difficulty here in identifying regions and in drawing the boundaries too narrowly. In some cases, cooperation needs to span the boundaries between conventional regions. Further problems arise with this criterion in those cases where one country falls into two or more regions. The solution may be to cooperate in whatever multidimensional way that includes neighboring countries.

The third criterion is to cooperate with navies that share similar national interests. While the recent fragmentation of larger states into smaller ones might suggest to some observers that a kind of tribalism is being rekindled, this diffusion of national power is also creating a similarity of certain security interests. This is particularly true for maritime interests.

Using the triple criteria of shared values, geographical proximity and shared interests, countries can develop a plan of multinational naval cooperation that includes both regional navies and distant navies with regional capabilities and interests.

The agenda for such cooperation could be nearly anything imaginable, but former United Nations Secretary-General Boutros-Ghali's "An Agenda for Peace" provides some very valuable ideas for consideration: preventive diplomacy, peacekeeping, post-conflict peace-building, and peace enforcement. In more specific terms, neighboring navies, sharing mutual values and complementary interests, could undertake such broad missions as

· providing humanitarian assistance;
· intervening to evacuate civilians at risk;
· making a show of force to stop a universally unacceptable action;
· conducting maritime peacekeeping operations;

- protecting sea and air traffic;
- controlling armaments and enforcing demilitarization;
- enforcing maritime agreements, and
- respond to a mutual threat.

Among these missions, there are some specific maritime tasks that could be shared by multilateral naval forces:

- protecting the maritime environment;
- regulating the use of maritime resources;
- preventing and controlling pollution;
- enforcing laws relating to fishing and sea bed use;
- controlling illegal immigration;
- interdicting illegal trade;
- suppressing piracy, and
- enforcing the UN Convention on the Law of the Sea.

These are some of the primary issues in the world today. Such tasks are difficult and complex to carry out at sea, often requiring advanced capabilities in surveillance, readiness, and specialized equipment for coordinating information as well as for command, control, and communications. The threats they involve are often regional, not national. All these aspects point again to the need for cooperative, multinational solutions.

In conclusion, sea power and sea control are increasingly important factors in contemporary affairs, but as such they have a new context. Navies, themselves, have changed, as have many of their most important future missions and tasks. Yet, because of the increased scale of naval proliferation, the expansion of maritime interests among coastal states, as well as by the mobility of naval forces and their multidimensional capabilities, the issues surrounding sea power and sea control continue to be important at present and there is every indication that they will become even more important for the future.

NOTES

This is a text of a lecture delivered at HMAS Creswell, the Royal Australian Naval College, on 22 August 1996. It was first published in the *Journal of the Australian Naval Institute,* vol. 23, no. 2 (April/June 1997), pp. 15–20.

1. *Jane's Fighting Ships, 1946–47.* (London: Sampson Low, 1946).

2. Captain Richard Sharpe, ed., *Jane's Fighting Ships, 1996–97.* (London: Jane's, 1996).

3. See Clark G. Reynolds, *Command of the Sea: The History and Strategy of Maritime Empires.* (New York: William Morrow, 1974), pp. 12–16.

4. The following is based on a draft version of Wayne P. Hughes, Jr., "Contemporary Naval Tactics" in *The Oxford Companion of Military History.* (New York: Oxford University Press, forthcoming).

5. See Jacob Børresen, "The Seapower of the Coastal State," *Journal of Strategic Studies,* 17 (March 1994), pp. 148–175, upon which this and the following paragraphs are a modification and interpretation.

6. The following is based on Admiral Angelo Mariani, Italian Navy, "Peacetime Patterns of Cooperation," in John B. Hattendorf, ed., *Thirteenth International Seapower Symposium: Report of the Proceedings of the Conference, 5–8 November 1995.* (Newport, RI: Naval War College press, 1996), pp. 37–48.

16

The Study of Maritime History

Maritime history is a broad theme within general historical studies that by its nature, cuts across standard disciplinary boundaries. A student who pursues the theme may approach it from a variety of vantage points and touch upon many other, related approaches, including science, technology, industry, economics, trade, politics, art, literature, ideas, sociology, military and naval affairs, international relations, cartography, comparative studies in imperial and colonial affairs, institutional and organizational development, communications, migration, intercultural relations, natural resources and so on. In short, maritime history is a humanistic study of the many dimensions in man's relationship with the sea.

Maritime history focuses on ships and the sailors who operated them, relating an identifiable segment of society to a specific range of technological development and to a hostile geographical area covering seven-tenths of the globe. The relative importance of maritime affairs varies from one period to another in general history; it stands out in some periods and in some cultures and not in others. For example, maritime affairs were an essential aspect of general European and European colonial history from the fifteenth century to the twentieth century. Only recently, in the twentieth century, have alternative means of communication and transport developed and displaced much of the technological, social, economic and industrial fabric that surrounded maritime affairs, although a number of aspects continue.

While the subject may seem to brighten and fade for the general historian, a specialist in the subject of maritime history must keep in mind the continuity of maritime development through all periods. Maritime affairs are rarely, if ever, absent in history. At the same time, ships and sailors are not isolated phenomena. They are very much a part of larger developments. In order to understand what happened at sea and to analyze the effect of those events, one needs to relate them and interpret them in the context of broad issues that were occurring on land. Maritime history is, in many respects, only an extension of events on land, but it does involve a variety of very technical and specialist issues, such as shipbuilding, navigation, naval gunnery and tactics, marine engineering, hydrography, and so on. In order to understand these elements, which are key factors in maritime history, maritime historians must explain them in terms of the broadest context, while at the same time, they must come to grips with the details and make sense of the specific developments within that special area.

One of the main problems for maritime historians is the need to see events at sea in terms of a variety of perspectives. For example, a ship that was built in a particular country was a product of certain national political, economic, social, technological and industrial factors. When the same ship sailed at sea, it entered a different realm with an international dimension that may involve such additional factors as wars, cross-cultural relations, imperial competition, scientific research, exchange of goods or accumulation of capital through international trade.

Additionally, when ships left land and the network of activities that prepared them, they spent long isolated periods at sea. This unusual experience produced a social dimension within the ships that, itself, became a new factor, creating microcosms of land-based societies while bringing them into various new environments and new experiences. These experiences, in turn, were reflected into landbased societies as sailors returned from the sea. In this area, as in others, maritime affairs typically acted as a conduit as well as a separate channel of development.

Although focusing on ships and sailors, maritime historians deal in the interrelationship of events on land and at sea, dealing simultaneously with integrated, parallel, and unique aspects. As a theme in general history, maritime history is not separate from other aspects of historical study. Nevertheless, it involves a wide range of specialized learning and knowledge that justifies the identification of maritime history as one of the many legitimate fields for historical research and writing. Identifying the field in this way, however, neither removes it from the accepted standards of the best historical scholarship nor creates any unique standards or exclusive prerogatives for those who follow it. It merely recognizes that the topic is broad enough to identify fully a range of specialization and that it is complicated enough to sustain the varied work of a number of scholars devoting their scholarly careers to working on differing aspects of the theme.

We cannot forget its national dimensions. We must be aware that sea history, maritime trade, and naval rivalry touch on several nations simultaneously. At the same time, it is a theme that brings together a spectrum of different view points and disciplines. Within it, one finds a dynamic interaction at a variety of levels. We can see relationships and trends between technological development and industry, the formation and growth of sciences, changing economic trends and financial instruments, politics, international relations, law, theories of economics and warfare, sociological and anthropological issues, along with reflections of cultural, intellectual, and religious impulses with additional perspectives to be found through art and literature. All of these subjects are worthy of study in their own right, but defining them through their relationship to men and ships at sea provides us with a distinct series of related themes that we can follow over long periods of history. This broad perspective justifies the academic pursuit of maritime and naval affairs as a subject. Lest there be a misunderstanding, it is important to emphasize that the subject is not a closed category of human activity. Its academic legitimacy is to be found not in isolation from other types of history, but rather in the breadth and range of historical interconnections which one can intelligibly make in following, over time, the varied developments surrounding ships, sailors, and their related enterprises.

At universities and in research institutions, it is appropriate to stress the academic value of the field and to discuss its state in terms of the highest historical scholarship. At the same time, however, there is a different level of attention to the subject that should not be ignored. Here, scholars must draw attention to the importance which seamen themselves place on naval and maritime history. Their focus is designed to serve the maritime and naval profession. In this sense, it differs somewhat in emphasis and in objectives from that of the academic, while at the same time it shares much. In one respect, it is a means of maintaining an institutional memory for the organizations involved. On a larger scale, however, the history of a profession—for a professional within it—is clearly part of the specialized body of knowledge relating to its professional skills and practice as well as a tool for promoting the profession's special interests.

Since the nineteenth century, navies in particular have cultivated this approach. Naval historians such a Sir John Knox Laughton, Sir Julian Corbett, Captain Alfred Thayer Mahan, and Admiral Sir Herbert Richmond were certainly among the founding fathers of this method in the Anglo-American world. Illustrating the professional mode, Sir Herbert Richmond identified "three classes of individuals to whom an acquaintance of naval history is needful: the general public, the statesman, and the sea officer."[1]

The public, he said, needs to understand the navy as an integral part of national and general history. For this audience, he stressed the need to promote an understanding of the Navy's role in maintaining a maritime country's security at sea.

The statesman, Richmond said, needs to understand how naval power has been employed, applied, and even misapplied. A statesman who understands these issues in history, Richmond argued, "Would be more capable of undertaking the tremendous responsibilities attached to policy, preparation and direction of war than one to whom naval history is a closed book."[2]

The sea officer will gain several things from a study of naval history. First, he will find an understanding of the elements of the use of sea power. From this he can develop a foundation upon which to build up knowledge of naval war, starting from a record of practical experience rather than futuristic speculation. The officer will find naval history a groundwork of strategical study and a mental stimulant that will serve as a guide to conduct. Moreover, Richmond suggested, a study of tactics from the age of sail could have practical value for the modern officer in the twentieth century, when naval weapons and equipment changed beyond recognition. Even though the tactics of earlier times are themselves of little practical use to the present, a study of them reveals "the principles of the use of force and human nature, which expresses itself in its methods of command."[3] For the professional naval officer, the study of naval history brings out the need for clear thinking on a wide range of professional issues, while at the same time providing illustration, stimulation, and guidance to officers on the nature and character of naval command.

In other words, from a professional point of view, the general public should know enough about the history of naval and maritime affairs to appreciate and support public expenditure on current programs; the statesman should maintain, guide, and use it appropriately; the sea officer, should understand the nature of issues he faces and absorb the ideals of the profession. Many of these points are ones which a professional academic would hesitate to endorse, seeking instead a broader and more dispassionate understanding of the maritime dimension in human affairs.

As one looks at the present state of maritime history, one finds a variety of situations, varying from country to country. In some, there are only a handful of professional seamen who are doing the heroic work of maintaining this field of historical work. Their work tends to center in the professional service academies, staff colleges, or in contributions from retired officers and merchant mariners. In other countries, the professional seamen have made links with academics and with research organizations that have helped to raise historical standards and to broaden understanding of events at sea. In other places, it is the museums that have taken the lead in research and writing, as well is in educating the public on the historical role of sea affairs. In a few places, maritime history has become a subject for research and courses at the university level. Although it has not fully reached the level we would like it to achieve, there is undeniably a resurgence and growth of well-founded studies that begun to develop within the field.

Overall, maritime and naval history is an area with tremendous potential for serious historical research, yet as a field, it has sometimes lacked methodological standards. Professional seamen have been the first to promote study in this area, finding it valuable for their own professional concerns. However, when interest in the field expands, too often it consists initially of only a fascination with ships or in some romantic notion of seafaring, rather than in broader, historical understanding. In order for the general study of maritime and naval history to reach a higher level, its focus must move beyond a confined, self-contained and self-referenced view to make links with events and trends of broad, general interest. Indeed, the best studies in naval and maritime history, up to this point, are those that specifically use naval and maritime affairs as examples, extensions or variations of already established general themes in the history of science and technology or economic, social, political, international or intellectual history. Yet, maritime and naval history affairs are more than just stray examples. Man's activities at sea involve complex interrelationships of many strands in human affairs. When seen together, they constitute a significant theme within general history that should be neither isolated nor ignored. The central issues maritime historical development lie in several key areas, including the technologies of ships, the range of the nautical sciences, the skills and character of seamen, as well as in trade, war, international law, art, and literature.

As a field, maritime and naval history is generally underdeveloped when compared to other historical topics. Nevertheless, some very important basic work has been done in laying the foundations for proper study: there are now available some important research guides to manuscript materials. Scholars continue to publish critical

editions of key documents,[4] and they are identifying, through bibliographies, the standard works which new research can test and expand upon.[5] In addition, a steady stream of new scholarly writing is
already apparent, establishing a series of monographs that give us
reason to believe that the field of maritime history is moving rapidly
toward higher standards.[6] Pressures from both within and without
the maritime community have opened its closed, self-referenced
shell that was originally so valuable for early professional development. The wider contacts and perceptions benefit equally the modern professional seaman as well as the historian who wishes to observe them. In order to use them effectively, however, those who work
in maritime and naval history must be more fully aware of progress
that is being made toward improving methodology in the field.

Teaching is the least developed of all. Aside from professional academies which sometimes still deal with the subject only in outmoded
hagiographic, romantic, or nationalistic styles, there are only a very
few serious academic courses that examine the broad historical implications of the subject. With a few exceptions, university courses have
tended to ignore the international and comparative perspectives that
maritime and naval affairs involve. Few have attempted to deal in the
alternative patterns to national history that such distinctive features
of the subject as ocean currents and the pattern of maritime trade
might suggest. Some of the rare academic chairs, designed to be filled
by scholars who should be leading the teaching and work in the maritime and naval field at great research universities, are unfilled or di-
verted to specialists in distantly related themes. At universities, both
undergraduate and graduate students approaching the broad spectrum of historical issues often entirely miss the maritime dimension.
Yet as the twentieth century comes to a close, there are clear signs
that this long-standing situation is now changing in maritime history as well as in its subspecialty of naval history.

There is a wide range of cognate issues in naval history that deserve consideration and that contribute to knowledge in naval affairs. Cognate aspects of naval affairs include such specialized areas
as theory, art, literature, social affairs and so on, that might also be
considered aspects of another broad theme, such as intellectual history, social history, art history, sociology, political science of science
and technology. Readers and practitioners of naval history must
avoid confusing the core and the cognate, but they should ignore neither the interrelationship nor disparage one over the other. When
seen along side a full appreciation of core naval history, cognate
naval history becomes particularly important in helping to define the
place of naval affairs within the broad context of general affairs.

Naval affairs, after all, are very often a special case of broader issues. On one hand, they fall under the broad rubric of maritime history; on the other, they relate to military issues. In general, however, we must work to rejoin the military and maritime aspects that have only recently become separated in North American and British practices of historical writing.

In terms of the military dimension of naval affairs, it is important to understand the navy as an instrument of national power, both in terms of the sources of its power and in its varying interrelationships to the nation's diplomatic, military, and economic policies, as well as to more specialized areas of strategy, operations, and tactics. Within this context, the subject of joint military operations has become increasingly important in the past fifty years and is forcing specialists in naval affairs to see their subject in terms that relate naval operations to those of the other armed services, but the scope of naval history is wider and moves beyond operations to larger issues. For navies, these broader issues lead naturally to commerce at sea, shipbuilding, seamen, labor conditions, port development and many other topics relating to finance, industry, transportation, technology, cultural and social conditions. This illustrates one of the most important patterns in the field of maritime history, showing the overlap and interconnection between the defense-related issues of naval affairs and the economic issues associated with merchant marine affairs. Although they are often treated separately in English-speaking countries and typically are founded in differing bodies of literature, differing types of analysis, and differing source materials, they are, nevertheless, closely connected topics within the single, larger field of maritime history. As further scholarly work continues, the fundamental connections between these subtopics within maritime history will, undoubtedly, become clearer.

Mankind's relationship to the sea is very much a part of history and this field of study is properly called maritime history. Within its variety of subtopics, naval history is a distinctive element of the larger whole. The current trends in our understanding show that scholars limit the value of their work and curtail the range of their understanding when they attempt to follow older patterns that pit one specialist theme within maritime history against another. For the coming generation of maritime historians, it will be far less important whether their special historical expertise lies in the specifics of naval, merchant marine, nautical science, overseas expansion, technological affairs, transportation, or some other topic. What will be important and what will contribute the most to historical understanding of maritime affairs will be for future scholars to see their expertise in the light of the broadest themes within general historical studies and to understand the fundamental nature of a field that cuts across the limiting and narrow boundaries established in previous generations. Those boundaries served a useful purpose in the past, when professional maritime studies were just beginning and when they needed careful nurturing. Maritime history is maturing and moving beyond the toddlers' stage. In the future, practitioners of sophisticated and well-developed maritime history, and the readers of their work, will no longer need to be concerned about a crisis of scholarly identity or a lack of scholarly standards. Those issues were certainly legitimate concerns in the historiography of the nineteenth and in the late twentieth centuries, but they may be safely left behind in the twenty-first century. With a new and broader vision of maritime history, applying the highest standards of historical understanding to the wide range of related themes that touch on human interaction with the oceans of the world, maritime historians will have much insight that bring new and deeper understandings to general history.

NOTES

This essay is a composite and a revision of elements that appeared earlier in the introductions to Hattendorf, ed., *Maritime History.* volume 1: *The Age of Discovery* (Malabar, FL: Krieger, 1995) , pp. xiii-xv, and to *Doing Naval History: Essays Toward Improvement,* (Newport, RI: Naval War College Press, 1995), pp. 2–6.

1. H. W. Richmond, "The Importance of the Study of Naval History," The Naval Review, 27 (May 1939), pp. 201–18, quote from p. 201. The article was reprinted in The Naval Review 68 (April 1980), pp. 139–50.
2. Ibid., p. 203.
3. Ibid., p. 212.
4. See chapter 6, above, for a discussion of naval documents. Similar studies could be done in the related subfields of maritime exploration, nautical science, and merchant marine affairs.
5. The fundamental bibliographical reference for books in English is Robert G. Albion's *Naval and Maritime History: A Bibliography.* 4th edition. (Mystic Seaport: Munson Institute, 1972), supplemented by Benjamin W. Labaree, *A Supplement to Albion's Naval and Maritime History: A Bibliography.* (Mystic Seaport: Munson Institute, 1988). An updated, comprehensive revision of this bibliographical work is currently in progress at the Munson Institute.
6. See Hattendorf, ed., *Ubi Sumus?: The State of Naval and Maritime History.* (Newport, RI: Naval War College Press, 1994), supplemented and expanded by Frank Broeze, ed., *Maritime History at the Crossroads: A Critical Review of Recent Historiography.* Research in Maritime History, no. 9. (St John's, Newfoundland: International Maritime Economic History Association, 1995).

Index

Page numbers in italics indicate an illustration.

Union of Soviet Socialist Republics. *See* Russia

United Kingdom, 39, 43; Admiralty, 25, 92; Royal Navy, 42, 43, 44, 72, 178, 187, 190, 193, 198, 231, 232, 255; in Anglo-American maritime strategy, 109–120. *See also* Committee of Imperial Defence

United Nations, 111, 112, 233, 259, 261, 263, 264

United Service, 11

U.S. Naval Institute, 2, 4, 5, 9, 44, 92, 155; *Naval Review,* 210, 211; *Proceedings,* 2, 6, 9, 11, 62, 149, 150, 152, 153, 223

Upton, Emory, 7–8

Veenendaal, A. J., 105–106n. 14

Veldkamp, B., 198

Vera Cruz, 32

Vogelgesang, Carl T., 40, 45

Walker, John G., 6

Wall Street Journal, 154–155

war-gaming, 25, 30, 37, 38, 50–51, 62, 220, 243, 245

war plans and planning, 35, 36, 39, 40, 82, 110, 115–117; Color Plans, 39; "The Maritime Strategy" (1983–1991), 119, 201–228; Plan Black, 40; Plan Orange, 39, 41, 117, 121–135; Rainbow, 124, 125; Sea Plan 2000, 205; Sea Strike, 205, 216, 220

war, principles of, 34, 50, 246–247

warfare, art and science of, 8, 9, 20, 34, 40, 41, 50; antisubmarine, 189, 211, 230; mine, 230, 237

wars, American Civil War, 2, 3, 6–8, 35, 92, 94, 100; American Revolution, 92, 100; Anglo-Boer, 231; Barbary Wars, 92, 100; Cold, 117–118, 193–194, 201–228, 230, 235; Crimean, 232; Franco-Prussian, 36; French Revolution and Napoleonic, 113, 231; Gulf, 230, 233, 248; Korean, 230; Kosovo, 230; Quasi War, 92, 100; Russo-Japanese, 116, 231; Spanish-American, 29, 33, 36, 51, 92, 116, 231; Spanish-Succession, 105–106n. 14, 128; Vietnam, 172, 202, 230; War of 1812, 5, 92, 100; World War I, 29, 51, 84–85, 116, 230; World War II, 23, 101, 111, 122–139, 165, 189, 230, 235, 245

Warsaw Pact, 193

Watkins, James, 211, 217–218, 222, 223

Weeks, Stan, 199, 216–218, 219

Welles, Gideon, 35, 100

West African Naval Symposium, 255

Western Pacific Naval Symposium, 255

West Indies, 111

Wevers, J. W. E., 198

Wilhelm II, Kaiser, 80

Williams College, 148

William III, King, 80, 110

Wilson, Woodrow, 47

Woolsey, James, 205

Wright, Carleton, 142

Wylie, Elizabeth, 216

Wylie, J. C., 73, 125, 137–159, 203, 219, 235, 246

Yale University, 148

Zumwalt, Elmo R., 163, 172, 177, 178, 179